Half in Love With Death

Managing the Chronically Suicidal Patient

∽

Half in Love With Death
Managing the Chronically Suicidal Patient

Joel Paris

McGill University

LEA

LAWRENCE ERLBAUM ASSOCIATES, PUBLISHERS

2007   Mahwah, New Jersey   London

Lawrence Erlbaum Associates, Inc., Publishers
10 Industrial Avenue
Mahwah, NJ 07430

Cover design by Kathryn Houghtaling Lacey

Library of Congress Cataloging-in-Publication Data

Paris, Joel, 1940-
Half in love with death: managing the chronically suicidal
    patient / Joel Paris.
        p.   cm.
    Includes bibliographical references and index.
    ISBN 0-8058-5514-9 (cloth : alk. paper)
    ISBN 0-8058-6081-9 (pbk. : alk. paper)
    ISBN 1-4106-1459-X (E book)
    1. Suicidal behavior—Treatment. 2. Suicide. 3. Young
        adults—Mental Health Services.   4. Chronic dis-
        eases—Treatment   I. Title.
    RC569.P37   2006
    616.85'844506—dc22   2006002686
                                                              CIP

Books published by Lawrence Erlbaum Associates are printed
on acid-free paper, and their bindings are chosen for strength
and durability.

Printed in the United States of America
10   9   8   7   6   5   4   3   2   1

This book is dedicated to my patients, who have taught me so much about the human condition.

Contents

Preface

〜

Darkling I listen; and, for many a time
I have been half in love with easeful Death,
Call'd him soft names in many a mused rhyme,
To take into the air my quiet breath.

—"Ode to a Nightingale" by John Keats

The Problem of Chronic Suicidality

John Keats's poem describes a state of mind we often see in chronically suicidal patients. Life becomes so painful for these people that they feel "half in love" with death.

Chronic suicidality is a difficult problem. I have written this book to help clinicians with treatment. Many authors have written about the clinical management of patients who threaten or attempt suicide. Yet there is a surprisingly small literature on chronic suicidality. Most books on suicide focus on the assessment of patients with episodes of depression lasting a few months. But chronically suicidal patients can think about suicide for years and often make multiple attempts.

Maltsberger (1994) described some of the problems in managing these cases:

Patients who threaten suicide in all seasons, self-mutilate, and who from time to time make serious suicide attempts tax and challenge clinical workers. Every hospital has its legend about the exploits of such a patient. When these patients die of suicide, a wave of sorrow and guilt follows. Many therapists exclude them from their practices; keeping clinical balance in working with them is difficult. Intractably suicidal patients require much time and great energy from those responsible for their care. They draw forensic attention and excite hospital administrators to action. Much of the anxiety they arouse comes from the question of whether they should be admitted to the hospital and, once they have come into the hospital, from the reciprocal: whether they should go out again. The increasingly litigious climate in the United States makes the treatment of such persons extremely difficult. (p. 199)

Therapists lack guidelines for dealing with such problems. And without guidelines, chronically suicidal patients are frightening. Our greatest fear is losing a patient to suicide. We try to do everything we can to prevent fatal outcomes, but most of us will experience a completed suicide sometime in our career.

It is, therefore, not surprising that some therapists attempt to avoid treating this population. Yet no one can practice for long without seeing chronically suicidal cases. And once patients are in treatment, we are obligated to help them. Thus, most of us struggle along, dealing with the situation the best we can.

On a purely human level, we care about our patients. It would be painful to lose someone with whom we have spent so many intense hours. On a professional level, suicide challenges our feelings of helpfulness and competence. Last, we have to be concerned about the consequences of a suicide. If a patient dies by his or her own hand, what will our colleagues think? Could we suffer a lawsuit by angry family members?

The following example illustrates some of these problems:

Colleen was a 25-year-old nurse who came to therapy after taking a large overdose of pills. The immediate precipitant was a break-up with a boyfriend. However, Colleen reported that since the age of 13, suicide had always been an option for her. She had taken her first over-

dose, 20 aspirins, as a ninth-grade student, after an argument with her mother. Colleen awoke the next morning feeling ill, but she went to school and never told her family what she had done. Over the coming years, Colleen continued to feel that her life was empty, although she achieved some degree of outward success. Colleen did well in nursing school and took on a demanding position at an intensive care unit. But in her adult years, Colleen found herself unable to find intimacy and happiness, and despair took command of her life.

Colleen was seen weekly in therapy over the next 3 years. Although she did not make another attempt, both Colleen and her therapist were always aware that she had the means to ensure that the next one would be fatal. For example, Colleen had access to vials of potassium chloride at work, which she kept at home, along with a syringe. Every session dealt with the possibility of suicide. The therapist could never be sure whether Colleen would survive to the next session. And if she did kill herself, the medical community would know of it.

Although clinical problems like this are difficult, this book suggests a way for therapists to approach such problems without being paralyzed by fear. This book also challenges conventional wisdoms about the management of suicidality. I suggest that most of the "classical" approaches in the literature are mistaken and even counterproductive when applied to patients who are chronically suicidal. But this book is not intended to be simply a polemic against misconceptions and bad practices. It offers a different approach to treatment, one I hope readers will find both positive and practical.

Acknowledgments

The concepts in this book expand on ideas originally presented in two journal articles: Paris (2002a) and Paris (2004b).

Roz Paris and Hallie Frank read earlier versions of this manuscript and made many useful suggestions for improvement. Judy Grossman helped me to find obscure references. Chapter 9 uses concepts developed by Deborah Sookman.

Introduction

∽

Challenging Conventional Wisdoms

The conventional wisdoms about the management of suicidality have misled us. We have long been taught that when patients are suicidal, therapists should be highly vigilant and intervene actively to prevent completion. This point of view usually leads to hospital admissions, which are assumed to save lives.

This book will show that there is little evidence for these assumptions. There are no data to show that hospitalization prevents suicide, even in patients who are acutely suicidal. Even if it were true that admission to a ward can prevent some people from committing suicide, hospitalization tends to be ineffective and unhelpful for chronically suicidal patients.

These ideas will probably encounter some resistance. Therapists believe that it is their responsibility to ensure safety for patients. This book suggests that "safety" is an illusion—and a dangerous one, in that attempts to protect patients from suicide cut them off from everything that makes life meaningful.

Instead, I suggest that giving up the idea of actively saving chronically suicidal patients actually liberates us to understand them and to work on their problems. Paradoxically, the most important thing therapists have to do when treating this population is to *tolerate* suicidality. This provides the basis for addressing the psychological issues behind suicidal ideas and behaviors.

The Four Major Points of This Book

1. The inner world of the chronically suicidal patient is one of pain, emptiness, and hopelessness; suicidality is an attempt to cope with these states of mind.
2. Chronic suicidality is not usually accounted for by depression alone but is associated with personality disorders.
3. Methods generally recommended for the management of suicidality are ineffective and counterproductive in chronically suicidal patients.
4. Effective therapy requires that therapists tolerate chronic suicidality while working toward healthier ways of coping.

The Inner World of the Chronically Suicidal Patient

Planning any form of treatment for suicidal patients requires an understanding of why they have become chronically suicidal.

The inner world of suicidal patients will be alien to most people. At the center of suicidal patients' experience is a paradox. Suicidality has become the center of their existence. Death has become a way of life.

Although it may be hard to imagine, patients can actually be comforted by suicidal ideas. These patients suffer a high level of distress and can only tolerate that distress if they know they can escape it. In this way, patients become "half in love with easeful death."

Chronically suicidal patients have only a faint hope that their lives will ever be happy or that they can do anything to change their situation. Yet because they can always choose not to live, they retain a strange power over their fate. That is the main reason why patients can think about suicide every day. When crises arise in their lives, they need not suffer passively but can do things that give them a feeling of activity and control: making suicide attempts by overdose, or cutting and burning themselves.

Behavioral patterns remain stable when they perform a function. In this way, suicidality can be seen as a coping strategy. In fact, most chronically suicidal patients do *not* end their lives by suicide. Herein lies the paradox. The only way for them to go on living is to maintain the option of dying. They threaten to die in order to stay alive.

This book considers some of the unique psychological issues that affect the emotional life of these patients. The first concerns *psychological pain*. The feelings that the chronically suicidal patient is trying to cope with are beyond the experience of most people. Empathizing with these states of mind requires some imagination.

We all know what it is like to be depressed and anxious. The level of such feelings tends to be unpleasant but manageable. Moreover, we generally anticipate that painful emotions will go away with time. Imagine, however, what it must feel like to experience severe and continuous distress. Chronically suicidal patients are rarely happy for more than a few days. Most of the time, their mood is depressed, anxious, or angry. This level of suffering is quantitatively beyond our experience, and that is what makes it qualitatively different.

The second unique emotion we see in chronically suicidal patients is *emptiness*. This state of mind is not the same feeling as depression. Patients who are depressed have a sense of loss. Patients who feel empty describe a sense of having nothing inside and of being nobody. As one of my teachers once put it, these patients have a sense not of "having been" but of "never was."

The third emotion associated with chronic suicidality is *hopelessness*. This state of mind also occurs in classical depression, but the difference lies in the time scale. If one cannot remember ever feeling content, there can be little hope for a return to happiness.

This is one of the reasons why chronic suicidality cannot be accounted for by depression. Most people are "down" from time to time. In the course of a lifetime, 1 out of 10 people will meet criteria for a clinical diagnosis of major depression. As long as this state lasts, nothing can cheer the patient up. But depression tends to be temporary. If it is not too severe, patients may remember better times and realize they are not quite themselves. Although many depressed people have transient thoughts about death, only a minority will act on these thoughts by making suicide attempts. And once depression lifts, suicidal ideation disappears.

What Kinds of Patients Are Chronically Suicidal?

At least half of chronically suicidal patients meet criteria for a personality disorder. Yet patients who are suicidal are often diagnosed only with depression, and many clinicians go no further in their diagnostic thinking. Actually, most people with suicidal ideas of any kind, not to speak of suicide attempts, tend to meet *Diagnostic and Statistical Manual of Mental Disorders (DSM)* criteria for major depression. But that diagnosis tells us little about why patients become suicidal.

Much of the confusion derives from the way depression is defined. *DSM* (4th ed., text rev.) lists eight criteria for a major depressive episode and requires that patients meet five of them. It is not very hard to earn this diagnosis. Almost anyone who is seriously unhappy for more than a couple of weeks can be diagnosed with major depression. This definition is based on too broad a concept and is particularly unhelpful in distinguishing chronically suicidal patients from depressed patients in an episode of mood disorder.

The chronicity of suicidality requires a diagnostic concept that reflects continuous dysfunction over time. Patients with major psychiatric diagnoses, such as bipolar disorder, melancholic depression, substance abuse, and schizophrenia, can also be chronically suicidal. I might have written another book about the problems these groups present. But in the majority of cases, the most useful diagnostic concept for understanding chronic suicidality is personality disorder. One is not likely to develop chronic suicidal ideas and actions in the absence of this kind of pathology.

Moreover, the largest literature on this clinical problem derives from studies of Axis II disorders, most particularly patients who meet criteria for borderline personality. These are the clients who give the most trouble to therapists and on whom this book focuses.

How Not to Manage Chronic Suicidality

Suicidology is a discipline in its own right. It addresses an important clinical problem by inspiring a large body of empirical studies examining the risk factors for suicide. Clinical guidelines for the assessment and management of risk identify patients who are, at least statistically, more likely to commit suicide. For example, completion is more common in men than in women, particularly among older men. Suicide is more likely to occur when patients have poor social supports and when they feel hopeless about the future. Patients who have previously attempted suicide are somewhat more likely to die by their own hand. Completion is an increased risk in a number of diagnostic groups, particularly melancholic depression, bipolar illness, alcoholism, and schizophrenia.

However, these risk factors are not at all useful in predicting whether any *individual* will die by suicide. This research suffers from a very large number of false positives (patients who have the risk factors but who never commit suicide). Moreover, there is little evidence from systematic research that identifying these risk factors helps to prevent completion.

Of particular concern, guidelines for managing suicidality have been applied to all patients who think about, threaten, or attempt suicide. Arguably, little harm will be done if one intervenes unnecessarily in patients with acute suicidality, because that condition is usually temporary. However, methods of assessment and treatment developed for acutely suicidal patients can be inappropriate, or even counterproductive, for chronically suicidal patients whose symptoms are in no way temporary. On the contrary, by providing reinforcement, these interventions tend to increase chronic suicidality. It does not make sense to treat all patients as if they were at immediate risk of losing their lives. Only a minority will eventually end their lives, and there is little to go on in predicting which patients are most likely to be completers.

To clarify these issues, this book makes some fundamental distinctions between several patterns, all of which have been called "suicidal." First, suicidal thoughts, common in many depressed states, must be distinguished from suicidal actions. Second, self-mutilating behaviors are not usually suicidal in intent. Finally, high-risk suicidal actions that are potentially lethal have a different meaning from actions such as minor overdoses. Although their functions overlap, each of these situations is different and needs to be managed differently.

Suicidal thoughts, given their high base rate in the population and their common appearance in depression, are not useful markers for completion. Suicide attempts, despite their relationship to completed suicide, are also not strong predictors of completion. Repetitive attempters and suicide completers are separate, albeit overlapping populations. Finally, self-mutilation does not predict suicide. Repetitive cutting is not even really "suicidal" behavior but rather a way that patients self-regulate dysphoric emotions.

In summary, this book will further argue that hospitalizing chronically suicidal patients accomplishes little and can do some harm. When patients are suicidal over long periods of time, "safety" is an ephemeral goal. Treatment approaches designed to prevent completion tend to reinforce the very behavior they are trying to contain. Hospitalization, however unproductive, tends to be repetitive. A vicious cycle is created in which therapy becomes virtually impossible.

This book maintains that treating chronically suicidal patients requires therapists to tolerate some degree of risk. Most patients will not complete suicide, even if some do. Clinicians are trained to believe that they must act to prevent suicide at all costs. If one could identify who is at risk, perhaps focusing on prevention would make sense. But we cannot identify these patients. The most rational approach to the chronically suicidal patient is to avoid unnecessary interventions and to proceed with therapy.

Managing Chronic Suicidality in Therapy

This book explains why the backbone of management for the chronically suicidal patient with a personality disorder is outpatient psychotherapy. Unlike many of my medical colleagues, I am skeptical about the value of currently available pharmacotherapy in this population. I will show that although drugs can "take the edge off" dysphoria, their therapeutic value has been both overrated and overstated. Although the future may provide us with better agents, at present one can only conclude that pharmacological treatment fails to produce remission of the disorders that cause patients to be chronically suicidal. In fact, there is better evidence of the efficacy of psychotherapy than for any pharmacological intervention in this population.

A more general principle is that therapists should avoid making unnecessary interventions and should focus their efforts on addressing the underlying causes of chronic suicidality. We have to address the real-life issues that make lives unbearable. Until patients develop new skills, and have new and more positive experiences, they will not readily give up their suicidality. The ultimate goal of treatment is to help the patient to "get a life."

Obviously, psychotherapy takes time. While awaiting an improved quality of life, therapists need to tolerate suicidality. Doing so is an essential part of the treatment strategy. Patients may need to be allowed to maintain a suicidal option because it is often their way to go on living. Later, when life satisfactions become more available, they can move away from a preoccupation with death and begin to solve the problems of living. In the meantime, patients can be taught to tolerate dysphoric emotions, to stand outside of them, and to reappraise the circumstances that bring them on.

Many of the questions examined in this book do not have unambiguous answers based on research data. I do not wish to join the ranks of authors who offer dogmatic opinions based on experience alone (often drawn from a very limited and unrepresentative clinical case load). Yet clinicians and their patients must not be expected to wait another 50 years for definitive answers to important problems. Thus, although I have not systematically tested every idea in this book, my clinical recommendations are informed by my experience as a researcher and are consistent with what the empirical literature shows.

How I Became Interested in Chronic Suicidality

As a young therapist, I often felt unsure about whether I was helping people. But if my patients were suicidal at the beginning of treatment, I would at least know if they were alive or dead at the end. I was also fascinated by the inner world of suicidality and energized by the clinical challenge it presented. I began to collect chronically suicidal patients in my practice.

It took me several years to understand that these patients could be diagnosed with severe personality disorders. I had learned about this form of pathology in my training but did not really understand it. Until the 1970s, there was little formal research on personality disorders. Then the field saw a dramatic growth, producing a large body of empirical data. Although I had little formal training in research, I became part of that movement, learning from colleagues how to conduct empirical studies and eventually publishing my own work on borderline personality disorder.

Although research became a major part of my professional life, it did not provide me with guidelines for treating chronically suicidal patients. But the findings of my studies of the long-term outcome of personality disorders helped me to feel more comfortable. Most of these patients, despite having been seriously suicidal for many years, eventually recovered and returned to a reasonable level of functioning.

These findings left room for a guarded optimism. I also learned that those who did commit suicide had not done so at the time when they were most threatening to their therapists but rather ended their lives at a much later point, usually when they were no longer in treatment. This observation greatly reduced my anxiety about treating young suicidal patients. I hope to produce the same effect on the readers of this book.

The Plan of This Book

Each chapter develops a theoretical perspective based on empirical data, and most are illustrated by clinical examples.

Chapter 1 distinguishes between the various types of "suicidality": thoughts, attempts, and self-mutilation. These distinctions help us to understand the relationship between suicidality and completed suicide.

Chapter 2 examines the inner world of the chronically suicidal patient, with particular focus on pain, emptiness, and hopelessness.

Chapter 3 shows how chronic suicidality can originate in childhood and adolescence, well before any clinical presentation. The chapter also presents a perspective on why the adolescent years are usually the time when overt suicidal behaviors first appear.

Chapter 4 examines the relationship between chronic suicidality and personality disorders, most particularly the category of borderline personality. The chapter questions the concept that chronic suicidality is primarily the result of depression.

Chapter 5 critiques the myth that suicide can be prevented using current methods of intervention. This chapter shows why hospitalization is not useful for patients with chronic suicidality and examines some of the alternatives.

Chapter 6 reviews the effectiveness of psychotherapy for chronically suicidal patients.

Chapter 7 reviews the effectiveness of pharmacotherapy for chronically suicidal patients.

Chapter 8 focuses on the problems therapists have in tolerating chronic suicidality.

Chapter 9 offers an approach to management, in which even the most alarming behaviors can be dealt with in a matter-of-fact, pragmatic fashion.

Chapter 10 discusses the risks of litigation in managing this patient population

The book ends with a brief summary of its main arguments, followed by an outline of their practical implications for treatment as well as future directions for research.

$\widehat{1}$

Suicidality
and Suicide
~~~

What is Suicidality?

When therapists talk to each other, they may refer to a patient as being *suicidal*. Yet it is not clear what using this term communicates. A single word can have many meanings. Understanding what is meant by *suicidality* is not just a problem in semantics: Ambiguity in language leads to confusion in practice. At best, when clinicians describe people as suicidal, the clinicians are expressing concern. It need not mean that patients are in mortal danger.

A standard text (Maris, Berman, & Silverman, 2000, p. 314) defines *suicidality* very broadly, including situations in which patients consider suicide, cut their wrists, take mild overdoses, or carry out life-threatening acts. The risk of completion is quite different in each of these situations, and each has to be managed differently. This chapter reviews research on these clinical problems and reviews to what extent suicidal ideas and actions are related to completion.

Suicidal Ideation and the Risk of Completion

What Does Suicidal Mean?

Most of the time, when therapists use the word *suicidal,* they are referring to thoughts that patients have of ending their lives. Clinicians have been trained to assess suicide risk by asking patients if they are considering suicide and to raise their level of concern if the answer is yes. Thus, the presence of almost any form of suicidal ideation can set off alarm bells.

Unfortunately, what therapists have been taught about suicide risk has little or no scientific basis. As we will see, stated intention has little relationship to completion. (Nor is the presence of suicide attempts a reliable marker for risk.) We should always be concerned about patients when they feel suicidal and acknowledge the level of distress that makes people think along these lines. But although there is nothing wrong with concern, the presence of suicidal thoughts can lead to a knee-jerk response, in which any suggestion that suicide is being considered is seen as life endangering.

Therapists are understandably anxious about losing patients to suicide. A buzzword that is often used to guide management is *safety*. Yet we do not really know what constitutes a safe environment for patients who are thinking about ending their lives. The answers suggested by empirical data do not correspond to current clinical practice.

The High Prevalence of Suicidal Ideation

Suicidal thoughts are very common. A large-scale American epidemiological study, the National Comorbidity Survey (Kessler et al., 1994; Weissman et al., 1999), reported the lifetime prevalence of suicidal ideation at all ages to be 17%. Thus, one of six people has contemplated suicide at some time in his or her life. And it is possible that older people may forget that about thoughts they had when they were young. In our own research, the prevalence of suicidal ideas in young adults was as high as 50% (Brezo et al., 2005).

This extremely high prevalence of suicidal ideation can be compared with prevalence of suicide completion, which is 11 per 100,000 (Grunebaum et al., 2004). Thus, the presence of suicidal ideas can hardly be a reliable way to assess the risk for completion. To some extent, ideation raises the risk for attempts: Although only 5% of the population will make an attempt of any kind over their lifetime, about 30% of those with suicidal ideation have made some kind of attempt (Kessler et al., 1994). Nonetheless, most people who think about suicide never make an attempt.

The reason why suicidal ideas are so common is that depression is common. Suicidal thoughts are very common when people are depressed. Accordingly, lifetime rates of depression decrease in much the same range as the prevalence of suicidal ideation: between 10% and 20% (Weissman et al., 1988). But because depression is an episodic condition, most suicidal thoughts are transient and go away when the depression lifts. Of course, this does not happen when patients are chronically suicidal.

Are Risk Factors for Suicide Clinically Useful?

Does suicidal ideation provide a better index of risk when combined with other risk factors? Clinicians have been trained to assess a set of predictors believed to increase the risk for completion in patients who think about suicide. Maris et al. (2000, p. 514) listed them, and they should not be unfamiliar. They include specific types of psychological symptoms (impulsivity, agitation, psychosis, violence), serious medical problems, high levels of stress, poor functioning, lack of social supports, and a family history of suicide.

Each of these risk factors is indeed associated with an increased probability of suicide. But most patients who have any one of these risks (or several of them) will never kill themselves. Thus, if we were to consider every patient who presents with these factors as being at risk for suicide, we would be faced with an enormous number of false positives.

Thus, statistical data obtained from large populations generate associations that are not of any practical use in a clinical setting. Applying these relationships to patients can be very misleading. As chapter 5 shows, even when we combine all of the risk factors in an algorithm and apply them to large groups of patients who are known to be suicidal, it has proven impossible to predict whether any individual patient will actually commit suicide (Goldstein, Black, Nasrallah, & Winokur, 1991; Pokorny, 1983). Although we sometimes have the impression, at least in retrospect, that suicide could have been prevented, we would have been unable to identify which individual patients are at the highest risk for completion.

Clinical Implications of Suicidal Ideation

If suicidal ideation is not a useful predictor of suicidal actions, it is actually misleading to refer to patients having these thoughts as being suicidal. This way of using words might conceivably be defended on the grounds that suicide is such a horrific event that it is better to be vigilant than to miss such a serious consequence, however rare. Yet as chapter 5 shows, there is hardly any evidence that clinicians can intervene in any meaningful way to prevent suicide.

Like preventive wars, attempts at suicide prevention can have unintended consequences. Allowing a large number of false positives can lead to improper management. As this book shows, treating all who have suicide ideation as if they were at risk of death is as likely to make them worse as better. This is a particularly important problem for chronically suicidal patients, in whom suicidal ideation does not take the same form or have the same meaning as in those who are acutely depressed.

Thus, suicidal thoughts, by themselves, should not be a cause for alarm and anxiety. They reflect mental states that may or may not be associated with actions. It is likely that anyone who suffers a depression of some severity will, at some point, think about the possibility of ending the pain. But if we were to treat all patients with suicidal ideation as if their life were at risk, hospital wards would fill up and would be unable to admit other cases. We would also be mistreating a large number of patients on the unproven assumption that doing so would allow us to save a few.

Again, this point of view should in no way be understood as encouraging clinicians to ignore suicidality. Even if suicidal thoughts are not harbingers of mortality, they can never be seen as unimportant. Ideas of death are a mirror of pain and distress. For that reason alone they should always be attended to carefully. Ultimately, suicidal ideation is a signal that something needs to be done to relieve psychological pain.

Suicide Attempts and the Risk of Completion

The Prevalence of Suicide Attempts

About 1 in 20 people in the United States will make some kind of suicide attempt during their lifetime (Kessler, Berglund, Borges, Nock, & Wang, 2005; Weissman et al., 1999; Welch, 2001). The ratio of ideas to attempts is therefore about 6:1. But the ratio of attempts to completions is 500:1.

These statistics, based on community data, may be somewhat misleading in that they include milder attempts (sometimes called "gestures") that may never come to medical attention. For this reason, there is a stronger relation of attempts to completion in hospital settings. Nonetheless, even in clinical populations, most patients who make attempts never complete suicide.

Differences Between Attempters and Completers

Research has consistently shown that suicide completers and suicide attempters are distinct populations (Beautrais, 2001; Kreitman & Casey, 1988; Linehan, Rizvi, Welch, & Page, 2000). Completers tend to be older, to be male, to use more lethal methods, and to die on the first attempt. In contrast, attempters tend to be younger, to be female, to use less lethal methods, and to survive (Maris et al, 2000, p. 285). Although these groups overlap to some extent, most cases in practice are distinct, and management draws on different principles.

Demographically, suicide attempters are more likely than completers to come from lower socioeconomic groups (Hawton, Harriss, Simkin, Bale, & Bond, 2001), although it is not clear whether that is a cause or an effect of their condition. Clinically, attempters constitute a large percentage of visits to medical emergency rooms, accounting for as many as 2.8% of all cases (Pajonk, Gruenberg, Moecke, & Naber, 2002). There is also a broad relationship between impulsivity and suicide attempts; large-scale surveys have found that attempters are highly likely to suffer from externalizing disorders (Hills, Cox, McWilliams, & Sareen, 2005).

Thus, attempters often suffer from both depression and substance abuse, and Hawton, Harris, et al. (2003) reported that problems with drugs have become more common among attempters. In addition, up to half of cases who present with suicide attempts also meet criteria for a personality disorder (Haw, Hawton, Houston, & Townsend, 2001), most particularly the borderline category (Forman, Berk, Henriques, Brown, & Beck, 2004; Suominen, Isometsa, Henriksson, Ostamo, & Lonnqvist, 2000). Because patients with borderline personality are highly treatment seeking (Zanarini, Frankenburg, Khera, & Bleichmar, 2001), this diagnosis is very common among suicide attempters seen in emergency rooms and outpatient clinics. About half of all clinic patients can be diagnosed with a personality disorder (Zimmerman, Rothschild, & Chelminski, 2005).

Of course, not every suicide attempter has a chronic mental disorder. This is reflected in the important differences between patients who make one attempt and those who make many. In general, repeated attempts are more predictive of completion than single attempts (Sakinofsky, 2000). Even so, most repetitive attempters do not end up completing suicide. In fact, the majority eventually give up this pattern of behavior. Maris

(1981) followed a cohort of repetitive suicide attempters and found that the behavior did not continue indefinitely but usually came to a stop after a maximum of four attempts. Although experienced clinicians will have seen patients who have made 10, 20, or more attempts, these cases are unusual.

How Often Do Attempters Commit Suicide?

Researchers have studied how often patients who are seen in mental health settings for suicide attempts eventually complete suicide. In a long-term, large-scale, follow-up study (ranging from 3 to 22 years) of all patients who presented with attempts to an emergency room in Oxford, England, Hawton, Harris, et al. (2003) identified 11,583 patients who had presented to a hospital with attempts. Of these, 3% eventually died by suicide. The rate for repeated attempters was twice that for single attempters (Zahl & Hawton, 2004). Nonetheless, because only 300 participants in this cohort actually completed suicide, predicting death from a repeated pattern of attempts would have led to a very large number of false positives.

Another large-scale study from England (Cooper et al., 2005) followed 7,968 patients with *deliberate self-harm* (a term that includes both overdoses and self-mutilation) over a 4-year period. The researchers reported 60 completed suicides (about 0.1% of the original sample). This is a very low rate, and the discrepancy is most likely due to the use of a sample that initially presented with less dangerous behavior.

Surveys in other countries have yielded higher rates of eventual completion: 5% in a study of 1,052 patients presenting to emergency rooms in Sweden (Skogman, Alsen, & Ojehagen, 2004), 6.7% in a follow-up of 1,018 emergency room patients in Finland (Suokas, Suominen, Isometsa, Ostamo, & Lonnqvist, 2001), and 5% in a Finnish follow-up of 1,198 patients with deliberate self-harm (Suominen, Isometsa, Haukka, & Lonnqvist, 2004). Some of the higher rates might reflect the higher overall prevalence of suicide in Scandinavia (England is more similar to North America).

A major methodological problem with these follow-up studies is that mild attempts tend to be mixed with life-threatening ones. If one begins with a sample with severe attempts, the rate of completion is bound to be higher. For example, Carter, Reith, Whyte, and McPherson (2005) found that multiple attempts with increasing severity were associated with a statistically significant higher rate of eventual completion (although the sample was too small for clinically useful prediction).

Another way to separate serious from less serious attempts is to focus on patients admitted to a hospital. In one of the first systematic follow-up studies, carried out in a Swedish hospital (Ettlinger, 1975), the overall completion rate for admitted patients was as high as 10%. Recently, a Finnish study (Suominen, Isometsa, Suokas, et al., 2004) found a similar rate: In a cohort of attempters followed for 40 years, as many as 13 out of 100 patients eventually died by suicide. This report noted that 8 of these died 15 years or more after the first attempt, raising the question whether longer follow-up periods are needed to determine the true rate of completion. On the other hand, Scandinavian rates of suicide could still be unusually high: In a well-designed large-scale study carried out in New Zealand (Gibb, Beautrais, & Fergusson, 2005), the rate of eventual completion for hospitalized patients after 10 years was only 4.6%.

The contradictions in this literature probably depend on the nature of samples. Everything depends on who gets admitted to the hospital. If only the most severely ill and psychotic patients are hospitalized, suicide rates will be higher. In settings where most attempters are routinely kept for a few days, rates will be lower.

Another way to separate patients at high and low risk is to differentiate between life-threatening attempts and mild overdoses. For example, in a 5-year follow-up of 302 patients who made medically serious attempts, Beautrais (2003) found that 6.7% had died by suicide. This rate is higher than that observed in the wide variety of attempters studied by Hawton, Harris, et al. (2003).

Perhaps the safest conclusion is that somewhere between 3% and 7% of attempters will eventually kill themselves. Yet even if we accept the high end of this range as accurate, its clinical application remains problematic. We cannot know whether patients were in imminent risk at the time of any previous attempt. Also, attempters who eventually kill themselves may have sought help for a previous episode but not for the one that actually leads to their death.

The Nature of Suicidal Intent

Assessing the nature of intent may be the best way to identify attempters most at risk for completion. Aaron Beck developed two scales for assessing suicidality, the Suicidal Ideation Scale (Beck, Resnick, & Lettieri, 1974) and the Suicide Intent Scale (Beck et al., 1974), to measure how seriously attempters intended to die. In a follow-up of Finnish attempters by Suominen, Isometsa, Ostamo, and Lonnqvist (2004), the Suicide Intent Scale was the only predictor (among many others that were used in the study) of completion; this finding was replicated in a study from England (Hariss, Hawton, & Zahl, 2005).

Another scale that has been widely used in research is the Reasons for Living Inventory (Linehan, 1983). This scale assesses intent from a somewhat different perspective: factors that make patients want to stay alive. However, none of these scales, even those that have been shown to predict completion with statistical significance, have been shown to be useful in making clinical decisions about suicidal risk. In other words, they identify populations at statistical risk, rather than the individuals who are most likely to die by suicide.

The most important factor in determining intent is the method used (Maris et al., 2000, p. 285). A patient who shoots himself is obviously more motivated to die than one who takes pills. But when patients overdose, the distinction between a lethal and a nonlethal action can be clouded by lack of knowledge about the effects of drugs (Beck, 1974), because not everyone knows which agents are most dangerous. Patients may overdose on benzodiazepines (which are rarely fatal), because the fact that they are prescription drugs can make them seem more dangerous than they really are. On the other hand, many people see over-the-counter drugs as harmless. They may not realize that a bottle of aspirin is enough to kill you.

Psychiatric Diagnosis and Suicide Attempts

Another factor in the risk associated with a suicide attempt is psychiatric diagnosis. Many mental disorders are associated with high suicide rates: Schizophrenia, melancholic depression, bipolar illness, and alcoholism all have completion rates as high as 10% (Inskip, Harris, & Barraclough, 1998), and borderline personality disorder (BPD) has a similar rate (Linehan et al., 2000; Paris, 2003).

Yet although diagnosis should always be considered in assessing risk, we are usually unable to determine whether the chances of suicide are high in any individual case or at any particular moment.

Number of Attempts

Another predictor of completion is the overall number of suicide attempts. A higher frequency of attempts has been consistently associated with an increased lifetime risk (Welch, 2001). In the Oxford study (Zahl & Hawton, 2004), the risk for completion after multiple attempts was 6%, twice that for single attempts. Even so, 94% of the patients with multiple attempts in the study did *not* commit suicide.

Can We Predict Completion From Attempts?

In summary, the findings reviewed here can be interpreted as showing that the cup is either half full or half empty. The majority of people who make suicide attempts decide to live, whereas a minority make a decision to die. Although one can identify risk factors that make a fatal outcome more likely, it is not possible to predict suicide completion from attempts in a clinically useful way. Two large-scale studies (Goldstein et al., 1991; Pokorny, 1983) that attempted to predict suicide, using algorithms based on all the risk factors described in the literature, were unable to identify any individual case of completion. This failure was entirely due to false positives (patients who have the risk factors for completion but who never actually commit suicide).

Why is prediction so difficult? The main reason is that completions are so rare relative to attempts. In addition, most deaths by suicide occur at the first attempt and are not preceded by unsuccessful actions (such as overdoses). In a survey by Maris (1981), the overall rate of suicide at first attempt was as high as 75%, with 88% of all completions over the age of 45 being first attempts. A large-scale Finnish study (Isometsa et al., 1996) obtained similar results, with 56% of completions being associated with a first attempt.

Of particular relevance to chronic suicidality, attempts have different meanings in different patients. In clinical populations, most occur during episodes of depression, which is usually either temporary or episodic. In chronic suicidality, however, most attempts are not intended to cause death but have an ambivalent motivation. Attempts that use nonlethal means (e.g., an overdose of benzodiazepines taken after a quarrel or a rejection) are particularly likely to occur in a communicative and interpersonal context in which significant others find patients and/or escort them to emergency rooms. These patients play a game of Russian roulette with fate, making death possible while leaving open the possibility that someone will come and rescue them in time.

Why Self-Mutilation is Not Suicidal Behavior

Of all the behaviors described in this chapter, self-mutilation is the least related to completed suicide. In fact, this kind of behavior should not be described as suicidal.

The literature has used multiple terms to describe this behavioral pattern, and this is a source of some confusion. Favazza (1996) defined *self-mutilation* as the deliberate nonsuicidal destruction of one's body tissue. *Self-injurious behavior* (Stanley, Gameroff, Michalsen, & Mann, 2001), also called *self-injury* (Osuch, Noll, & Putnam, 1999) or *self-wounding,* is essentially equivalent. *Deliberate self-harm* (DSH) is a term that has been widely used in the suicide literature. It is defined as "the intentional injuring of one's own body without apparent suicidal intent" (Hawton & van Heeringen, 2000, p. 1501). Actually, DSH is a broader concept because it includes both self-mutilation and overdoses, and this usage is a problem because it conflates nonsuicidal with suicidal actions. Recently, Hawton's group (Harriss et al., 2005) suggested redefining the term more simply as *self-harm* (after consumer groups complained that the term *deliberate* might be seen as stigmatic!). Finally, *parasuicide,* defined as "any nonfatal, self-injurious behavior with a clear intent to cause bodily harm or death" (Comtois, 2002, p. 1138), is also a broader concept that includes both self-mutilation and overdoses.

Self-mutilation is the narrowest and most clearly defined of these concepts. It was first described in the psychiatric literature 40 years ago (Pao, 1967). Typically, the pattern involves superficial cuts on the wrists and arms, actions not associated with serious danger to life. Although one occasionally sees dangerous slashes in patients who cut, most incidents consist of either "delicate cutting" or skin-deep cuts without damage to nerves, tendons, or blood vessels. Although the most common site tends to be the wrists, some patients will cut their arms and legs in relatively invisible places to avoid commentary from others.

The prevalence of self-mutilation in the general population (including single incidents) is similar to that for suicide attempts (i.e., about 4%; Klonsky, Oltmanns, & Turkheimer, 2003). But unlike attempts, this pattern does not have any consistent relationship to suicide completion. In fact, this behavioral pattern can have meanings that lie outside any clinical context. Thus, although self-mutilation in patients is generally seen in young women, it has long existed in religious groups and is also not uncommon in male prisoners (Favazza, 1996).

Although self-mutilators can go on to make suicide attempts, the intent of these behaviors is distinct (Gerson & Stanley, 2002; Winchel & Stanley, 1991). A study comparing two groups of patients with BPD, one with suicide attempts and the other with nonsuicidal self-injury (Brown, Comtois, & Lineham, 2002), found that both stated that their behaviors were usually intended to relieve negative emotions. However, whereas suicide attempts were frequently described as intended to leave others better off, self-mutilation was reported as performing other functions: to express anger, to punish oneself, to generate normal feelings, or to distract oneself.

This research, supported by other reports (Favazza, 1996; Gerson & Stanley, 2002; Leibenluft, Gardner, & Cowdry, 1987; Linehan, 1993; Simeon et al., 1992), suggests that cutting serves a psychological function, by providing short-term regulation of intense dysphoric affects. Its very success in achieving this goal may explain why self-mutilation tends to be repetitive and why chronic cutting can come to resemble addictive behavior (Linehan, 1993). Because some patients are in a dissociated state when they cut and feel little pain (Herpertz, 1995; Leibenluft et al., 1987), cutting can be highly reinforcing.

The main way that self-mutilation regulates dysphoria is by providing a distracter, substituting physical for mental suffering (Linehan, 1993). This mechanism is not unique to humans: Self-injury as a response to stressful circumstances has been observed in other species, such as dogs and nonhuman primates (Crawley, Sutton, & Pickar, 1985).

Self-mutilation can also communicate distress to other people (Paris, 2002a). Significant others (and therapists) will usually learn about the behavior and be alarmed by it. Although patients may initially be secretive about self-injury or be socially embarrassed by visible scars or burn marks (particularly in the summer months), the pattern eventually comes to the attention of other people. Gunderson (2001) also suggested that self-mutilation can be used to express emotions in a symbolic fashion: self-punishment related to guilty feelings, or a way of expressing anger that cannot be communicated in another way. Finally, self-mutilation is particularly associated with BPD (Gershon & Stanley, 2002), a relationship that is discussed in chapter 4.

Patterns of Suicide Completion

Completed suicide is the 11th most frequent cause of death in the American population (Maris, et al., 2000). Although the overall prevalence of suicide has not changed dramatically (van Praag, 2003), it does show some degree of variation over time. Thus, a recent survey (Grunebaum et al., 2004) noted that the overall rate of suicide in the United States increased by about 30% between 1957 and 1986 (from 9.8 to 12.9 per 100,000) and then decreased by 13% (to 10.7) by 1999; this decrease was twice as great in women than in men.

The explanation for changes in suicide rates over time is far from clear, although there has been a great deal of speculation. Moreover, responses to these statistics are not always disinterested. When suicide rates go up, the press reacts with alarm, and mental health professionals call for more action and more resources. When rates go down (as they have recently), the change may not even be reported in the press, whereas mental health professionals tend to believe they reflect the effectiveness of their work.

As discussed in chapter 5, the relationship between the availability of treatment and the frequency of completion remains controversial. We need to remain humble about the value of our interventions: Although human resources in mental health services have increased, making therapy more available to the population, doing so has not markedly reduced the number of people who end their own lives.

From a long-term perspective, suicide rates are fairly stable over time. One reason for this relative stability may be that most patients who complete suicide tend either to not seek help or to avoid it. This pattern has been identified by psychological autopsy studies in which family members are carefully interviewed (Cavanagh, Carson, Sharpe, & Lawrie, 2003). As already noted, most completed suicides occur on the first attempt, usually because the means used are likely to be fatal. Even among young adults, a large-scale study using psychological autopsies (Lesage et al., 1994) found that among 75 patients who died by suicide between ages 18 and 35, less than a third were in treatment at the time of their death, fewer than half had seen a therapist during the previous year, and a third had never even been evaluated. In a review of 174 suicides in young adults under age 25, Hawton, Houston, and Sheppard (1999) reported very similar findings.

The demographics of suicide completion are notable. In almost all locations in the world, men are much more likely to commit suicide than women (Maris et al., 2000). The main exception is China (Eddleston & Gunnell, 2006), where there has recently been an epidemic of suicide among women in rural areas (related to the availability of insecticides, which are often fatal when taken impulsively).

Suicide rates tend to increase with age, and the highest prevalence has always been in the elderly. But in the 1960s, suicide rates in the cohort ages 15 to 24 began to increase in several highly developed countries, including the United States (Murphy & Wetzel, 1980), Canada (Solomon & Hellon, 1980), and Australia (Morrell, Page, & Taylor, 2002). This increase in youth suicide was the subject of much discussion in the media, and entire books (e.g., Sudak, Ford, & Rushforth, 1984) were written to explain it.

However, the overall relationship between age and suicide completion continued to be largely linear. The increase in youth suicide was a "blip" that has leveled out in recent years (Maris et al., 2000). By the beginning of the 21st century, suicide among the young was no more common than it had been 20 years previously, even if the problem was not going away.

Suicide completion is more common in lower socioeconomic groups (Kreitman, Carstairs, & Duffy, 1991), although this relationship may only hold for men, not women (Morrell, Page, & Taylor, 2002). But almost all medical illnesses are more common among the poor as opposed to the rich (Lynch, Smith, Harper, & Hillemeier, 2004). Again, it is not clear whether lower social class is a causal factor in suicide or the result of the mental disorders associated with completion.

The prevalence of suicide completion is definitely affected by social context. For example, youth suicide is more common in specific cultures, most particularly in indigenous societies, where there have been dramatic increases in suicide and suicide attempts over recent decades (Kirmayer, Brass, & Tate, 2000). These populations, which are undergoing rapid social change associated with a disruption of traditional social structures, no longer provide meaningful roles for young people (Paris, 1996). However, these relationships are not universal. For example, African American populations have a surprisingly low rate of completed suicide (Willis, Coombs, Drentea, & Cockerham, 2003). Thus, the issue is not primarily one of social disadvantage but rather one of the availability of social roles and the strength of social networks.

Conclusions

Many types of behavior have been called "suicidal." But few of them are clinically useful predictors of whether people will kill themselves. Thinking about suicide, no matter how intense the ideation, is too common to be of any use for prediction of risk. Attempts such as overdoses can range from the trivial to the near-lethal, and most attempters never die by suicide. Self-mutilation is usually more disturbing than dangerous and should not even be thought of as suicidal behavior.

In summary, it is a mistake to treat all forms of suicidality as if they were one problem. Nor can suicidal behaviors be managed with any single tool. It has been said that if one has a hammer, everything looks like a nail.

$$\left(\,2\,\right)$$

The Inner World
of the Chronically
Suicidal Patient

~

It takes imagination to enter the inner world of a chronically
suicidal patient. Many of us have gone through depression
from time to time. Yet however painful that experience is, we
know it will not last forever. And when we recover from periods of depression, even when life continues to be difficult, we
remain engaged and motivated.

This is not the case for the chronically suicidal patient.
Locked into hopelessness, the patient finds that the idea of
death comes to dominate life itself. Maintaining suicide as an
option becomes a kind of identity, a way of defining oneself
outside the boundaries of the living world. Yet paradoxically,
keeping the exit door open can allow people to bide their time
and remain alive while awaiting a change of fortune.

The desire for death reflects powerful inner feelings. Again,
it takes imagination to empathize with the pain that underlies
chronic suicidality. Everyone knows what it feels like to be unhappy. But few of us have experienced dysphoria on a daily ba-

sis for months or years on end. It is also difficult to imagine the intensity of emotions that these patients feel.

Poets and novelists, some inspired by such experiences, help us understand this state of mind. Although the title of this book quotes Keats, I could just as easily have made use of Sylvia Plath, a poet who wrote brilliantly about suicide and who ended her life at age 30. Her story, well documented in biographies (Stevenson, 1988) and memoirs (Alvarez, 1971), illustrates the attraction of death for a sensitive poet. Plath was an intelligent woman who had considered suicide since childhood. She described this experience memorably in her poem *Lady Lazarus*, (Plath, 1966) remarking sardonically:

> Dying
> Is an art, like everything else.
> I do it exceptionally well.

Unfortunately, science has not shed much light on these states of mind. Thus we must turn to the clinical literature, based on the experience of therapists who have treated suicidal patients. Surprisingly, even here, the number of publications is sparse, although there have been a few insightful articles.

In one of the earliest contributions to the literature, Schwartz, Flinn, and Slawson (1974) described a group of patients with a "suicidal character." The authors suggested that chronic suicidality is not a short-term symptom but rather a central aspect of a patient's outlook on the world. As explained in chapter 4, this clinical picture cannot be accounted for by depression. A long-term pattern of suicidal behavior does not reflect a temporary change in mood but a way of life rooted in personality structure.

In a subsequent article, Schwartz (1979) went on to suggest that chronic suicidality has specific purposes. "There are some suicidal people for whom suicidality has become a means of securing nurturance from the interpersonal world. The usual 'crisis response' to suicidality reinforces such patients in their suicidal styles. Increased long-term risk becomes the price of short-term nurturance" (p. 194): The implication is that patients are reluctant to give up being suicidal unless they can find another way to gain support and care.

Fine and Sansone (1990) described clinical implications of the idea that suicidality is rooted in personality structure. If suicidal ideas perform important functions, they cannot easily be removed. Thus treatment must go beyond symptoms and address underlying personality issues. The authors also emphasized that approaches designed for the management of acute suicidality must be modified to treat chronically suicidal patients. Fine and Sansone (1990) suggested that "clinicians treating borderline individuals need to carefully discriminate 'acute' from 'chronic' suicidal states. For 'acute' suicidal situations, traditional management approaches are appropriate. However, for 'chronic' situations, common among borderline individuals, traditional management approaches may be therapeutically counterproductive" (p. 160).

Maltsberger (1994a, 1994b) has contributed greatly to our understanding of chronic suicidality. Like Fine and Sansone, he emphasizes that patients can use suicidality to obtain nurturance. What is different about his approach is an emphasis on the "aggressive" aspect of suicidality, which Maltsberger sees as a strategy that can be used to force other people to respond in specific ways. The danger for the therapist is that doing what the patient seems to want (i.e., providing more nurturance) can be countertherapeutic.

Maltsberger and Buie (1974) wrote an influential article emphasizing the danger of withdrawing from chronically suicidal patients in response to their demands. But this does not mean that therapists have to provide "reparenting" experiences in therapy or that they should routinely accede to demands, explicit or implicit, to hospitalize patients every time they feel suicidal. On the contrary, Maltsberger (1994a) suggested that chronically suicidal patients require therapists to take "calculated risks" as opposed to smothering patients with overprotective responses and unhelpful treatment strategies.

Psychic Pain and Chronic Suicidality

To account for the inner world of chronically suicidal patients, I next describe four essential elements of their experience: intense psychic pain, emptiness, hopelessness, and the need for control. I then discuss the interpersonal context of chronic suicidality.

High intensity of psychic pain is a crucial factor driving suicidality (Schneidman, 1973). Dying is a way of escaping these unbearable feelings. At the same time, patients who are chronically suicidal have a lower threshold for psychological pain, corresponding to the personality trait of neuroticism (see chapter 4).

Case Example

Anne was a 28-year-old woman who came to therapy complaining of chronic depression over many years. Currently she was in her second marriage and was completing advanced professional training.

Anne was a bright woman from a working class family in a small town who had worked her way up in the world. Her parents had never shown great interest in her, because they were preoccupied with her chronically ill younger brother. Anne moved away to study and never returned to her home. She was never really happy and had many periods of depressed mood but kept hoping that the future would bring her a different life.

At the university Anne met her first husband, Robert, a quiet man who focused on his own work. Anne experienced her husband as unsupportive and often attacked him, mainly to get a response, but doing so only led him to withdraw further. They did not have children and divorced reasonably amicably after a few years.

Anne chose a very different sort of man the second time around. Sam worked in the same area as Robert but had a more flamboyant character. Although he had a tendency to drink too much, Anne found Sam exciting. Due to Sam's ambition, they moved together to a new city where neither had a social network. It was in this context that Anne sought therapy. Although not initially suicidal, Anne became so as her new marriage began to unravel. Following their separation, Anne became chronically suicidal. She also took one serious overdose in the course of treatment but arranged it so that Sam would come home and rescue her.

Therapy proved to be long and arduous. Anne would usually walk into the office upset and leave without having experienced any relief. Her mood ranged from intense sadness, with convulsive weeping, to angry sarcasm, often directed at the therapist, who was seen as unhelpful. As was the case in her outside life, Anne rarely felt understood. She would describe how difficult it was for her to get through the day; at night, her sleep was restless and disturbed. One of her most frequent comments was: "You don't really know I feel. Or if you do, you don't seem to care very much."

This case illustrates the centrality of psychic pain for the chronically suicidal patient. Many of Anne's problems derived from emotions that were both powerful and unstable, and she met criteria for BPD, the prime diagnosis associated with chronic suicidality. As emphasized by Linehan (1993), dysphoric emotions in BPD are unusually intense and require more time to return to baseline, a pattern that has been termed *emotional dysregulation*. Research on BPD also shows that moods shift rapidly, associated with high levels of sensitivity to stressors (Gunderson & Phillips, 1991).

Thus, patients with BPD tend to respond with strong emotion to almost any life event, and their mood can vary, not by the week, but by the day or even by the hour. There can be a wide range of emotions, shifting from one to another within a very short time. Patients may be anxious in the morning, depressed in the afternoon, and angry in the evening. Although they can sometimes have periods of euphoria and excitement, these states rarely last more than a few hours, and the most prominent affect is anger (Koenigsberg et al., 2002). All these experiences are associated with continuous and intense psychological pain.

Although psychic pain in central to understanding suicidality, there has been surprisingly little formal research on this phenomenon. In one of the few publications on the subject, Orbach et al. (2003) proposed a classification of the different forms of mental pain: experiences related to feelings of irreversibility, loss of control, narcissistic wounds, emotional flooding, freezing, estrangement, confusion, social distancing, and emptiness. However, these categories were not studied systematically, and they are not really separate but rather are coexisting and overlapping.

The clinical literature on psychic pain is richer. Schneidman (1973), a pioneer suicidologist, provided a clear description of the unbearable experience of what he called "psychalgia." However, Schneidman was mainly interested in understanding why people may not want to go on living and did not consider the possibility that psychic pain might actually be *relieved* by suicidal ideas and behaviors. That mechanism has been documented in patients who report that suicidal ideation and actions can be comforting (Brown et al., 2002). The reason is that suicide offers an option of escape, providing a greater sense of control. In these patients, one of the functions of suicidality is to regulate psychic pain.

Case Example

Sonia was a young woman who held a job looking after mentally retarded patients in an institution. She came to therapy after an overnight stay in the emergency room, following an episode of self-cutting.

Sonia had been cutting on a regular basis since her adolescence and had also taken several overdoses. In one life-endangering incident, she set fire to her bed. However, when she was interviewed, Sonia showed a striking lack of overt distress. Instead, she had a chipper manner and a light sense of humor, describing her suicidality as a series of madcap escapades. Yet when Sonia was questioned more closely, it became clear that each of these episodes was initiated by intense emotions. For example, setting fire to the bed occurred after a major rejection, after which she had been weeping for hours. When this state continued for long enough, Sonia would begin to hear voices telling her to destroy herself, which she then acted on.

Again, this case demonstrates how suicidality can function (however maladaptively) as a way of coping with intense and shifting emotions. One of the main tasks of psychotherapy in this population is to provide alternative ways of managing intense and unstable moods.

Emptiness and Chronic Suicidality

A second important aspect of the inner experience of the chronically suicidal patient is emptiness.

What is the difference between emptiness and depression? Again, it requires some imagination to empathize with what it feels like to be empty. Yet many patients will tell you about it. Even those who are psychologically unsophisticated will spontaneously use the word *empty*. (I also have treated people in French, and patients have told me that what they feel inside is *une vide*.)

The feeling of an inner void is distinct from depression. When we are depressed, we experience a sense of loss. If only we could get back what has been taken away, all would be well. Thus, many states of depression resemble prolonged and intense grief and mourning.

In contrast, emptiness describes a more profound feeling of disconnection. It involves a sense that one barely exists in any meaningful way. In contrast to depression, the sense of emptiness is associated with the feeling that one has never had anything and never will.

Case Example

Mona was a university student with a strong academic record. Yet she described all her accomplishments as unreal, as an act she put on for the sake of her parents. Mona often insisted that behind this mask, there was nothing at all. The therapist was tempted to ask, "Then who am I talking to?" But Mona would reply, "Maybe you think you know me, but you don't. It wouldn't really matter if I were dead, because I've never been alive. People are fooled by me, but I'm nobody and have nothing to offer them."

This patient had a profound sense of disconnection from other people, which made her feel totally unreal. In many ways, people do not feel real without a sense of connection, either with intimates and friends or with life commitments. In the personality disorder literature, this state of mind has been called "borderline aloneness" (Adler & Buie, 1979; Gunderson, 2001; Pazzagli & Monti, 2000). The inner states of depression associated with BPD have also been shown to be distinct from those seen in classical depression (Leichsenring, 2004; Rogers, Widiger, & Krupp, 1995; Wixom, Ludolph, & Weston, 1993). The difference concerns the prominence of aloneness and emptiness, as well as a lack of identity and a purpose in life (Wilkinson-Ryan & Westen, 2000). Although these patients often seem to search for connections, they do not often find them, so that life itself becomes meaningless.

Hopelessness and Chronic Suicidality

A third aspect of the inner experience of the chronically suicidal patient is hopelessness. This experience is far from unique to chronically suicidal patients. Researchers find hopelessness to be an important correlate of suicidality in depressed people and have shown that its presence predicts suicidal actions (Beck, Resnik, & Lettieri, 1974). The difference in the chronically suicidal patient is that the feeling of hopelessness cuts much deeper.

These are patients who cannot remember ever being happy, or not for long. The current quality of their lives is also low: Many are unemployed, and many have relationships characterized by conflict and turmoil. In this state, one cannot fall back on happy memories and hope for a return to a lost Eden.

When one feels no hope, one searches for a sense of control. Again, when one is not in control of one's life, dying, or at least the threat of dying, can be an attractive alternative.

Case Example

Marlene was a 30-year-old woman who had made several suicide attempts by overdose. In the past, she had held a job as a speechwriter for a politician but felt little attachment to this work, or to any other. A long-term relationship with a boyfriend had ended with Marlene being abandoned, as she had always feared.

For the next 5 years, Marlene thought about suicide every day. She could not see any way out of her predicament. Marlene had no further hopes or ambitions for her career and did not believe that any man could stand her. Even friends were seen as a disappointment. Marlene's childhood had been marked by multiple moves generated by her father's career in industry. Her only meaningful relationship was with her parents, who acknowledged having neglected her in the past and who were making some efforts at reparation.

This case is a fairly typical example of how chronic suicidality turns hopelessness on its head. Threatening to die gives the patient a sense of control through the option of exiting life. This state of mind can last for years and can sometimes seem to be interminable and irreversible. Yet long-term follow-up studies of patients with BPD (see review in Paris, 2003) who had suffered from chronic suicidality show that in most cases, hopelessness can eventually decline with time. But, as chapter 9 shows, this can only happen when the patient's life begins to improve. Thus, most patients who have recovered are working, and about half also achieve some kind of stable relationship (although fewer raise children). Developing these life commitments aids recovery by providing meaning and connection. When patients achieve a healthy mastery over their lives, they become less hopeless and no longer need to be masters of death.

The Need for Control and Chronic Suicidality

The fourth function of chronic suicidality is that it provides a sense of control. In addition to needing an escape from psychic pain, emptiness, and hopelessness, many people with this clinical picture experience their lives as entirely out of control. Although patients contribute to their own problems, their subjective perspective tends to be that bad things happen for no good reason. Having suicide as an option becomes a way of reasserting control in a world that seems uncontrollable and chaotic. At the same time, suicidal thoughts can have an aggressive quality, revenging oneself on a hostile world by "resigning" from life.

Case Example

Paula was a 21-year-old woman working for an Internet pornography company. She claimed to have little conflict about this line of work and maintained a long-term relationship with a boyfriend who tolerated her lifestyle. However, whenever he was absent and out of touch, Paula became panicky, cut herself, and threatened to die. When the boyfriend learned of this behavior, he became much more available, leading to a vicious cycle.

In therapy sessions Paula had great difficulty allowing herself to admit that she needed anything; her typical attitude was one of challenge, dismissal, and devaluation. Paula used anger to hide her sadness, although this defense often proved brittle. Walking through life with the proverbial "chip on her shoulder" gave her the illusion of control in a life that was actually quite out of control.

In this patient, the illusion of control was sustained by her defiant life style. Other patients who are chronically suicidal may feel more helpless and hopeless. Yet even when people seemed locked into a position of dependency, their suicidality functions as an attempt at control: of significant others in the patient's life and/or caretakers in the mental health system.

The Interpersonal Context of Chronic Suicidality

Chronic suicidality does not exist in a vacuum. Even in patients who feel profoundly disconnected from other people, the wish to communicate and connect with the world remains intact. Thus, chronic suicidality can function to communicate distress to other people. Suicide attempts express despair in situations in which patients do not expect to be attended to in any other way. Sometimes the message is for a lover, and sometimes it is for a therapist. In either case, patients believe they have to turn up the volume to be heard. This way of looking at things is consistent with the ambivalent nature of many attempts. It is also consistent with the observation that completions in chronically suicidal patients tend to occur, not when patients are communicating their distress in dramatic ways but when they are hopeless, alone, and no longer actively engaged in treatment (Paris, 2003).

As pointed out by both Schwartz et al. (1974) and Maltsberger (1994a), suicidality can often be directed at other people who are seen as not likely to provide nurturance without the extreme pressure of suicidal threats and actions. This is the communicative function of suicidality (Paris, 2002a). The communication may be directed at a parent, a lover, or the therapist. The message is, "You are not taking proper care of me, and that makes me want to die." The implication is that the other person will be more supportive if suicide is an option. This may turn out to be the case for a while, although the effect is usually temporary.

Case Example

Lara was a university student who presented for therapy because of chronic self-cutting. Most of these episodes occurred when she perceived her boyfriend as neglectful or when he paid too much attention to other women.

This pattern had begun many years before, in relation to immigrant parents who were seen as preoccupied and unavailable. On one memorable occasion, Lara cut her wrists fairly deeply while her parents were having a party for relatives and friends. Blood dripped down the stairs from Lara's room, causing a dramatic uproar in the house. Although Lara certainly succeeded in getting her family's short-term attention, there was little long-term benefit for her. Instead, the parents packed her off to a psychiatrist to get her "fixed," that is, to behave properly. Lara remained defiant and her symptoms continued for several years. But when she moved away to attend a university, the target of the communication shifted to her boy-friend. One of the reasons Lara entered therapy was that every time the two of them socialized, she would become intensely jealous of other women, perceive him as rejecting her, sometimes ending the evening with an overdose.

In this example, although the intent of suicidal behavior was fairly obvious to others, the patient was not consciously aware of any motive to communicate suffering and would probably have resented such an interpretation. In her mind, suicidal actions were something almost outside herself that mysteriously took possession of her. It took much tactful therapeutic work to show the patient the connection between interpersonal situations to which she was sensitive and her behavioral responses.

Empathy and the Inner World

Although the experiences described in this chapter are unusual, they are not totally alien to common human experience. One can find very similar emotions expressed in popular culture, from songs to cinema.

Thus, the therapist's first task, as with any other type of inner feeling, is to empathize with feelings and to validate them. Although we want patients to change, this process cannot begin without a therapeutic alliance based on understanding and respect. Also, the process of empathic communication counters many of the mechanisms discussed previously. Empathy helps to relieve psychic pain, provides a sense of connection that combats emptiness, and confronts hopelessness by demonstrating that the patient in not completely alone.

The fact that the same scenarios can be enacted in the context of a therapist–patient relationship need not be a great cause for concern. One need not necessarily interpret these phenomena as transference; doing so is often counterproductive, leading patients to feel demeaned and dismissed for having negative feelings about therapists (Piper, Azim, Joyce, & McCallum, 1991). Instead, the clinician simply needs to proceed with the treatment plan, in the very face of despair and negation. This approach to therapy is described in chapters 8 and 9.

Finally, empathy for the inner world of the chronically suicidal patient implies respect for the need to retain death as an option. This kind of respect is implicit when we focus on conducting therapy and avoid repeated hospitalization in an attempt to "save" people. Respect can also be communicated directly: For example, when patients share thoughts about ending their life, the therapist might respond, "You need to know that if things don't get better, there is always a way out." This type of reflection on suicidal ideation also communicates the therapist's implicit belief that the situation is not hopeless and can indeed get better with time. As later chapters suggest, chronically suicidal patients should not be expected to give up the option of death until they develop enough life skills and commitments to make suicide unnecessary.

3

Suicidality in Childhood and Adolescence

~

Patients who are chronically suicidal often date their first attraction to death to their childhood and adolescence. And even those who have never been suicidal before adulthood usually describe having had psychological symptoms earlier in development.

Yet little formal research has been carried out on the childhood precursors of chronic suicidality. Lacking precise information, we can still draw on some general principles. Both genetic and environmental factors should influence the development of chronic suicidality. Biological vulnerability is associated with suicidal ideas and actions, although we do not know the precise nature of these predispositions. At the same time, adverse childhood experiences can increase the risk for developing suicidality later in life.

Adolescence appears to be a watershed in the development of suicidal ideas and actions. Suicidality is rare before puberty, whereas suicidal ideas and attempts often have an onset in the early adolescent years. We need to understand why this stage of development is associated with increased suicidality and determine which factors make these ideas and actions more likely.

The Developmental Origins of Suicidal Behavior

It has long been known that suicide completion runs in families; what is less well known is that suicidal ideas and attempts also have a genetic component (Joiner, Brown, & Wingate, 2005). Three large-scale twin studies (Fu et al., 2002; Glowinski et al., 2001; Statham et al., 1998) showed that the heritability of both suicidal ideas and attempts is in the range of 40% to 50%. This is similar to the level of genetic influence on most mental disorders (Jang, Livesley, Vernon, & Jackson, 1996).

Although the precise mechanisms by which the risk for suicidality is transmitted are unknown, it could be associated with personality traits, which are, in turn, influenced by genes. As chapter 4 suggests, personality profiles characterized by emotional instability and impulsivity often underlie suicidality. Moreover, variations in personality traits are associated with differences in neurotransmitter activity; much of the research on impulsivity and suicide has focused on abnormalities of the serotonin and dopamine systems (Joiner et al., 2005).

Yet trait predispositions need not lead to psychopathology. To understand how mental disorders develop, we should make use of a stress-diathesis model (Monroe & Simmons, 1991), a theory that has obtained strong empirical support in a wide range of disorders (Paris, 1999). The model states that temperamental vulnerability makes disorders more likely to develop but that psychopathology does not usually emerge without exposure to stressful circumstances. Thus, the crucial factors in the cause of mental disorders derive from *interactions* between genes and environment. These interactions are also dose-related: The higher the vulnerability, the less stress is needed to produce symptoms; when exposure to stress is greater, vulnerability may play less of a role.

The stress-diathesis model has been supported by some rather striking findings emerging from research in a large, longitudinally followed, birth cohort in New Zealand. These reports demonstrate that genetic variations associated with an increased risk for mental disorders *only* lead to depression (Caspi et al., 2003) or to antisocial behavior (Caspi et al., 2002), when environmental stressors are also present. The childhood origins of suicidality are, no doubt, equally complex and multidimensional.

One hypothesis about childhood precursors of suicidality is that those who are most vulnerable experience internal distress (which drives suicidal ideas) and also have a tendency toward impulsive action (which drives suicidal actions). This concept parallels a fundamental distinction in child psychiatry: between externalizing and internalizing symptoms (Achenbach & McConaughy, 1997). These same dimensions have been shown to underlie most forms of adult psychopathology (Krueger, 1999).

Internalizing and externalizing symptoms do not always develop in the same sequence. Many patients tell us that they were quietly miserable during childhood but only began to make suicide attempts after puberty. This scenario may correspond to the well-known observation that impulsivity (as demonstrated by antisocial behavior and substance use) increases dramatically at puberty (Brent et al., 2003). Other suicidal adult patients tell us that they were reasonably happy until age 13, after which "all hell broke loose." In this scenario, externalizing symptoms may have either been absent, or at least manageable, during childhood.

Suicidality and Adolescence

Research has documented that suicidality greatly increases in the adolescent years, when a much higher frequency of suicidal ideation and attempts becomes apparent (Brent, 2001). This change could be due to developmental factors, such as hormonal shifts that change brain function and influence responses to stressors, leading to the characteristic moodiness of the adolescent (Nelson, Leibenluft, McClure, & Pine, 2005). It might also be associated with the social challenges of the adolescent years, which may be particularly problematic in Western cultures.

There is evidence that both kinds of factors play a role. The importance of temperamental factors is supported by the observation that suicide attempts are more common in adolescent patients with a family history of suicide completion (Brent et al., 2002, 2003) as well as by the heritability of all forms of suicidality (Joiner et al., 2005). The importance of environmental factors is supported by studies showing that suicidal adolescents are exposed to higher levels of psychosocial stressors than adolescents who have never thought of suicide (Fergusson, Woodward, & Horwood, 2000). Again, most cases probably reflect interactions between genes and environment.

We are still left with the question of whether vulnerability to suicidality, overtly expressed during adolescence, has measurable effects before puberty. To address this issue, we need prospective data from cohorts of children followed into adolescence and adulthood. This type of research is unfortunately rather rare. We are left depending on retrospective studies, in which adults with suicidal symptoms are asked about their childhood.

In one such study (Rudd, Joiner, & Rumzek, 2004), the childhood diagnosis most associated with suicide attempts in adulthood was anxiety. This observation points to the importance of internalizing symptoms. However, anxiety is hardly specific as a precursor to suicidality, because it precedes many other symptoms. Moreover, making a suicide attempt involves action, not just inner suffering. This suggests that impulsivity should be a temperamental risk factor for adult suicidality. Since the seminal work of Robins (1966), we have known that children with conduct disorder tend to go on to develop antisocial symptoms as adults. Caspi, Moffitt, Newman, and Silva (1996) found that this outcome could be predicted prospectively by observing children as early as age 3. But whereas children with severe impulsivity would be expected to develop behavioral problems, lower levels of this trait might not produce any clinical symptoms in childhood. Then, when the adolescent individuates and receives less protection from the family, the impulsive pattern may emerge and become clinically apparent. This is what our research group found in a prospective study of children; the results showed that behavioral problems before puberty predicted suicidality in the adolescent and young adult years (Brezo et al., 2005).

A large-scale prospective study conducted by Fergusson et al. (2000), drawn from a longitudinal study of a birth cohort of 1,265 children born in New Zealand, also provided data supporting the importance of interactions between genes and environment. By the age of 21 years, 28.8% of the participants reported having thought about killing themselves and 7.5% reported having made a suicide attempt. The study found that temperamental and diagnostic measures predicted both forms of suicidality. Personality assessment showed that participants with suicidal ideas and/or actions had high levels of both neuroticism and novelty seeking—personality traits associated with, respectively, internalizing and externalizing symptoms. The most common psychiatric diagnoses associated with suicidal thoughts and actions were depression, anxiety disorders, substance use disorder, and conduct disorder (personality disorders were not assessed in this study). Finally, participants who reported suicidal ideas and behaviors also described a number of environmental risk factors: socioeconomic adversity, marital disruption, poor parent–child attachment, and exposure to sexual abuse. Adolescents with suicidality also described more current stressful life events.

These findings support the overall concept that suicidality emerges from a matrix of temperament, unique life experiences, and social circumstances. Suicidality is best explained by a stress-diathesis model, in which adolescents are predisposed to develop internalizing and externalizing symptoms, which emerge clinically when life stressors are present.

One might think that an early onset for suicidality, beginning in adolescence, might make chronicity more likely to develop. Joiner (2002) suggested that once suicidal behavior is initiated, it has some tendency to continue. In some cases, suicidality might develop "a life of its own" over the course of adolescence and youth. If suicidal ideas initially develop as an attempt to solve problems that are perceived as insoluble, patients could be tempted to return to the same "solution" at later points of crisis in their lives. However, as later chapters will show, chronic suicidality tends to remit with time, particularly when young adults develop sustaining life commitments such as work, relationships, and children. Thus, the development of suicidal ideas and actions in adolescence need not carry a grim prognosis. But we do not fully understand why some individuals become chronically suicidal whereas others do not,

Worrying About Adolescent Suicide

Suicidality in adolescence has been a source of great concern over the last few decades (Brent, 2001), both for clinicians and for the general public. As of 2003, the U.S. rate for suicide completions between the ages of 15 and 24 was 9.7 per 10,000. Worldwide rates (Pelkonen & Marttunen, 2003) for this age group are similar (American Association of Suicidology, 2006). Rates for males are about four times higher than for females.

Yet completed suicide remains rare before the age of 18. What is not generally understood is that all the statistics describing elevated rates in "adolescence" are heavily weighted with completions among 18- and 19-year-olds. The way these statistics are presented is confusing and misleading. Most suicides occur between 18 and 24, that is, in young adults, and not in adolescents between 15 and 17.

Nonetheless, an alarm was raised when research showed that between 1960 and 1980, young adults in America had a sharp increase in suicide completions (Murphy, & Wetzel, 1980; Sudak, Ford, & Rushforth, 1984). Although in previous decades, suicide rates always increased linearly with age (they are still highest in the elderly), one began to see a distinct "bump" in the young adult years. But these increases have leveled off in the last decade, (Grunebaum et al., 2004), and suicide rates in this age cohort remain at about the same level or even somewhat lower than they were 20 years ago (Gould, Greenberg, Velting, & Shaffer, 2003).

Most observers consider that rapid shifts in the prevalence of mental disorders over time (cohort effects) must be due to social change. However, the reasons for the recent decline in youth suicide are unclear, because social conditions are not obviously less stressful than they were 30 years ago. Interestingly, crime rates increased and then decreased dramatically in young people over the very same period (McDowall & Loftin, 2005). We also do not know whether recent reductions in suicide could be due to better treatment.

Even if suicide completion is uncommon before age 18, suicidal ideas and attempts in adolescents remain a serious clinical problem. And we do not know if suicidal behavior has shown the same decline as has been seen for completion. Although the crime rate is down, we do not have evidence for reductions in drug abuse and depression, conditions that increased in young people after World War II (Rutter & Smith, 1995) and which are both associated with suicide attempts (Brent, 2001).

Also, some evidence suggests that suicidal thoughts are also common (although not necessarily worrisome) in young people that mental health professionals do not see. Community samples show that as many as a third of adolescents and young adults report at least transient thoughts of ending their lives. In the large-scale National Comorbidity Study, Kessler, Berglund, Borges, et al. (2005) reported that the highest risk of initial suicide ideation and plans in the general population occurs in the late teens and early 20s. In our own study (Brezo et al., 2005), half of all young adults reported periods of suicidal ideation since adolescence.

Social Influences on Adolescent Suicidality

The increase in youth suicide that began after 1960 has now leveled off, but it still requires an explanation—particularly if it should turn out that suicidal ideas and attempts have not declined. I believe the evidence supports the concept that adolescent suicidality and the mental disorders associated with it constitute markers for social instability.

Epidemiological research has documented changes in prevalence of several mental disorders in adolescents and young adults between World War II and the 1990s. Specifically, substance abuse, antisocial behavior, and depression increased, both in North America and Europe (Millon, 1993; Paris, 1996; Rutter & Smith, 1995). These cohort effects paralleled documented increases in the prevalence of parasuicide among young adults (Bland, Dyck, Newman, & Orn, 1998), suicidal attempts during adolescence (Hawton, Fagg, Simkin, Bale, & Bond, 1997), and completed suicide in late adolescence and in the early 20s (Maris et al., 2000).

Although it is difficult to explain such complex phenomena in any simple way, there are reasons to believe that adolescence has become a more difficult time than it has ever had been in the past, due to social changes that make it more difficult for young people to find an identity and a social niche (Paris, 1996). This situation may be in part particular to modern (or modernizing) societies.

Cross-cultural studies suggest that the clinical problems of youth suicidality, depression, and substance abuse have been less frequent in other societies in the past but have been increasing with modernization (Paris, 1996, 2004d). For example, in India, suicidality among the young, once rare, has been increasing, as has the clinical presentation of BPD (Pinto, Dhavale, Nair, Patil, & Dewan, 2000).

The mechanism driving these changes relates to social structure and social cohesion, which can influence the prevalence of mental disorders. Social scientists have long made a distinction between traditional societies, which have high social cohesion, fixed social roles, and intergenerational continuity, and modern societies, which have lower social cohesion, fluid social roles, and less continuity between generations (Lerner, 1958). Through history, most social structures have been traditional. Today, although there are few societies left in the world that can still be described in this way, some are more traditional than others.

Disorders that vary from one society to another can be described as *socially sensitive* (Paris, 2004d). In particular, conditions characterized by impulsivity tend to be less prevalent in traditional societies, which tend to contain impulsive actions through their social structures. For example, Taiwan (Hwu, Yeh, & Change, 1989) and Japan (Sato & Takeichi, 1993) have a relatively low prevalence of substance abuse and antisocial personality among the young. The increasing prevalence of these disorders among young adults in modern societies might be explained if some individuals cannot easily cope with the expectations of contemporary society and are therefore at risk for mental disorders. These mechanisms would apply to a vulnerable minority, even if many (or most) young people are thriving under these conditions.

Socially sensitive disorders would also tend to have their onset in adolescence and youth, when the protective influence of families is reduced and when social demands for autonomous behavior increase. Although biological puberty is a universal, adolescence as a separate developmental stage is largely a social construction. Throughout most of history, young people assumed adult roles at this stage. Moreover, these roles were prescribed, fixed, and socially supported. This was a world in which most people lived in extended families, villages, and tribes and rarely traveled far. Those who did not fit into existing social structures had to leave and search for a niche elsewhere. The majority stayed put, doing the same work as their parents and their grandparents. Moreover, most people did not have to search very far to find intimate relationships. Marriage was arranged early in life, with partners chosen from the same or from neighboring communities.

Adolescence as a stage of life emerged in modern societies that expect the younger generation to postpone maturity in order to learn more complex skills. In traditional societies, adolescents were provided with jobs and entered into arranged marriages. In modern societies, young people have to find their own work and their own intimacy and develop a unique identity. Adolescents must give up the protection of assigned roles and networks and spend many years learning how to function as adults. Young people rarely do the same work as their parents and must learn necessary skills from strangers. Families may not even understand the nature of their children's careers. Instead of identifying with family and community values, young people are expected to find their own, often identifying more with peers who are better attuned to the demands of a changing world. Young people are also expected to find their own mates. Because there is no guarantee that this search will be successful, the young need to deal with the vicissitudes of mistaken choices, hurtful rejections, and intermittent loneliness.

In summary, we live in a highly individualistic society, where people have to find their own work and their own relationships. Although most people cope with these demands, vulnerable individuals have difficulty. Not everyone is cut out for the challenge of modern society, and adolescence is a stressful time for those who are vulnerable to stress.

Contemporary culture values individualism, and most of us would be thoroughly miserable in a traditional society. But temperamentally vulnerable people may not be in a position to cope with the expectations of the modern world. How can impulsive adolescents choose a career without structure and guidance? How can moody adolescents deal with the cruelty and rejection of peers without social supports? How can unusually shy adolescents find intimate relationships when they can barely introduce themselves to a stranger?

Which Adolescents Are at Risk?

Although suicidal ideation is common in adolescence, most teenagers never seriously consider suicide. Suicidal ideation probably reflects the moodiness associated with this stage. And when suicidal attempts occur, they are not necessarily life threatening.

Young people who eventually kill themselves have more serious psychopathology that those who only think about it or attempt it. In the San Diego study (Rich, Fowler, Fogarty, & Young, 1988), in which psychological autopsies were carried out on a large number of suicides among young adults, a combination of depression and substance abuse was much more strongly associated with completion than either factor alone. Lesage et al. (1994) found that almost one third of youth suicides can be diagnosed with BPD.

Some researchers have also obtained follow-up data on adolescent patients who present with depression, to see which individuals are likely to commit suicide later in life. In one report (Fombonne, Worstear, Cooper, Harrington, & Rutter, 2001), 245 adolescents admitted for depression to Maudsley Hospital in London, England, were followed 20 years later; 44% of these patients had made a subsequent suicide attempt. However, only 2.5% (i.e., 6 patients) had completed suicide (at a mean age of 24). Fergusson, Horwood, Ridder, and Beautrais (2005), following an adolescent cohort with suicidal ideas and ideation to age 25, found that participants were at risk for continued suicidality (as well as substance abuse) but did not report any completions. Thus, although serious depression in adolescence is a marker for many later difficulties, the ultimate suicide rate, even if elevated above that for the general population, is not high enough to make prediction a practical possibility.

Substance Abuse and Adolescent Suicidality

It is hardly surprising that many suicidal adolescents meet criteria for depression. What may not be so widely recognized is that adolescents who complete suicide, who make suicide attempts, or who have suicidal ideas are likely to have serious problems with substance abuse (Esposito-Smythers & Spirito, 2004). And when depression and substance abuse co-occur, the risk of completion is greater (Lewinsohn, Rohde, & Seeley, 1995).

Three psychological autopsy studies have demonstrated an association between substance abuse and completion in adolescents. Shaffer et al (1996) found that among 120 completers, 35% met criteria for either alcohol or drug abuse (six times the frequency of a community control group). Brent et al. (1993) reported similar findings in the United States in 67 completers, among whom 27% met criteria for substance abuse; in a Finnish cohort, Marttunen, Aro, Henriksson, and Lonnqvist (1991) found almost the same rate (26%).

Similar findings emerge from studies of adolescent attempters. Vajda and Steinbeck (2000) found about one third of adolescent attempters with either drug or alcohol abuse. Spirito, Valeri, Boergers, and Donaldson (2003), in a younger sample (mean age of 15), still noted a prevalence of 12%. Pfeffer et al. (1991), who prospectively followed a sample of 106 patients and 101 nonpatients, observed that among those who went on to make a suicide attempt, half had substance abuse and adolescents with substance abuse have a markedly increased rate of suicide attempts (Esposito-Smythers & Spirito, 2004).

Three mechanisms underlie these relationships. One is that drugs, especially alcohol, lower inhibitions and make suicide actions more likely to occur (Hufford, 2001). A second is that depressed or anxious young people use drugs for self-medication (Hufford, 2001). Finally, substance abuse is a marker for other forms of psychopathology; young people who are depressed or having serious problems with school, work, and relationships are more likely to have substance abuse, and abusing substances tends to make their problems even worse (Esposito-Smythers & Spirito, 2004; Hufford, 2001).

When depression and substance abuse are associated with suicidality in young people, another diagnostic construct, a severe personality disorder, helps explain their co-occurrence.

Borderline Personality Disorder in Adolescence

BPD usually begins in adolescence, and its symptoms involve suicidal behavior, including overdoses and self-mutilation. BPD has a mean age at first clinical presentation of 18, with a standard deviation of 6 years (Zanarini et al., 2001), although most patients only come to clinical attention after several years of symptoms. Unlike conduct disorder and antisocial personality, BPD is more prevalent in females (Paris, 2003), so that girls who eventually develop BPD may not have enough symptoms in childhood to merit clinical attention.

BPD is a common diagnosis among chronically depressed adolescents (Kasen et al., 2001; Lewinsohn et al., 1995; Pepper et al., 1995). One longitudinal community study (Crawford, Cohen, & Brook, 2001a, 2001b) found that early adolescents who presented with a combination of externalizing and internalizing symptoms were likely to develop Cluster B personality disorders (including BPD) as young adults.

Adolescents who present with suicidality may also have earned a diagnosis of conduct disorder at some point. However, conduct symptoms present somewhat differently in females (Moffit, Caspi, Rutter, & Silva, 2001), that is, with less criminality, and with more promiscuity and runaway behavior. Thus, although conduct disorder in boys is a precursor of antisocial personality, in adolescent girls conduct disorders can be a precursor for a variety of adult personality disorders, including BPD (Rey, Singh, Morris-Yates, & Andrews, 1997). Personality disorders are also more likely to develop when conduct disorder is accompanied by depression, and this pattern is seen more often in females (Crawford et al., 2001a).

There is nothing *normal* about personality disorder symptoms at this point of development. One sometimes hears that all adolescents can be "a little borderline" or that adolescent turmoil is just a stage. No one denies that moodiness and some degree of experimentation are common in this age group. But most teenagers never become seriously troubled or rebellious. As shown in a classical large-scale study of normal adolescents by Offer and Offer (1975), the vast majority do not experience adolescent turmoil but focus their life on school and friendship, and most describe a healthy identification with their parents.

Moreover, failing to recognize personality disorders in adolescence on the grounds that adolescents are too young to make such diagnoses can be a mistake, particularly if pathology is seen as less severe (Kernberg, Weiner, & Bardenstein, 2000). In fact, absolutely typical cases of BPD can be observed during adolescence (Paris, 2005b).

Consider the following clinical example.

Ellen was a 16-year-old high school student who asked for treatment after the death by suicide of her best friend (who had suggested a suicide pact for the two of them). The friends had often talked about suicide, and both had been wrist slashers over several years. Ellen, who decided to live, had nonetheless retreated into an intense fantasy life, hearing the voices of characters in this world asking her to join them through death.

Ellen had a very traumatic life history. At age 16, she was living with her older sister, after running away first from her alcoholic mother and then from a father who incestuously abused her. Ellen had made a first suicide attempt at age 10, leaping from a first story balcony after a quarrel with her mother. This episode had led to Ellen's first clinical presentation.

Ellen was treated with weekly outpatient psychotherapy and attended regularly until age 18. Despite a stormy course, with two brief hospitalizations, Ellen gradually recovered, going on to hold a job and raise a family in adulthood. However, Ellen continued to have periods of distress and fragility and returned to her therapist for several more courses of treatment over the next 20 years.

One could hardly describe a more prototypical case, because all the features associated with BPD are present. The atypical aspect was an early and sustained recovery. Actually, we do not know whether adolescent-onset cases have a better or a worse prognosis that those that present later, although remissions are common in the young adult years (Gunderson et al., 2003; Zanarinini, Frankenburg, Hennen, & Silk, 2003).

Suicidality in Childhood

Suicide completions are very rare before puberty. That is the good news. The bad news comes in two ways. The first is that children can think about suicide and occasionally attempt it. The second is that childhood suicidality can continue into adulthood.

Again, statistics on the relationships between age and completed suicide are reported in a confusing way. Rates are recorded by age cohort, but the cohorts are divided into age groups of 5 to 14, 15 to 24, 25 to 34, and so on. Unfortunately, these cutoff points do not necessarily correspond to meaningful divisions between developmental stages such as childhood, adolescence, and young adulthood. (Notably, adolescence is split down the middle and combined with early adulthood.)

Nonetheless, these statistics show that suicide before 14 is rare: The 2003 rate for completed suicide in the United States in children between ages 5 and 14 was 0.6 per 100,000 (American Association of Suicidiology, 2006). This low level of completion before puberty is similar in many other countries (Pelkonen & Marttunen, 2003).

Although children rarely complete suicide, they can consider it and occasionally attempt it. Unfortunately, there has been some confusion in the literature in that suicidality is described as occurring in "children" (Pfeffer, 2000), which obscures the fact that almost all studies concern adolescents. (Prepubertal children with suicidal ideas have not been subject of much research.) Thus, although everyone under 18 is *legally* a child, we should not get the impression that suicide in children is more frequent than it really is.

Although completions and attempts are rare, we do not know how frequent suicidal thoughts or attempts are prior to puberty. One confounding factor is that the meaning of suicidality can be different in prepubertal children than it is later in life, because the concept of death as an irreversible event has not yet developed (Pfeffer, 2000).

The following clinical example illustrates these issues:

Magda was an 8-year-old girl living in a foster home because her substance-abusing parents were unable to look after her. She came to clinical attention because of frequent tantrums associated with threats of suicide. Other serious problems included poor performance at school and quasi-hallucinatory experiences in which she heard the voice of her brother talking to her (he was in another foster home, and she saw him rarely).

Magda was clinically depressed and probably talked about suicide out of a sense of desperation and abandonment. She may also have heard about this possibility, as her mother had been hospitalized at one point for a suicide attempt. Despite a history of poor attachment, Magda's fantasy was that her family would one day be reunited. For her, suicidal ideas were a communication of distress, and she never made an attempt.

Suicidality in High-Risk Children

In severely disturbed children, suicidal ideas form part of a larger pattern of psychopathology. Thus, when distress is high, stressful events are responded to with impulsive actions or threats of action.

Our own research team has studied children with this pattern. This clinical population has been described as suffering from "borderline pathology of childhood" (Guzder, Paris, Zelkowitz, & Feldman, 1999; Guzder, Paris, Zelkowitz, & Marchessault, 1999; Paris, 2000). The use of this term reflects a resemblance between symptoms seen in these children and the clinical picture of adult BPD. Like adult BPD patients, these children suffer from affective instability and a wide range of impulsivity. These are children who frequently threaten to kill themselves, and we found that suicidality was crucial in discriminating "borderline" cases from a comparison group of other children attending the same day treatment center (Paris, 2000). But unlike adults with personality disorders, children who were suicidal almost always made threats, not actions.

The following clinical example gives the flavor of these patients:

Boris was a 9-year-old boy who had been referred for day treatment at a children's hospital. There had been a series of incidents in which Boris had become aggressive and uncontrollable, disrupting his class, and threatening to kill himself when sent to the principal. Additional symptoms included mood swings from sadness to anger as well as quasi-psychotic experiences (such as seeing ghosts in his house).

Boris was being raised entirely by his mother; his father, who had a criminal history, had long since been out of the picture. He received inconsistent discipline at home and had few outside friends. Boris had shown difficulties of this kind from an early age but presented clinically when he was unable to be managed in a school setting.

Our group began studying this population in the hope of determining the childhood precursors of personality disorders. However, it must be emphasized that borderline pathology of childhood is not a precursor of any specific personality disorder. First, as is true of all child psychiatry cohorts, most of the patients were boys. BPD in adult clinical populations is a largely female condition that males less frequently develop, even in community samples (Torgersen, Kringlen, & Cramer, 2001). Second, a long-term follow-up study of a similar cohort of children (Lofgren, Bemporad, King, Lindem, & O'Driscoll, 1991) showed that by age 18, these patients (also mostly boys) tended to develop personality disorders, but not BPD. Our own follow-up study (Zelkowitz, Paris, Guzder, Feldman, & Rosval, 2006, submitted) elicited similar findings. Thus this clinical picture may not help in predicting whether patients who are suicidal in childhood become suicidal adults.

My research group has also analyzed longitudinal prospective data on a large sample of children from the community to identify predictors of suicidality in young adulthood (Brezo et al., 2005; Brezo et al., in press). Again, our hypothesis was that chronic suicidality reflects a combination of externalizing and internalizing symptoms, Externalizing symptoms are found in children with conduct disorder, oppositional defiant disorder, and other conditions characterized by impulsive behavior patterns. Internalizing symptoms are associated with depression and anxiety. A combination of the two is seen in adults with BPD (Paris, 2003; Siever & Davis, 1991).

We made use of a cohort studied at the University of Montreal, where the lead researcher, Richard Tremblay, has been following 2,000 normal children from age 7 to young adulthood (Coté, Tremblay, Nagin, Zoccolillo, & Vitaro, 2002). At age 21 to 24, we assessed suicidal ideation, as well as the presence of suicide attempts, in the cohort. We also examined whether these patterns could be predicted by patterns of behavior during childhood that had been rated yearly by their teachers. The findings (Brezo et al., 2005) demonstrated a link between childhood aggression and adult suicidality. Unfortunately, since the study had originally been designed to predict antisocial behavior, not suicide, we had very little baseline data on childhood depression and anxiety.

Another way to study the relationship between childhood symptoms and adult suicidality is to follow a high-risk group of children. This approach would test more precisely the hypothesis that externalizing and internalizing symptoms in childhood predict suicidality later in life. However, the practicality of such a procedure is limited by the fact that many children who go on to become suicidal in adolescence and adulthood report no contact with the mental health system during childhood. Thus, high-risk studies of children might not pick up individuals who only show the effects of risk later in development. Moreover, most chronically suicidal patients in adulthood are women, and girls are vastly outnumbered by boys in child clinics. As has long been known, boys are much more likely to present with overt behavioral problems that lead them to be assessed and treated, whereas girls are more compliant, both at school and at home, at least until they reach adolescence.

Zanarini et al. (2001), in a study of (mainly female) patients with BPD, confirmed what many clinicians have observed: Patients who are chronically suicidal in adulthood may describe having had the same ideas early in life, even if they never sought treatment for them. In some cases, patients state that they often thought about suicide as children but never told anyone. They describe themselves as having been somewhat unhappy during childhood but as having felt significantly worse after puberty. This finding also supports the hypothesis that children who later become chronically suicidal have more internalizing symptoms before adolescence but only develop clinically significant presentations associated with an increase in externalizing symptoms during adolescence.

High-risk samples exposed to psychosocial adversities should also be studied to determine their vulnerability to suicidality, but such research is rare. One study followed children subjected to well-documented abuse and neglect over a 20-year span (Horwitz, Widom, McLaughlin, & White, 2001), and the results did show that these children are more likely to develop mental disorders. However, this research did not examine whether suicidality is an outcome of childhood maltreatment, as has been suggested by retrospective studies (Yen et al., 2004).

Thus, we are left with many unanswered questions about the childhood origins of chronic suicidality. Although prospective studies are needed to address the issues, that kind of research is rare and expensive. Moreover, studies of normal samples may not find enough adults with serious symptoms. For example, a large-scale study of children in the Albany–Saratoga area led by Pat Cohen of Columbia University attempted to assess the childhood precursors of personality disorders (Johnson et al., 1999a). However, the researchers could not find more than a handful of diagnosable cases. As a result, the analyses could only report associations with the total number of personality disorder symptoms. What they were able to show was that these symptoms were associated with suicidality (Johnson, Cohen, Skodol, et al., 1999) and that abuse and neglect during childhood made suicidality in young adulthood more likely (Brown, Cohen, Johnson, & Smailes, 1999). Despite their limitations, the findings of prospective studies of children point to a link between personality, adversity, and an outcome of suicidality.

Reports of Childhood Experiences in Chronically Suicidal Adults

Although prospective studies are ideal, much of the research in the literature has taken a more direct approach, by asking chronically suicidal patients to describe what their childhood was like. There have been a large number of studies of this kind on patients with BPD (see review in Zanarini, 2000). But there is a problem with retrospective methods. Do adults remember their childhood accurately, or are they influenced by their current state? Most of the data are based on reports from adult patients in clinical samples who are asked to remember their childhood while in a serious state of dysphoria. Thus, all findings are inevitably colored by recall bias, that is, the tendency to see the past in the light of the present (Maughan & Rutter, 1997). This means that the sicker the patient is as an adult, the worse tends to be his or her view of childhood experiences. Conversely, when patients improve, they tend to find more good things to say about their past.

With this caveat in mind, it is still useful to examine the large literature on the recollections of childhood experience in patients with BPD, a diagnosis strongly associated with chronic suicidality (see reviews in Paris, 1994; Paris, 2003; and Zanarini, 2000). In our own work (Paris, Zweig-Frank, & Guzder, 1994), about two thirds of patients reported adverse events during childhood: About one third described major adversities, such as consistent child abuse (sexual and physical), emotional or physical neglect, and serious family dysfunction, whereas another third reported less serious problems (such as single incidents of abuse). Even so, another third of patients described a relatively normal childhood, although they developed serious psychopathology during adolescence.

These findings raise two questions. First, to what extent are traumatic experiences responsible for suicidality in adolescence and adulthood? Correlational data cannot address that issue. Some patients become suicidal without undergoing any major traumatic experiences. Moreover, most children exposed to adverse experiences never become suicidal. These discrepancies suggest that other risk factors must be involved (see review in Paris, 2000). The most likely explanation is that children who later become suicidal adults also have temperamental vulnerabilities and that these predispositions interact with, and amplify, the effects of life adversities (Paris, 2003).

Second, how can we take into account recall bias affecting retrospective reports? The most conservative view, backed up by some research evidence (Robins, Schoenberg, & Holmes, 1985), is that patients give reliable reports about the facts of their life stories but are not so reliable when one asks about "softer" data such as family atmosphere. For example, in another study, when we asked a group of older patients who had recovered from BPD about their early experiences (Zweig-Frank & Paris, 2002), they still reported a large number of traumatic events during childhood but took a much more sanguine view of their relationships with their parents, contrary to what is reported by patients with active symptomatology.

In summary, although childhood trauma and adversity play some role in the development of chronic suicidality, there is no simple causal relationship. Some suicidal patients have had an untroubled childhood. Most people with a troubled childhood manage to develop normally in adulthood and never become suicidal (Paris, 2000b).

Clinical Implications

We know too little about the roots of suicidality to come to firm conclusions about its roots in childhood. The pathways to suicidal ideas or attempts, not to speak of chronic suicidality, are complex, and researchers need decades to understand them. As clinicians, we are often too quick to explain adult symptoms by childhood adversity. The mistake involves failing to take into account the high base rate in the community of trauma, neglect, and dysfunctional families. Most children are resilient enough to survive such stressors and go on to a reasonably productive adult life. This is why biological vulnerability is crucial; it explains why the majority survive stress, whereas a minority do not. Therapists need to keep this point in mind, so as to avoid playing a "blame game" with patients.

This being said, we know too little about vulnerability to apply these concepts directly to the clinical situation. Although most work with suicidal patients involves psychotherapy, we do not have data about environmental risks in childhood to apply them in practice to our patients. Given the lack of clear causal links between risk and outcome, this book recommends that therapists not spend too much time on "working through" childhood traumas but concentrate on finding ways to improve current life situations.

Finally, the onset of suicidal symptoms in adolescence has led many to conclude that we should devote more effort to treating this population. Although I do not disagree in principle with this idea, enthusiasm is not enough. Large-scale programs designed for early intervention in suicidal adolescents should not be undertaken until we have a strong evidence base showing that such treatments are consistently effective.

4

Chronic Suicidality and Personality Disorders

~

Patients who are chronically suicidal may not see their thoughts and behaviors as alien. In fact, suicidality has become an essential part of their sense of self. This can only be explained by understanding chronic suicidality as a feature of a personality disorder. Once we see chronic suicidality in this way, it is more clearly distinct from the acute suicidality associated with mood disorders. Consistent with the early onset and chronicity of suicidality, personality disorders begin early in life and exert broad effects on functioning over many years.

The overall definition of a personality disorder in the *Diagnostic and Statistical Manual of Mental Disorders* (4th ed., text rev. [*DSM–IV–TR*]; American Psychiatric Association, 2000) describes long-term dysfunction in a variety of domains, including the way people think, the way they feel, and the way they behave. Patients with these disorders typically have long-term difficulties with work and intimate relationships. In the absence of basic life satisfactions, people are more likely to consider suicide.

The diagnosis of BPD is particularly associated with chronic suicidality. Although not all chronically suicidal patients have BPD, a large percentage of patients with BPD are chronically suicidal. A day in and day out obsession with suicide over many years in a nonpsychotic patient immediately suggests this diagnosis. BPD is a disorder that begins in adolescence and produces a wide range of problems, including unstable mood, impulsive behavior, and highly unstable interpersonal relationships. Some of these patients also hear voices telling them to kill themselves, but they do not delusionally elaborate these experiences.

Chronic suicidality is one of the defining features of BPD. This condition is marked by mood instability, widespread impulsivity, unstable relationships, and micropsychotic phenomena (Paris, 2005d). These features make suicidal thoughts and behaviors more likely, and chronic suicidality is listed as one of the criteria for diagnosing BPD in *DSM–IV–TR*. Moreover, this is the feature that makes borderline patients so difficult to manage.

To illustrate this point, let us return to the case example presented in the Introduction.

Colleen was a 25-year-old nurse who presented with chronic suicidality and who seriously considered killing herself for many years. In addition, Colleen's mood was highly unstable, shifting in response to the events of the day. She could wake up depressed and anxious but later on go into a rage in response to any frustration, usually a slight or a rejection. Colleen also suffered from a wide range of impulsive behaviors, including excessive use of marijuana, sexual promiscuity, and binge eating. Her relationships were highly unstable and her choices dubious. In fact, Colleen had a repetitive pattern of involvement with criminals and on several occasions had helped boyfriends hide from the police. Finally, although Colleen did not initially describe any psychotic symptoms, she developed a dramatic micropsychotic episode, with hallucinations and delusions lasting several days, following her decision to recontact an alcoholic father who had abandoned her as a child. This incident occurred during the course of therapy and led to a brief hospitalization.

This case is a typical example of the clinical picture associated with borderline personality. Much of the research on chronic suicidality has been conducted on patients meeting criteria for this disorder. Of course, not every patient who is chronically suicidal meets criteria for BPD, and some BPD patients are only intermittently suicidal. Nonetheless, the link is quite strong. This chapter therefore examines personality disorder research that illuminates the phenomenon of chronic suicidality.

Does Depression Account for Chronic Suicidality?

Before reviewing research on personality disorders, let us consider to what extent chronic suicidality can be accounted for by depressed mood. I suggest that this way of understanding patients is misleading.

When suicidality is associated with depression, it usually has a time-limited course. Typically, patients suffer from an illness that dramatically changes their normal state of mind. When depression is not too severe, patients openly recognize that they are "not themselves." When patients recover, they may feel ashamed of having even considered ending their lives. Moreover, acute suicidal ideas can usually be reduced by rapidly effective treatment. Thus, suicidality is in no way intrinsic to the depressed person's sense of self. Although mood disorders can also be chronic, even in these cases, suicidality is more episodic than continuous.

Patients with suicidal ideas generally acknowledge that they are suffering from depression. Therapists may see the problem in the same way. Yet depression itself is a surprisingly slippery concept. In the mental health field, we tend to take the reality of diagnoses for granted—particularly major depression. Clinicians who apply this category to patients on a daily basis see it much like a medical disease. And physicians often consider major depression real enough to prescribe antidepressants to almost anyone who meets *DSM* criteria for the disorder.

Actually, the construct of major depression is little but a shorthand way of describing a common clinical presentation. Depression defines a state of mind in which lowered mood causes significant functional impairment. Yet it is not a disease. There are many ways to be depressed, and this makes the term *depression* fuzzy and heterogeneous.

Depressed mood, as a symptom, is seen in many different clinical diagnoses. What *DSM–IV–TR* (American Psychiatric Association, 2000) calls major depression requires the presence of only five out of eight symptoms, each of which describes one of the common psychological or physical consequences of lowered mood. As is the case for most *DSM* categories, the cutoff point for making this diagnosis is quite arbitrary. No one has ever shown that patients meeting five criteria are different from those who have only four (or six).

The other requirement listed in *DSM–IV–TR* is that a mood disturbance must be present for at least 2 weeks. This is a very short time frame. Using this duration, we may fail to distinguish between depressive disease and normal unhappiness. Many people who suffer a loss have symptoms for 2 weeks or more and recover without treatment. This definition is much too broad to separate normality and pathology. Like the number of symptoms, a cutoff of 2 weeks is arbitrary and has the effect of putting too many people with different problems in the same category. We also do not know whether patients who recover in a few weeks have the same illness as those who take months to get better.

Another result of the rather lax definition is that epidemiologists have reported high lifetime prevalence for this diagnosis in the community. Major depression has been estimated to affect between 10% and 20% of the population over a lifetime (Kessler, Berglund, Borges, Nock, & Wang, 2005; Weissman, Bland, Canino, & Faravelli, 1996). Depression has sometimes been called "the common cold of psychiatry." And like a common cold, it is ubiquitous but can arise from a variety of causes.

The broad concept of depression in *DSM* describes the common disturbances of mood we all experience, as opposed to the catastrophic effects of a melancholic or a psychotic depression. The validity of classifying relatively normal reactions along with life-threatening illness is questionable (Parker, 2005).

The category of major depression is also heterogeneous: It includes people who are sad after suffering a loss as well as people who suffer from depression in its most severe forms. Moreover, depression is a syndrome that overlaps with many other diagnoses, including anxiety disorders, eating disorders, and substance abuse (Horwitz, 2002). This phenomenon has been called *comorbidity,* but that term is misleading. People who meet criteria for more than one *DSM* diagnosis do not necessarily have more than one disease; comorbidity is actually an artifact of a diagnostic system that encourages multiple diagnoses. Nonetheless, this overlap between categories helps account for the fact that treatment with antidepressants is by no means specific to depression; these agents are effective for a very wide range of psychological symptoms (Healy, 1997).

In current clinical practice, the concept of depression has become *reified.* We see major depression as a "real" entity rather than a label having some practical use for clinical communication. Some writers (e.g., Akiskal, Chen, & Davis, 1985) even seem to believe that depression is *more* real than other diagnoses and dismiss more complex constructs such as personality disorder. Their concept is that the clinical features of personality disorders can entirely be accounted for by changes in mood, either by depression itself (Akiskal, et al., 1985) or by atypical forms of bipolar disorder (Akiskal, 2002). The problem with this approach is that it fails to account for the difference between mood instability in response to environmental changes and abnormally lowered (or elevated) mood that does not respond to changes in the environment (Gunderson & Phillips, 1991; Paris, 2004a).

It is important to distinguish between depressions that are, or are not, associated with personality disorders. About half of all patients with major depression are comorbid for at least one Axis II disorder (Hirschfeld, 1999; Mulder, 2002; Mulder, Joyce, & Luty, 2003). And when depression is chronic, the comorbidity for personality disorder is still higher (Pepper et al., 1995).

Another argument for the concept that mood trumps personality is that the current diagnostic classification of personality disorders has serious conceptual problems. For example, there is great overlap between, and heterogeneity within, Axis II categories. There are indeed serious concerns about the validity of the Axis II categories in the *DSM* system (Livesley, 2003). Yet these problems are probably no greater than those involved in a diagnosis of mood disorder itself.

The *DSM* system is really a rough and ready way of organizing the chaotic world of mental illness. Psychiatric diagnoses are nothing but convenient ways of summarizing information for clinical practice. At present, the categories in *DSM–IV–TR* are, almost without exception, syndromes, not diseases. Unlike diagnoses in medicine, they are not rooted in an understanding of anatomy, physiology, and biochemistry. And even from a purely psychological point of view, *DSM* diagnoses do not "cut nature at its joints." Thus, psychiatric diagnoses only describe symptoms that cluster together but may or may not derive from common pathological processes. We do not know enough about these processes to consider mental disorders in the same light as cancer or heart disease.

Valid disease entities in medicine have a specific set of causes and respond in a predictable way to therapy. Some mood disorders are like medical diseases: Classical bipolar illness and recurrent severe unipolar depression probably represent discrete disease processes, and each of these conditions has a fairly specific response to treatment. But for most patients meeting criteria for major depression, we can identify neither a specific cause nor a specific treatment.

In fact, a diagnosis of major depression is not a particularly good guide to treatment response. Despite all the hype about antidepressants, these agents only produce full remission in about half the cases of major depression for which they are normally prescribed (McIntyre & O'Donovan, 2004). Although there are several reasons for this variation in response to drugs, one is that many patients who meet criteria for depression also suffer from personality disorders. (So many patients who are depressed also have some form of personality disorder that researchers find that pure cases of depression are hard to find.)

For this reason, antidepressants are less likely to be effective when depression is chronic and associated with a personality disorder, and such cases may also fail to respond to psychotherapy (Shea et al., 1990). Although some patients with Axis II diagnoses respond to antidepressants (Mulder et al., 2003), those with more severe disorders, such as BPD, are likely to respond partially or not at all (Paris, 2005d; see chap. 7, this volume). A recent meta-analysis (Newton-Howes, Tryer, & Johnson, 2006) confirmed that the treatment of depression is much less successful in the presence of a personality disorder.

The literature has described a phenomenon of *treatment-resistant depression* (Trivedi & Kleiber, 2001). But we need to ask, resistant to what kind of treatment? This term is generally used to refer to patients who respond poorly to medication. Yet a fair number of depressed patients do not respond to any drug. This observation reflects the syndromal nature of major depression.

Thus, in chronically suicidal patients, we should not see depression as an alien force that takes over the mind but rather as a result of the way a patient's mind is structured. And that is exactly what we mean by *personality*. This is a more complex way of looking at patients that explains much more about suicidality.

The Origins of Personality

Personality is a crucial concept in psychology. It refers to consistent patterns of emotion, thought, behavior, and relationships that characterize individuals. Personality trait profiles explain why different people respond very differently to the same situations in life. For example, when stressed, an introverted person tends to withdraw, whereas an extroverted person tends to seek stimulation or "act out."

Personality traits are often called *dimensions* because they can be measured quantitatively as continuous variables (i.e., given a score). In research, the dimensions of personality have usually been identified through factor analysis of questionnaire data in normal populations. It is generally assumed that personality disorders are extreme versions of these normal traits.

A large body of research has examined the sources of individual variation in personality. These traits reflect both temperament and experience. Behavior genetics is a method that allows us to sort out the effects of heredity and environment. The most frequent procedure is to compare the similarity of traits in monozygotic versus dizygotic twins. Thus, when concordance (i.e., similarity) for any trait dimension is greater in identical than it is in fraternal twins, it must be heritable. These studies have consistently shown that personality trait dimensions have a moderately large genetic component, usually accounting for about 40% of the variance between individuals (Livesley, 2003; Plomin, DeFries, McClearn, & Rutter, 2000).

Behavior genetics has also shed light on the environmental factors affecting personality. In twin studies, one can separate the effects of genetic vulnerability, of environmental factors derived from being brought up in a specific family, and of environmental factors that are not related to having the same family. Thus, to the extent that children brought up in a family are similar on any trait, one can describe the effect of a *shared environment*. To the extent that children brought up in the same family are dissimilar, the environmental contribution must be unique to the individual and is therefore described as *unshared*. Surprisingly, research has consistently shown that shared environment contributes little or nothing to personality and that its environmental component is almost entirely unshared. Thus, siblings are likely to have completely different personality profiles and are no more similar to each other in this way than perfect strangers.

These findings present a serious challenge to classical theories in child development and in psychoanalysis (Paris, 2000). The large effect of unshared environment can be explained in a number of ways. One is that different children can receive different parenting. However, the causes of differential treatment in families may also lie in personality. Reiss, Hetherington, & Plomin, (2000), in a large-scale study of adolescent development, found that parenting with different siblings in the same family was largely driven by temperament. In other words, parents react to their children as a response to unique temperamental qualities.

Another part of the explanation may be that environment is not something that "just happens" to a child. Children often select their own environments, based on their personality trait profiles (Scarr & McCartney, 1983). This has been called an "evocative" gene–environment correlation. (The other types of correlation are "passive," in which parental treatment reflects genes in common with children, and "active," in which parents respond in accordance with children's temperamental qualities.)

But there is still another explanation of the unshared environment, one that presents the greatest challenge to classical ideas in child development. It comes from the possibility that environmental influences from outside the family may be more important than influences inside the family (Harris, 1998). In this view, peer groups and social networks might be as important in shaping personality as parents themselves. Whether or not this is so, it seems clear that the influence of parents has been somewhat exaggerated. Parents themselves often know this, after trying unsuccessfully to mold their children in one direction or another. And if they have two children, they discover that the same parenting can produce entirely different results.

Classifying Personality Traits

Trait psychologists classify personality dimensions in order to measure them. There are several schema used to assess and score personality traits, but the most widely studied (and the most influential) is the Five-Factor Model (FFM; Costa & Widiger, 2002). The FFM describes five broad trait dimensions in personality. The first is Extraversion, describing a need for social interaction and stimulation (in contrast to introversion, in which individuals prefer solitary activities). The second dimension is Neuroticism, which describes how easily people get upset or anxious. The other three factors are Conscientiousness, Agreeableness, and Openness to Experience. Four of these five factors (Extraversion, Neuroticism, Conscientiousness, and Agreeableness) more or less parallel those identified by other dimensional schema (Cloninger, Svrakic, & Pryzbeck, 1993; Livesley, Jang, & Vernon, 1998).

The most important personality dimension for clinical work is Neuroticism. This trait is associated with a predisposition to mood and anxiety disorders (Costa & Widiger, 2002). (At the other extreme, psychopaths are unusually low in neuroticism.) It may not matter quite as much whether one is an extravert or an introvert, because either can work for the individual under the right circumstances. But if one is high in Neuroticism, symptoms are more likely to develop when stressful circumstances occur, particularly symptoms associated with internalizing disorders that present as disturbances of mood and anxiety (Kahn, Jacobson, Gardner, & Kendler, 2005).

Although Openness is not usually related to psychopathology, two other dimensions in the FFM are clinically important. Low levels of Conscientiousness are associated with impulsivity, whereas high levels are more associated with compulsivity. People who are low on Agreeableness are more likely to develop antisocial or narcissistic traits, particularly if they are also impulsive. People who are high on Agreeableness may be easy to get along with, but they run the risk of being insufficiently assertive with other people.

These five broad dimensions of personality interact to create profiles for each individual that define vulnerability to psychopathology, both on Axis I and Axis II. There is a strong relationship between trait profiles and the type of Axis I disorder that people develop (Krueger, 1999). For example, Trull and Sher (1994) found that many Axis I disorders are associated with a very similar profile: Extraversion, high Neuroticism, high Openness, low Conscientiousness, and low Agreeableness.

Personality Dimensions and Personality Disorders

Personality trait profiles determine the type of personality disorder that any individual can develop. Thus, people will not develop antisocial personality or BPD unless they are already low in Conscientiousness, and people will not develop avoidant or compulsive personality disorder unless they are already low in Extraversion.

It should not be surprising to see that personality disorders tend to fall into groups that reflect these underlying trait dimensions. Thus, Cluster B disorders (antisocial, borderline, histrionic, and narcissistic), as described on Axis II of *DSM–IV–TR* (American Psychiatric Association, 2000), reflect high levels of Extraversion and low levels of Conscientiousness (i.e., high levels of impulsivity). In Cluster C disorders (avoidant, dependent, compulsive), the most prominent feature is a high level of neuroticism leading to social and interpersonal anxiety. Borderline personality is a more complex condition that seems to reflect both high Neuroticism (affective instability) and Impulsivity (Siever & Davis, 1991). Finally, Cluster A disorders (schizoid, schizotypal, and paranoid) lie in a broadly defined "schizophrenic spectrum" (Paris, 2003).

Similarly, personality disorders also reflect broader dimensions of psychopathology that cut across Axis I and Axis II in the *DSM* system (Krueger, 1999). Thus, Cluster B disorders fall within the externalizing dimension, whereas Cluster C disorders fall within an internalizing dimension (Paris, 2003). Cluster A, related to cognitive function, is not accounted for by the schema.

Clinicians should also be aware that many cases of personality disorder do not fall into the categories (or the clusters) described in the Axis II system. The overall definition in *DSM–IV–TR* (American Psychiatric Association, 2000) indicates that one can diagnose patients with a disorder if (a) functioning is significantly affected by maladaptive personality traits, and (b) dysfunction begins early in life and continues over many years. Patients who meet these criteria but who do not fall in any of the Axis II categories suffer as much dysfunction as patients who do fall within these categories (Johnson et al., 2005). In a recent large-scale study of psychiatric outpatients (Zimmerman et al., 2005), 31% of all patients met criteria for one of the Axis II categories, and when personality disorders "not otherwise specified" (i.e., those meeting overall but not specific criteria) are added, the prevalence goes up to 45%. Finally, personality disorders, as defined by Axis II of the *DSM* system, are very common in the community, with an overall prevalence of at least 10% (Grant et al., 2004; Samuels et al., 2002; Torgersen et al., 2001).

Clearly, therapists who do avoid diagnosing personality disorders do so at their own risk. Understanding the more chronic aspects of patients' psychopathology may be crucial for management.

Personality and Psychotherapy

Therapists have long been interested in understanding the personality structure of their patients. The psychodynamic tradition always promoted this point of view. Psychoanalysts saw symptoms as surface phenomena that could shift over time, whereas personality was viewed as deep and lasting. Forty years ago, it was virtually a truism that depression and anxiety emerge from underlying personality conflicts.

Today, these ideas have fallen out of favor. In the last few decades, we have seen a dramatic decline in the influence of psychoanalytic ideas within psychology and psychiatry (Paris, 2005a). The psychodynamic approach has either been drastically modified for practical application in therapy or replaced by cognitive models and pharmacological approaches, both of which tend to focus more on symptoms and less on personality.

At the same time, diagnosis has become a central focus for clinicians, particularly since the development of a series of *DSM* manuals culminating in the current edition, *DSM–IV–TR* (American Psychiatric Association, 2000). The prominence of the *DSM* system sometimes leads clinicians to assume that diagnosis is a guide to treatment. Actually, the manual has nothing to say about therapy. *DSM* only provides a common language to describe psychopathology. In any case, most treatment methods target symptoms, not diagnoses.

None of this has prevented clinicians from believing that any patient meeting criteria for major depression should receive an antidepressant. Many (if not most) patients that therapists see today are on medication. And it is not only psychiatrists who believe in the sovereign power of psychopharmacology. Psychologists and other nonmedical therapists may insist that their patients be evaluated for, and receive, drug treatment. If you cannot prescribe yourself, you may be even more susceptible to the pharmacological mystique.

Of course, many drugs have established effectiveness for mental disorders. There can be no doubt that schizophrenic patients improve on neuroleptics and that bipolar patients stabilize on lithium. But the situation is less clear for the more commonly prescribed drugs, most particularly antidepressants. Many patients with symptoms of anxiety and depression, particularly those who also suffer from personality disorders, respond poorly to these agents. Psychopharmacology has filled a gap in therapy for many patients but should not always be considered a primary form of treatment. Unfortunately, the current mental health system actually discourages the practice of psychotherapy. And in the American system of managed care, therapy for Axis II disorders is not even insured.

When patients today receive any type of psychological treatment, it is most likely to be cognitive-behavioral therapy (CBT). The concreteness and practicality of CBT are its strong points. Moreover, CBT is a method that is based on systematic research and that has proven to be effective for a wide variety of mental disorders. Aaron Beck, the founder of CBT, wrote a book on the treatment of personality disorders, now in its second edition (Beck & Freeman, 2002). Chapter 6 discusses the work of Marsha Linehan and other cognitive therapists who have developed new ways of treating personality disorders. However, CBT was developed to treat anxiety and depression, and not all its practitioners are interested in personality issues. In contemporary practice, both pharmacological and psychological interventions tend to be focused on symptoms rather than underlying pathological processes.

Personality and Suicidality

Personality profiles have specific associations with suicidality. For example, neuroticism defines an individual's vulnerability to dysphoric affects. In a study of suicide attempts among adolescents and young adults, Fergusson et al. (2000) found that suicide attempters had significantly higher levels of this trait. In other words, patients with emotional dysregulation are more likely to think about suicide.

In addition to trait profiles, suicidality is associated with diagnosable personality disorders that represent exaggerated and dysfunctional versions of traits (Livesley, 2003; Paris, 2003). These are chronic conditions that begin early in life and have continuous effects over many years. Personality disorders are expressed in several ways: through abnormalities in affect regulation, through impulsivity, through cognitive patterns, and through serious problems in work and relationships. Because BPD is the Axis II diagnosis most strongly related to chronic suicidality, we can use the larger body of data on its treatment and outcome to understand this problem.

Soloff, Lunch, Kelly, Malone, and Mann (2000) documented the course of suicidality in patients with BPD. In a study comparing inpatients with depression and no personality disorder with inpatients who were both depressed and diagnosed with BPD, the patients who had BPD made suicide attempts with similar potential lethality but had significantly more attempts. The mean number of attempts for BPD patients was three, and the subjects in the study might have gone on to make more attempts if they had been followed for a longer time.

But we can look at this relationship another way—how common are personality disorders in patients who carry out repeated suicide attempts? It has long been known that repeated attempters have more psychopathology and meet criteria for more psychiatric diagnoses than do single attempters (Rudd, Joiner, & Rajab, 1996). However, few researchers have examined the frequency of personality disorders in this population. A recent exception, a study of repeated attempters (Forman et al., 2004), showed that as many as 41% of people presenting to clinics and emergency rooms with multiple attempts had a diagnosis of BPD. Of course, BPD did not account for all cases; many patients had severe depression with psychotic features. However, because Forman et al. did not report on the overall frequency of personality disorders in their population, it is possible that up to half of their repeated attempters might have earned a diagnosis for at least some form of Axis II disorder.

The psychopathology seen in BPD is a combination of several domains or dimension, most particularly two traits: affective instability and impulsivity (Siever & Davis, 1991). When Yen et al. (2004) examined which specific characteristics of borderline patients are related to suicidality, it was found that a high level of affective instability was the most significant predictive factor for suicidal actions.

In *DSM–IV–TR*, affective instability is defined as "a marked reactivity of mood (e.g., intense episodic dysphoria, irritability, or anxiety usually lasting a few hours and only rarely more than a few days)." Affective instability is a characteristic symptom of BPD and a feature shown to distinguish it from other personality disorders (Koenigsberg et al., 2002). Linehan's (1993) term (derived from research on emotions) *emotion dysregulation* refers to the same phenomenon and is one of the broad dimensions of personality, similar to Neuroticism in the Five Factor Model of Livesley et al. (1999). Emotion dysregulation might be described as a specfic form of Neuroticism in which mood is both unstable and chronically dysphoric.

As described by Linehan (1993), emotions are dysregulated when they are unusually intense and take longer to return to normal levels, and these phenomena have been documented in patients with BPD (Koenisgberg et al., 2002). There have also been attempts to measure this phenomenon in the laboratory (Herpertz, Kunert, Schwenger, & Sass, 1999).

Thus, borderline patients can be characterized by very high Neuroticism, that is, a "thin-skinned" pattern in which they are easily upset by a variety of environmental stimuli. Cloninger et al.'s (1993) dimension of *harm avoidance*, describing a tendency to be overly concerned about the negative consequences of one's actions, is a similar concept.

However important the role of emotion dysregulation, one cannot understand BPD on the basis of mood symptoms alone. The other important trait in suicidality is *impulsivity*. This term refers to an inability to control behavior; patients who are impulsive might be described as having a defective "braking system." In the Five Factor Model of personality, this would correspond to low Conscientiousness.

Impulsivity is a complex construct, but it helps to account for why patients move from suicidal ideation to suicidal attempts. Some actions (such as self-mutilation or substance abuse) can be as much planned as carried out on the spur of the moment. However, this trait describes a tendency to use action as a way of dealing with upset feelings. Because impulsive traits are often expressed through aggressive actions, a predominant research paradigm has been the construct of *impulsive aggression* (Coccaro et al., 1989).

A large body of research has found links between high levels of impulsivity associated with suicidal attempts and completions. More than one third of completed suicides have a history of substance abuse (Cavanagh et al., 2003). In BPD, the suicide completion rate approaches 10% (Paris, 2003), and substance abuse increases the risk (Links & Kolla, 2005). Even in antisocial personality, an impulsive disorder in which patients have often been assumed not to suffer very much, the suicide rate is 5% (Robins, 1966).

There are a number of reasons to support the concept that impulsivity is central to BPD (Links, Meselgrace, & van Reekum, 1999). First, long-term outcome is best predicted by impulsive traits (Links et al., 1999). Second, relatives of BPD patients often have other impulse spectrum disorders, such as antisocial personality and substance abuse (White, Gunderson, Zanarini, & Hudson, 2003). Third, the biological correlates of BPD are strongly and consistently related to this trait (Moeller, Barratt, Dougherty, Schmitz, & Swan, 2001; Paris et al., 2004).

Impulsivity involves difficulty in delaying responses or considering their consequences, the converse of Conscientiousness in the FFM. Impulsivity can be formally assessed by self-report questionnaires such as the Barratt Impulsivity Scale (Barratt, 1985). It can also be measured in the laboratory using neuropsychological tests such as the Go-NoGo task (Leyton et al., 2001) or the Continuous Performance Test (Conners, 1994).

There is a very large biological literature on impulsivity. This trait is related to the activity of the prefrontal cortex, responsible for executive function (O'Leary, 2000). It is also the only psychological trait that has been shown to be related to levels of a neurotransmitter. Consistent findings indicate that low serotonin activity in the brain is associated with impulsive traits (Coccaro et al., 1989; Paris et al., 2004). There may also be a relationship between genetic variability and impulsivity. The serotonin transporter gene, which helps control serotonin activity, comes in two forms (alleles), one short and one long. The somewhat less effective short allele tends to be associated with a variety of impulsive behaviors (Mann, Brent, & Arango, 2001).

In summary, a combination of dysfunctional personality traits is associated with chronic suicidality. Affective instability or emotion dysregulation creates constant psychic pain leading to suicidal ideation but does not account for suicide actions. Impulsivity leads patients to actually carry out their intentions and make suicide attempts.

Suicidality and the Outcome of Personality Disorders

The long-term outcome of BPD sheds light on how often patients with chronic suicidality attempt suicide and under what conditions they eventually give up their patterns of suicidal behavior.

Patients with personality disorders, particularly the young, are at some risk for suicide. In psychological autopsy studies of late adolescents (Rich et al., 1988) and of adults aged 18 to 35 (Lesage et al., 1994), BPD was found in nearly one third of cases. In psychological autopsy studies of patients of all ages, both Cluster B and Cluster C personality disorders are common (Cavanaugh et al., 2003).

Yet Maris (1981), in his follow-up study of suicide attempters, found that most patients stop making repetitive suicide attempts by early middle age. This research did not examine diagnosis, but several groups of researchers have studied suicidality as an outcome of BPD. This is, after all, a disorder in which we see young patients making multiple attempts. What happens to them, and why do we see fewer cases after middle age?

McGlashan (1986) examined outcome for patients with BPD who had been treated at Chestnut Lodge (a private hospital near Washington, DC). Stone (1990) followed a similar group of patients from New York State Psychiatric Institute, a hospital associated with Columbia University. Our own group (Paris, Brown, & Nowlis, 1987) studied BPD patients who had been treated at a general hospital in Montreal.

All three studies examined outcome 15 years after initial treatment, and all found that patients with a BPD diagnosis usually get better with time. However, there was a significant amount of completed suicide. The lowest rate (3%) was obtained in the Chestnut Lodge group, whereas the New York and Montreal groups both reported rates of 9%. But completed suicides were also close to 10% in samples from Toronto (Silver & Cardish, 1991) and Norway (Kullgren, 1988). In a 7-year prospective follow-up from Hamilton, Canada, Links et al. (1993) found that 7% of BPD patients had completed suicide, a rate that might have increased to near 10% if the sample had been followed for another 7 years.

Our own research group went on to study the same cohort of BPD patients 27 years after their first clinical presentation, by which time the mean age of the sample was 50 (Paris & Zweig-Frank, 2001). The patients had improved even further, but the suicide rate had risen to nearly 10%, and another 8% had died prematurely from medical causes. Clearly, personality disorders carry a significant risk for long-term mortality.

However, in recent years, two groups of researchers have conducted prospective studies of patients with BPD suggesting a much better prognosis. A large-scale study, the National Institute of Mental Health Collaborative Study of Personality Disorders, has been examining the outcome of several groups of patients with Axis II diagnoses. The overall findings are consistent with previous research in that most patients tend to get better with time. But the rate of recovery in this sample has been surprisingly rapid, and only half the patients still met BPD criteria after 5 years (Grilo, McGlashan, & Skodol, 2000). On the other hand, most patients continued to have similar difficulties with functioning, even when they no longer could be diagnosed with BPD (Skodol et al., 2005). Their apparent improvement may have mainly been due to a reduction in suicidal behavior. As patients become less impulsive, they no longer meet BPD criteria but may still meet criteria for an overall personality disorder as described in *DSM–IV–TR*. Although it is too early to determine what the final suicide rate will be in this group, it has thus far been closer to the 3% rate described by McGlashan than to the higher rates described by other researchers.

In a second study, Zanarini et al. (2002) followed a group of patients with BPD who had been admitted to McLean Hospital, a psychiatric facility linked to Harvard University. A rapid rate of recovery, similar to the National Institute of Mental Health study, was observed on 6-year follow-up, although most patients remained in regular treatment. The suicide rate in this sample was 4%, again lower than has been observed in most other studies.

These findings raise a question about the "true" suicide rate in patients with BPD. If it is indeed 10%, then these patients are at high risk, that is, they are as likely to commit suicide as patients with bipolar illness, severe depression, or schizophrenia. If the rate is 3% to 4%, we might be somewhat less concerned (although hardly sanguine).

The main methodological issues that need to be considered in addressing this question concern methods of follow-up and differences between samples. The studies conducted by McGlashan, Stone, and Paris were all "follow-back" studies. In other words, patients were identified from chart records and then located. The validity of this method depends on how many patients are actually located. McGlashan and Stone both found nearly all (85% to 90%) of the people they were looking for. (Our group did not do anywhere as well as that, failing to locate half of the original group, although results were about the same.) The limitation of the follow-back method, however, is that one cannot determine what variables to measure at baseline; one is at the mercy of what was written down in the patient's chart.

Thus, prospective methods have a number of important advantages. One can choose evaluations made at baseline, examine the progress of patients at various points over the course of their lives, and determine potential predictors of outcome. But there is an important limitation for prospective research in relation to generalizability. Most patients do not sign up for these studies. This is particularly the case for difficult, chronically suicidal patients with a diagnosis of BPD. Thus, one ends up with a sample that is not fully representative, consisting of more compliant patients who agree to and continue to maintain their participation in research. These are patients who are probably more likely to recover and less likely to commit suicide.

Moreover, most of the patients in the prospective studies were in regular treatment. There are important differences between patients who stay in treatment and those who do not.

Most patients with a diagnosis of BPD drop out of psychotherapy within a few months (Gunderson et al., 1989; Skodol, Buckley, & Charles, 1983). Patients in research studies who attend therapy with some regularity and are also on medication do not represent this larger group.

In this respect, the follow-back method may actually be more representative of clinical reality, because it includes the large number of patients who are not compliant but who can still be found and assessed. It is therefore likely that the higher suicide rates seen in the follow-back studies in New York and Montreal reflect a certain truth about chronic suicidality.

Perhaps the most clinically important finding of these outcome studies of BPD concerns the age at which suicide occurs. In the 15-year follow-ups by Stone (1990) and Paris et al. (1987), the mean age of suicide was about 30. But in our 27-year follow-up (Paris & Zweig-Frank, 2001), the mean age went up to 37, with a standard deviation of 10. (In fact, we saw very few suicides before age 30.) Thus, the age at which suicide threats are most intense and most alarming, that is, the early 20's, is not the same as the age when suicide completions happen. The time to be most concerned about suicide in this population is after age 30. One of the reasons why suicide completions in personality disorders occur at a later age is that they happen when patients fail to recover and when they give up after a series of unsuccessful treatments.

Knowing these outcome findings could help therapists to feel calm in the face of suicidal threats, however blood-curdling, from their younger patients. The cases that frighten us the most, young people who threaten suicide in clinics and emergency rooms, are not the ones at highest risk. This is not to say that they never kill themselves, but that the risk is lower.

There are, unfortunately, few strong predictors as to which BPD patients will commit suicide and which will go on living (Paris, Nowlis, & Brown, 1989). The strongest predictor, found in two of the studies (Links et al., 1993; Stone, 1990) was substance abuse. Alcohol and drugs are well-known risk factors for suicide completion in all patients; probably people who drink or take drugs are more likely to act on their impulses (Cavanagh et al., 2003).

In summary, long-term studies of BPD show us an up side and a down side. On one hand, most chronically suicidal patients with personality disorder recover over time. On the other hand, up to 1 in 10 of these patients will eventually complete suicide. The next chapter examines whether this outcome is preventable.

5

Myths of Suicide Prevention

∽

Suicide is an emotional issue. Death by one's own hand is almost always a tragedy. For this reason, virtually every article written on the subject of suicide makes at least a gesture toward prevention. It would be good if we actually knew how to prevent suicide. But we do not.

Therapists who treat highly suicidal patients often believe that they have cases in which they have actually saved lives. I have sometimes thought so too. It is hard to discount the experience of intervening with a patient who threatens suicide and seeing him or her gradually give up the option of death. One gets very little credit as a therapist, and these situations provide a rare chance to feel good about one's work.

Yet it is not possible to know whether any individual patient would actually have died without our interventions. This chapter shows that empirical evidence on the prediction and prevention of suicide suggests that clinical impressions about prevention do not reflect reality.

This conclusion should not in any way lead to the dismissal of a patient's wish to die or justify a *laissez faire* attitude to care. Suicidality always has to be taken seriously. That is because suicidal thoughts and actions communicate profound suffering and hopelessness. This is a message that has to be received, understood, and acknowledged.

Can Suicide Be Predicted?

To prevent suicide, it must first be predicted. This is the crux of the question—do we know which patients are most likely to go on and commit suicide? It is one thing to say that we can identify patients who have risk factors associated with completed suicide. It is quite another thing to say that we actually know which patients are going to kill themselves and that we can use this information to save them.

A large amount of research has addressed this problem. These studies have attempted to predict suicide in people who are depressed or who have made previous attempts. For example, we know that patients who make repeated attempts are more at risk than those who have made only one (Zahl & Hawton, 2004). Yet most patients with repeated attempts never commit suicide (Goldney, 2000).

This difficulty bedevils all attempts at prediction in medicine, particularly when the outcome under question is relatively uncommon. Even when research has shown that risks have a statistical relationship to outcome, most people with the risk do not have the outcome, and most people with the outcome do not have the risk. For example, even if it could be convincingly shown that a poor diet raises the risk for heart disease, most people eating such a diet die of other causes, and most people who die of heart disease will not have had a poor diet.

Thus, identifying a population as being at statistical risk for suicide completion is not really useful in the clinical setting. There are always too many false-positive cases. Most patients who have the risk factors do not kill themselves. This applies to almost any of the risks for suicide. Patients who make more lethal attempts, who are older, who lack social supports, and who abuse substances are more likely to commit suicide. We can come to the same conclusion about the other common risk factors (discussed in chap. 1): impulsivity, psychosis, serious medical problems, high stress, poor functioning, lack of social supports, and a family history of suicide. Most people with these risks will not die by suicide. The vast majority will always be false positives. There are also false negatives, because patients who do kill themselves can lack the most commonly identified risk factors.

As Goldney (2000, p. 585) concluded, "The sobering reality is that there has not been any research which has indicated that suicide can be predicted or prevented in any individual." Note the crucial phrase "in any individual." We can establish a statistical risk for completion that applies to large groups of patients. But in any single case, we do not know whether or not suicide will occur.

Let us examine two important studies (Goldstein et al., 1991; Pokorny, 1983) that attempted to predict suicide in very large populations of patients admitted to a hospital, who were then followed long-term. Both studies failed to show that we know how to identify which patients are most likely to die by suicide. In both cohorts, algorithms consisting of well-established risk factors were applied to determine whether completion could be predicted. Although some factors were statistically associated with completion, the algorithms failed to predict *any* individual case of completed suicide.

Thus, given present knowledge, even within a high-risk sample of patients admitted to a hospital for mental illness, it is not possible to predict suicide with any degree of accuracy whatsoever. Reviewing a meta-analysis of several other studies that also failed to demonstrate that completion is predictable, Von Egmond and Diekstra (1990), concluded, "Suicide prediction research has made little progress over the last 25 years." Nothing has happened in the last two decades to modify this conclusion.

Can Suicide Be Prevented?

If suicide cannot be predicted, it cannot be prevented. There is currently little evidence that any specific therapeutic intervention can be used to prevent suicide. As Wilkinson (1994, p. 861) concluded, "The reality is that there is no convincing evidence that education, improved social conditions and support, or better training play a substantive part in preventing suicide." One recent review article (Mann et al., 2005), which summarized much of the research in this area, expressed a hopeful view of the possibility of prevention. However, the evidence is just not there. In a systematic review of the suicide prevention literature, Gaynes et al. (2004) could only conclude that although there is evidence for the effectiveness of treatment for "intermediate outcomes" such as depression and hopelessness, there is no solid evidence that suicide completion itself can be treated.

These are sobering conclusions, but we must face reality. Good intentions are not good enough. The situation could change when we understand the causes of suicide better. But that lies far in the future.

Despite all the effort therapists spend on prevention, the psychological interventions of mental health professionals have never been proven to save lives. This observation may explain an apparent paradox. There has been a dramatic growth in the numbers of therapists over the last 50 years, leading to a much greater availability of treatment for the population, yet suicide rates, although showing some degree of variability over time, have not shown any dramatic change (Maris et al., 2000).

Given the evidence for the efficacy of psychotherapy, there can be little doubt that mental health professionals do a lot of good. But this does not translate into suicide prevention. Nor did increases in access to therapy prevent the increase in suicides that occurred in young adults between 1960 and 1980 (Solomon, & Hellon, 1980). Although therapists continue to believe that they sometimes prevent suicide, research has never been able to demonstrate this effect empirically.

The same conclusions apply more generally to suicidality. In a large-scale survey of the American population, Kessler, Berglund, Borges, et al. (2005) found no change over the last 10 years in the frequency of suicidal ideation, suicidal gestures, or suicidal attempts. This finding is very striking, because suicidality has remained stable despite notable increases in the availability of both psychological and pharmacological interventions.

There have only been a few prospective studies of suicide prevention, and they do not lead to useful clinical generalizations. Although many studies have found that interventions can reduce the frequency of attempts (Sakinofsky, 2000), there is little evidence that completion can be prevented in this way.

A major point of confusion for clinicians derives from a failure to distinguish between suicidality and completed suicide. Many interventions have been shown to decrease the frequency of suicidal attempts. This goal can be accomplished by psychotherapy (Brent, 2001; Hepp, Wittmann, Schnyder, & Michel, 2004; Linehan, 1993) as well as by the prescription of antidepressants (Verkes & Cowen, 2000). Thus, we can do something about attempts, even if we do not know how to prevent completion.

Even if we were able to carry out prevention in acutely suicidal patients, it would not follow that applying the same procedures to chronically suicidal patients would be effective. Trying, at all costs, to prevent an action that patients have been considering for many years (and may continue to consider for some time to come) requires a different approach.

Psychopharmacology and Suicide Prevention

A current point of controversy in suicide prevention concerns the usefulness of psychopharmacology. There has been evidence in recent years suggesting that in some conditions, drugs can reduce suicide completion. The most convincing data come from studies of patients with bipolar disorder. Thus, long-term follow-up studies (Goodwin et al., 2003) and national registry studies (Kessing, Vedel, Søndergård, Kvist, & Andersen, 2005) have shown that patients who take lithium have a lower suicide rate than those who do not, and these findings have been supported by a comprehensive review (Cipriani, Pretty, Hawton, & Geddes, 2005). There are also data suggesting that patients with schizophrenia who take clozapine (but not any other antipsychotic agent) have a reduced rate of suicide (Meltzer & Okayli, 1995).

Yet even here, we have a problem in determining causality. Patients who are compliant with pharmacological regimes may be less likely to commit suicide than those who are not. Thus, the finding might not be a drug effect but a selection bias. Moreover, patients attending clinics providing pharmacological treatments usually receive monitoring and psychosocial support. Thus, we cannot say that prescribing drugs definitely prevents suicide in patients with mental disorders.

The case for antidepressants as preventives is even more controversial. Some authorities (Van Praag, 2003), considering the frequency of prescription of these drugs and the relative stability of suicide rates, have wondered why these agents have failed to reduce suicide rates in any dramatic way. Others (Gould et al., 2003; Grunebaum et al., 2004) have suggested that recent decreases in suicide might be accounted for by the prescription of serotonin reuptake inhibitors

Evidence supporting an effect of antidepressants mainly comes from Scandinavia. In an autopsy study in Sweden, patients with depression were less likely to die by suicide (compared with other causes) if they had taken antidepressants (Isacsson, Bergman, & Rich, 1996). It has also been found in Swedish rural communities that suicide rates decreased at about the same time that family doctors began to prescribe antidepressants (Isacsson, 2000). Finally, a program to educate Swedish family doctors about depression was followed by a reduction in mortality from suicide (Philgren, 1995). However, this finding was not replicated in a recent British study (Morriss, Gask, Webb, Dixon, & Appleby, 2005), which failed to show that education of primary care physicians about the treatment of depression had any effect on completion rates.

A related approach involves the education of "gatekeepers," that is, nonprofessionals who are in contact with potentially suicidal individuals and in a position to direct them to treatment. The best-known study of this intervention, conducted in the U.S. Air Force (Knox, Litts, Talcott, Feig, & Caine, 2003), examined suicide rates before (1990–1996) and after (1997–2002) measures were instituted to identify personal problems and reduce stigma in servicemen. A 33% reduction in suicide was observed in the second period, a very encouraging finding. However, this methodology does not establish a relationship between intervention and outcome.

The problem is that associations do not prove a causal relationship. Other factors could be responsible for decreases in mortality rate. For example, association between increased prescription of medication and decreases in suicide rates might only be a coincidence.

Suicide rates have decreased in developed countries in recent years, including the United States, where Grunebaum et al. (2004) reported a 13% decrease (particularly among women) after 1987, as well as in Britain (Gunnell & Ashby, 2004), Grunebaum et al. noted that the decrease occurred at the same time as the widespread prescription of specific serotonin reuptake inhibitors (SSRIs) and suggested that the completion rate might have decreased even further if patients who did not seek help before committing suicide had been administered SSRIs. However, in the absence of large-scale clinical trials, conclusions like these, based entirely on temporal associations, are speculative and impossible to validate.

Paradoxically, there has been a recent storm of concern that antidepressants might actually increase the rate of suicide, particularly in adolescents (Lapierre, 2003). This controversy may be based on a misunderstanding. Contrary to what has been written in the media (which always confuses suicide with suicidality), it has never been shown that adolescents taking these agents are more likely to kill themselves. (As discussed in chap. 3, suicide remains a rare event in that age group.) Moreover, there has been a decrease in the suicide rate among adolescents (Gould et al., 2003), which is even more striking in communities where antidepressant prescriptions are more common (Olfson, Shaffer, Marcus, & Greenberg, 2003).

It is true, however, that patients can become more agitated when given specific serotonin reuptake inhibitors, and this agitation may, at least in certain subgroups, lead to increased suicidal thoughts, as well as attempts. Actually, these side effects are not specific to adolescents. It has long been known that patients who become more active on medication before their depression lifts may commit suicide; this phenomenon was described many years ago, at a time when tricyclic antidepressants were commonly prescribed to depressed adults (Tollefson et al., 1993).

Access to Means of Suicide

Surprisingly, the best evidence that suicide can be prevented comes from interventions that have *not* been carried out by mental health professionals. One of the key factors in completion is access to fatal means (Clarke & Lester, 1989; Pirkola, Isometsa, & Lonnqvist, 2003). Suicide rates are distinctly higher in countries with lax gun control. Also, the fact that physicians now prescribe benzodiazepines (which are unlikely to be fatal) instead of barbiturates (which are very likely to be fatal on overdose) has prevented many deaths (Jenkins & Singh, 2000).

One of the most striking lowering of suicide completion rates occurred when Britain changed the content of natural gas provided to homes to reduce the content of toxic fumes (Clarke & Lester, 1989). Another example comes from Asia. Recently there has been an epidemic of suicide among women in rural China (Ji, Kleinman, & Becker, 2001) as well as in Southern India (Aaron et al., 2004). These suicides would most probably not have occurred if it were not for ready access to highly fatal means: insecticides used in farming.

Reductions of completion rates that result from restricting access to fatal means stand in contrast to the relative ineffectiveness of volunteer organizations that were specifically designed for suicide prevention. The Samaritans are a British group that pioneered hot line services for suicidal patients. The Samaritans were undoubtedly helpful to many people; we know that suicidal individuals are lonely and often benefit from almost any contact. But the efforts of the Samaritans had no effect whatsoever on suicide rates. Studies comparing completion rates at locations where the group was active with those where they were not found no differences at all (Jennings & Barraclough, 1978).

Maintaining Patient Contact

One study has suggested that maintaining contact with patients might make a difference in preventing completion. Motto and Bostrom (2001) studied a large group of patients who had been hospitalized for depression but who refused follow-up after discharge. These researchers conducted a randomized controlled trial (RCT) in which the treatment consisted only of sending patients a letter four times a year indicating that the team was interested in their progress. Compared with a control group who did not receive such letters, this simple intervention reduced completion. However, the effect was small (21 suicides in the control group and 15 in the contacted group), and the difference only remained significant for the first 2 years of follow-up.

Thus, although these findings are suggestive, they are not yet convincing, and have not been replicated.

Hospitals and the Illusion of Safety

Chronic suicidality takes a toll on clinicians. Many years ago, Maltsberger and Buie (1974) described how chronic threats tend to wear down therapists to the point that they withdraw (at least emotionally) from patients. But there is another, even more frequent, scenario that can also be damaging. Anxiety about losing a patient to suicide often leads to the decision to send patients to the hospital every time they threaten to end their lives.

The assumptions behind the practice of hospitalizing chronically suicidal patients are wrong on several counts. First, is it true that patients are likely to commit suicide if sent home (and will not do so if admitted to a hospital ward)? No one has ever shown this to be the case. As we have seen, predicting completion from ideation or attempts is virtually impossible. When a patient is admitted to a hospital (and comes out alive), therapists tend to get the impression that they have just carried out a life-saving intervention. But an acute crisis is rarely the scenario for completion. If patients had not been admitted, they would most probably have not committed suicide. The only difference is that the therapist would have been less anxious.

Second, in what way is a hospital environment truly safe? Admitting suicidal patients is often rationalized on the grounds that we must ensure safety. But there is no such thing as a safe place for patients who are seriously suicidal. In order to physically prevent suicide in a hospital environment, nursing procedures have to become extreme. Patients may be put on a suicide watch, with someone hired to sit with them 24 hours a day. Even so, they have been known to kill themselves on hospital wards despite all precautions. This is particularly likely to happen in psychotic patients with schizophrenia or severe mood disorders (although this scenario is rare in chronically suicidal patients).

Third, the hospital environment can be toxic for the chronically suicidal patient. Understanding the problem requires us to embrace a paradox. Some people with chronic suicidality are pleased to be on a ward. When beds are short, some people must be held over in the emergency room in rather uncomfortable circumstances, yet we can often see them happily chatting with other patients. The point is that this environment, however unappealing to us, is less lonely than a patient's own apartment. Moreover, nurses and doctors check on them regularly.

It has sometimes been suggested that patients in difficult social circumstances need to be in a hospital for a "respite." But we do not know whether such experiences are therapeutic, either in the short run or the long run. When a patient is discharged, the situation tends rather quickly to go back to square one. And a reinforcement pattern has been set up that often leads to further hospitalizations. M. M. Linehan (personal communication, October, 2003), a behaviorally trained researcher, suggested wryly that if a patient must be hospitalized, the environment should be made as *unpleasant* as possible.

Moreover, there are quite a few reports in the literature of patients worsening in response to hospitalization. The scenario has sometimes been called *malignant regression* (Dawson & MacMillan, 1993). This concept describes a sequence in which patients become more suicidal (not less) in the hospital. To consider one example, wrist slashing can escalate on a ward despite precautions. Although nursing procedures involve removing sharp objects from the patient's possession, it is almost impossible to prevent this behavior entirely. One can even see overdoses, particularly on open wards where there is no real way to prevent patients from walking across the street to buy over-the-counter medication at a drug store.

What is the explanation for malignant regression? Simply put, suicidal behavior is reinforced on hospital wards. If we apply classical behavioral principles, the more pleasant the environment in the hospital, the more likely it is that suicidality will continue, or even increase (Linehan, 1993). One of the main reasons for this reinforcement mechanism is that the more suicidal patients are, the more time they are given by staff. For patients with poor social supports, a week on a ward, or even a night in an emergency room, provides a highly reinforcing level of social contact. Second, in the environment of a psychiatric ward, patients who cut themselves or who carry out parasuicidal actions receive more, not less, nursing care.

In this way, a ward can become a place for attachment and connection. Chronically suicidal patients can talk to nurses and students who may take a special interest in them, and patients may also form relationships with other patients, usually those with similar problems. I have even heard patients claim they are "making friends" on the ward. If the hospital environment is sufficiently reinforcing, patients may be afraid of discharge, with its inevitable return to a lonely and difficult life on the outside. To avoid this feared outcome, suicidality may escalate. Where there is no limit on length of stay, patients may end up spending months (or even years) on hospital wards.

Thus, what appears to be a safe environment may not be safe at all. In this way, hospitalization is a two-edged sword. It creates an environment that reinforces the very behaviors that therapy is trying to extinguish. Most clinicians will recognize the scenario in which patients escalate suicidal or self-mutilating behaviors in the hospital.

A patient who recovered from BPD (Williams, 1998) published a brief article in *Psychiatric Services* based on her experiences as a consumer. Williams described how repetitive hospital admissions made her worse: "Do not hospitalize a person with borderline personality disorder for more than 48 hours. My self-destructive episodes—one leading right into another—came out only after my first and subsequent hospital admissions, after I learned the system was usually obligated to respond." Williams (1998) went on to say,

> When you as a service provider do not give the expected response to these threats, you'll be accused of not caring. What you are really doing is being cruel to be kind. When my doctor wouldn't hospitalize me, I accused him of not caring if I lived or died. He replied, referring to a cycle of repeated hospitalizations, "That's not life." And he was 100 percent right! (p. 174)

I agree with the views of this former patient and have said so at many conferences and symposia. It can be difficult, however, to convince clinical staff that hospitalization is unnecessary and unproductive. After all, this is what they do. Also, many will often point to a recent suicide as a warning, even if they cannot show that such events could have been prevented.

Reassuringly, many if not most experts on the treatment of personality disorders agree with my views. I can include on this list Linehan (1993), Kernberg (1987), and Livesley (2003). Gunderson (2001) also believes that hospitalization is usually unhelpful for chronically suicidal patients, although he is reluctant to refuse admission to patients who insist on it. His view is that when hospitalization is understood to be ineffective, refusing it to the patient can lead to a power struggle. In his book on borderline personality, Gunderson (2001) proposed a paradoxical intervention in which a therapist agrees to hospitalize the patient for suicidality, while letting the patient know that doing so would not be helpful (with the hope that the patient will then elect to decline the offer). Both Gunderson (2001) and Kernberg (1997) also recommend that therapists tell patients that in the long run, they cannot take responsibility for their survival, and recommend informing the family of the situation. (Ways to involve families are discussed in chap. 9.)

Yet some experts continue to advocate hospitalization for patients with personality disorders who threaten suicide. This conclusion found its way into the American Psychiatric Association Guidelines for the treatment of BPD (Oldham et al., 2001). I regret that this report, based on recommendations of members of a committee with highly disparate views, kept faith with the conventional wisdom and did not consider the lack of evidence for its position.

Actually, I was consulted on the text of these guidelines, although few of my suggestions were taken into account. I must also give credit to the senior author, John Oldham, for editing the final version, which was much more evidence-based than earlier drafts. The problem with clinical guidelines generally is that conclusions are often based on expert consensus rather than hard evidence. All members on the committee get to have their say, whether their ideas are based on data or on clinical experience. In this case, no one took into account the absence of controlled trials to establish the value of hospitalization for these patients.

To publish my disagreement, I edited a special issue of the *Journal of Personality Disorders* in 2003, in which the guidelines were criticized from several aspects by various authorities. The most cogent critic was Tyrer (2002), a British personality disorder researcher, who wittily described the APA guidelines as "a bridge too far," that is, going far beyond empirical evidence while justifying clinical tradition. In another article (Paris, 2004c), I focused on the lack of evidence for hospitalization in this clinical population.

To assess the value of hospitalization, we need to go back to basics. The standard approach to evaluating suicidality in clinical practice consists of eliciting suicidal ideation and surveying known risk factors for completion. Then, if the risk is considered high, the patient is sent to a hospital. But these procedures, even if they are useful in acute suicidality (and they may not be), have never been tested for chronic suicidality.

Hospital admission of chronically suicidal patients may help therapists feel better, even if it does little for patients. The underlying principle seems to be what might be called *the rule of fear*. Patients are admitted because therapists are afraid they will kill themselves. The question of whether hospitalization actually saves lives or changes the course of illness is an empirical question that has not been addressed.

Hospitalization is expensive. These scarce and valuable resources must be used to carry out specific treatment plans that can be provided only in a hospital setting. Moreover, patients should be admitted for indications that are well supported by empirical evidence. For example, in acutely psychotic patients, the rationale for admission is clear. We have a treatment for them, and it usually works within a short time. Nor would anyone doubt the importance of hospitalizing suicidal patients with a classic melancholic or psychotic depression. In such cases, the efficacy of treatments, ranging from high-dose antidepressants to electroconvulsive therapy, is well established, and again we often see results within weeks (or even days). It makes some sense to bring patients into the hospital to carry out these interventions and I would not disagree with instituting suicide precautions to make sure the patient does not die before the treatment takes effect.

In this context, patients with acute suicidality may benefit from a restrictive hospital environment as a temporary expedient. But in patients with chronic suicidality, buying time is not very helpful. The problem is not likely to be resolved in a short time. Successful treatment will require months to years of work. Hospitalization would be justified if, as is the case for mental disorders such as schizophrenia and bipolar illness, it provided an opportunity to administer effective pharmacotherapy. However, medications for chronically suicidal patients, particularly those with BPD, have not been shown to yield the specific effects one sees with drugs for schizophrenia or severe depression; although a number of pharmacological agents have some effectiveness, their most consistent effect is an overall reduction in impulsivity (see detailed review in chap. 7). Also, although pharmacological interventions can be useful options for many patients, they do not necessarily require a hospital setting for their administration.

Is hospitalization ever useful in chronic suicidality? To answer this question, we can consider the most common reasons why patients with BPD are hospitalized (Hull, Yeomans, Clarkin, & Goodman, 1996). These include psychotic episodes, serious suicide attempts, suicidal threats, and self-mutilation.

In my view, it is logical to admit a patient for treatment of a brief psychosis. In such cases, one can provide a specific treatment (neuroleptic medication) to control symptoms. I would also support the admission of a patient after a life-threatening suicide attempt. Even if no active treatment is conducted in the hospital, a brief admission can provide an opportunity to assess precipitating factors and review treatment plans.

But these are not the most frequent reasons why chronically suicidal patients are admitted. The most frequent scenarios involve suicidal threats, minor overdoses, and self-mutilation. The value of hospitalization for these problems is difficult to justify. There is no specific treatment for these symptoms that can be offered on a ward that cannot be provided in another context. Often, the chronically suicidal patient simply sits there, being monitored and observed. Clinicians sometimes assume, without any evidence, that this constitutes suicide prevention.

Links & Kolla (2005) argue in favor of retaining an option for hospitalization on the grounds that crises can represent a scenario Links terms *acute on chronic suicidality*, that is, an acute episode raising the immediate risk in a patient over a baseline of chronic suicidality. However, the evidence that interventions for acute suicidality are useful in patients with chronic suicidality has not been tested. In fact, because chronically suicidal patients can have frequent "acute on chronic" episodes, Links' guideline leads directly and inevitably to repetitive hospitalizations.

In this population, one always needs to take into consideration the negative effects of hospitalization. One of my American colleagues suggested to me that the best thing that ever happened to patients with BPD is managed care, because it prevents psychiatrists from prescribing a treatment that is bad for them.

Linehan (1993), applying the principles of behavioral psychology, has discouraged admission for patients with BPD, tolerating at most an overnight hold. A brief stay in an emergency room is usually less regressive than a full admission to a ward. A researcher in suicide once suggested to me that an overnight hold might be useful in a crisis, "as long as the patient does not go upstairs." The scenario of admission only to an emergency room has become common for another reason: Beds are scarce, and holding patients overnight in the emergency room is often the only alternative to sending them directly home.

However, there are problems with overnight holds. Some patients will agree readily to go home in the morning. But others will not. The outcome sometimes depends on emergency psychiatrists who do morning rounds on patients held over from the night before. These physicians need to be fairly tough. If they are not, the patient may indeed "go upstairs."

In a recent incident at one of the hospitals at my university, two experienced emergency psychiatrists, both of whom understand chronic suicidality and personality disorders, went on vacation during the same week. When they returned, the emergency room was full of chronically suicidal patients who had been staying there for several days, admitted and held by replacement physicians with less emergency experience. These psychiatrists, each of whom only took on a short shift, had simply passed on the decision to each other, with predictable results.

For these reasons, I do not favor a policy of holding over patients with chronic suicidality, even if they are in crisis. I cannot prove I am right, because I have not done a controlled trial (and it is not likely that anyone ever will). But I am not convinced of the necessity of keeping these patients in an emergency room overnight, for any other reason than reducing the anxiety of the physician on call. I worked for 25 years in the emergency room of a busy general hospital and almost never admitted anyone for this reason. Sometimes patients left the emergency room in a rage, warning me, "You will hear about this on the evening news." But it never happened that patients went home and killed themselves. And I have never heard of this occurring when anyone else was on call. What was really happening was a scenario of engagement and help seeking, however angry and chaotic, as opposed to the hopeless disengagement of patients who commit suicide. Because the intent of their behavior was communicative and not truly suicidal, these patients did not complete suicide.

Full hospitalization carries even more risks, making patients more suicidal, not less, and cutting them off from their social and occupational networks. Ironically, this may be why restrictions on hospitalization of psychiatric patients (based on the policies of health maintenance organizations in the United States, as well as major reductions in overall hospital beds in Canada and other countries) may have benefited this patient population. And if, as so often happens, the patient becomes suicidal again shortly after discharge, little has been accomplished. Although being in a hospital provides temporary relief, it is not unusual for chronically suicidal patients to have a return of ideation when they have to re-enter the outside world. In this context, using a hospital ward as an asylum provides no framework for solving the problems that make patients suicidal in the first place.

Clinicians should be particularly concerned about long admissions. The longer hospitalization continues, the more likely it is that the patient will not be able to return to work or maintain links with other stabilizing influences in their out-side life. What leads to long admissions is the rule of fear. Most therapists will be familiar with the scenario in which patients spend months on a ward but are not seen as "dischargeable" as long as they continue to threaten suicide. In one case that I was consulted on, a patient spent 5 years on a unit designed for acute care. Every time discharge was brought up, the patient would announce that she would throw herself in front a sub-way train. Yet this patient eventually left the ward and never committed suicide.

Another problem is that once hospitalization is intro-duced, admissions tend to be repetitive. This is a malignant (and unfortunately common) pattern. Many patients fall into cycles in which they are in and out of hospital for years. Their charts, containing several volumes, can barely be lifted. With this scenario in mind, Dawson and MacMillan (1995) took the position that chronically suicidal patients should never be hospitalized. Although one should never say "never," admissions are generally ineffective and counterpro-ductive.

Reviewing the various scenarios described in chapter 1 un-der the broad term *suicidality* helps us to understand why hos-pital admission does not address the problems of chronically suicidal patients. Suicidal threats should never be dismissed or not taken seriously. They communicate a state of severe dis-tress, and therapists have to acknowledge and deal with that distress. Yet by themselves, these threats do not constitute a sufficient reason for hospitalization.

Similarly, although suicide attempts are one of the main reasons why patients are admitted to a hospital, there is no evi-dence that doing so provides effective treatment. We also need to consider the nature of the suicidal act. Many attempts in chronically suicidal patients consist of small overdoses related to interpersonal crises, with low intent. One does see, none-theless, overdoses that are potentially lethal, and in such cases we need to be more concerned. This is why I accept this scenario as one of the few justifications for hospitalization. But there is no evidence that hospitalizing patients prevents them from repeating attempts, whether they have been lethal or nonlethal. We should be particularly concerned when patients are hospitalized for self-mutilation. As discussed in chapter 1, self-cutting is not a suicidal action at all but a way of regulating dysphoric emotions.

Ultimately, the problem with hospitalization is that it interferes with the main treatment for chronic suicidality: outpatient therapy. It may not be possible to carry out effective management in these patients when frequent and repetitive hospitalizations interrupt the course of therapy. This point is well made in a classic article by Schwartz et al. (1974, p. 204), who were the first to point out that chronic suicidality is a unique clinical problem and that interventions appropriate for acute suicidality may be inappropriate or even counterproductive in this group.

> The management of the person for whom suicidality has become a way of life requires a willingness to take risks and an acceptance of the fact that one cannot prevent all suicides. Those are two qualities which not all therapists have. Once one has concluded that the only way to strive toward the ultimate reduction of lethality is to accept the risk of suicide in the interim, one next needs to determine to what degree the patient and the other people important in the patient's life are ready to accept those risks and to share the responsibility for treatment.

In this light, therapists who treat this population benefit from having some personal characteristics. If they want to help these patients, they need to give up the idea of being a savior. One can remain optimistic without being omnipotent. One may not be able to treat these patients unless one accepts taking what Maltsberger (1994a) called a "calculated risk." Maltsberger agreed that repetitive admissions are not helpful and concluded that one cannot treat chronically suicidal patients without accepting some risk of completion. This paradox lies at the center of the clinical problem.

Day Hospitals and Chronic Suicidality

Hospitalization is not the only alternative when outpatient management is unable to handle suicidal crises. When therapy spirals out of control and the clinician needs the help of a specialized team, partial hospitalization is useful. Unlike full admission, day treatment has been empirically demonstrated to be effective in two cohorts of patients with personality disorders (Bateman & Fonagy, 1999; Piper et al., 1991). One of the positive outcomes in both studies was a reduction in suicide attempts.

One reason why partial hospitalization is effective is that it provides a highly structured program. Patients with BPD typically show increased pathology in an unstructured environment (Gunderson, 2001). In this respect, day hospitals contrast with the environment of a ward, where there are large amounts of unstructured time and where acting out may increase on evening shifts when there are no activities at all. In a partial hospital program, where activities are scheduled every hour, little time remains to slash one's wrists. Regression is further limited by the fact that the patient goes home at night. Given that there is no evidence that full hospitalization prevents suicide completion, suicidal risk is not a contraindication for day hospital treatment.

Unlike full hospitalization, day treatment is an evidence-based treatment for this population. Controlled trials on a mixed population of Axis II disorders (Piper, Rosie, & Joyce, 1996) and on patients with borderline personality (Bateman & Fonagy, 2004) have shown effectiveness in this setting. We do not know the precise mechanism by which day treatment works. These programs combine many types of intervention, including individual therapy, group therapy, family therapy, occupational therapy, and psychopharmacology.

Time is another factor in partial hospitalization. The day programs examined in the RCTs by Piper et al. (1996) and by Bateman and Fonagy (2004) lasted at least 6 months. Over this period, improvement could occur through the therapeutic effects of a milieu or through social and occupational rehabilitation. However, these longer (and more expensive) stays may not be necessary; no one has compared them with briefer periods of treatment. One of the day hospitals in the university where I work has an 8-week program, and I have rarely been disappointed with the results.

Unfortunately, many locations lack day treatment entirely. This is most unfortunate, given the evidence base for its effectiveness and the fact that it has been around for a long time. (The first day hospital in North America opened in Montreal in 1944.) Mental health services can become dependent on hospital beds, whether they were useful or not. Whereas everyone complains about closed beds, few lobby for the opening of day treatment centers. We have a good alternative to the wasteful and harmful practice of hospitalizing patients every time their suicidality goes out of control. The main problem with day programs is access: It is rare that one can rapidly get patients from the clinic or the emergency room into partial hospitalization.

Outpatient Therapy: Accepting Calculated Risks

Most chronically suicidal patients are followed in outpatient therapy. If therapists have any hope to address the root causes of suicidality, they must accept a degree of risk. There is also evidence that outpatient therapy works. Studies of several psychotherapeutic methods, including dialectical behavior therapy (Linehan, 1993) and mentalization-based treatment (BMT; Bateman & Fonagy, 2004), have shown that they are effective in reducing both self-mutilation and suicide attempts, without providing any time in a hospital. What we lack is follow-up data to determine whether completed suicides are less likely in patients treated with these methods.

The management of chronic suicidality requires a unique set of principles. Unlike patients with psychosis or melancholia, patients with personality disorders who are chronically suicidal rarely commit suicide while in the hospital. Although some completions can occur soon after discharge, most patients can be expected to remain alive but chronically suicidal. Treatment will take time, and we have no strategies that provide a quick fix for the problem.

Kernberg (1984) agreed that chronic suicidality requires patience and tolerance and also suggested that therapists need to maintain the frame of therapy and avoid going out of their way to "prevent" suicide at all costs. Kernberg stated (1984, p. 261) that he might tell a patient "that he would feel sad but not responsible if the patient killed himself," would avoid unusual measures to prevent completion, and would routinely inform the family of his management plan. This rationale is similar to that of Rachlin (1984), who pointed out that attempts to save lives in suicidal patients tend to deprive patients of their quality of life. As Williams (1998, p. 174) put it,

> When you as a service provider do not give the expected response to these threats, you'll be accused of not caring. What you are really doing is being cruel to be kind. When my doctor wouldn't hospitalize me, I accused him of not caring if I lived or died. He replied, referring to a cycle of repeated hospitalizations, 'That's not life.' And he was 100 percent right!

Another crucial point is that it is difficult to conduct effective treatment in an atmosphere of constant turmoil. For this reason, an excessive focus on suicide prevention prevents us from doing our job. When clinicians spend too much time worrying about suicide completion, problem solving takes a back seat. And when clinicians feel forced to do almost anything to prevent suicide completion, the therapeutic relationship becomes characterized by "coercive bondage" (Hendin,

1981), in which the patient controls the behavior of the therapist, and the quality of the patient's life becomes
compromised by overzealous concern.

Implications for Managing
Chronic Suicidality

We live in a world where prevention of illness is highly valued.
Every morning one picks up the newspaper and reads about
risk factors for various diseases. Sometimes one gets the impression that almost everything (including milk and coffee) is
potentially dangerous. But all of this media hype supports the
illusion that we are in control of the universe. We seem to believe that we need never die as long as we follow a proper regime of diet and exercise. In this mindset, death by one's own
hand should be even more preventable.

Research shows that almost everyone who commits suicide
suffers from some form of mental disorder (Robins, 1981).
Moreover, most suicides are associated with depression, which
is usually treatable. Why therefore should we not be able to
prevent suicide?

Unfortunately, the situation is not so simple. Suicide exists
in every society and has been with us as long as historical records have been kept. Its frequency fluctuates over time, and
between one society and another, but it is never absent. As we
have seen, most people who end their own lives do so under
circumstances in which prevention would not have been possible. The only suicides we can hope to prevent are those in
which a patient gambles with death and loses. And it has not
been shown that we have any consistent way of preventing
that kind of fatal outcome.

Yet even if we cannot prevent patients from committing
suicide, we need not accept an attitude of therapeutic nihil-
ism. Most of the patients we see who are considering suicide

will not kill themselves. And most can benefit from treatment. Once we move beyond trying to "prevent" suicide, we may actually be liberated to accomplish more. Worrying about suicide is understandable, but it does not help patients and does not help therapists to carry out their tasks.

6

Psychotherapy Research and Chronic Suicidality

～

Psychotherapy is the treatment of choice for patients with chronic suicidality. This chapter reviews empirical studies on various forms of therapy, drawing on research findings rather than on clinical reports.

There is a large literature on the treatment of suicide attempts (see Cochrane report by Hawton, Townsend, et al., 1999), but these studies do not concern chronic suicidality. On the other hand, research on the therapy of personality disorders is highly relevant to management, so that most of the data reviewed in this chapter derive from studies of patients with BPD.

Some General Principles of Psychotherapy

Before we examine specific applications to suicidal patients, let us take a broad look at the empirical literature in psychotherapy. Several broad principles have been supported by research data that apply to all forms of psychological treatment.

First, we know that psychotherapy works. In an influential and widely quoted meta-analysis of the psychotherapy research literature, Smith, Glass, and Miller (1980) examined 475 studies measuring the outcome of many forms of therapy and found a considerable difference between treatment and no treatment. Every review of the literature since then has led to a similar conclusion (see reviews in Lambert, 2004). As Smith et al. (1980) put it, "Psychotherapy benefits people of all ages as reliably as school educates them, medicine cures them, or business turns a profit" (p. 183).

Second, the mechanisms by which psychotherapy works are not that unique to any particular method. Seventy years ago, Rozenzweig (1936, p. 412), wittily quoted Lewis Carroll to conclude that comparisons between different forms of therapy elicit a "Dodo bird verdict" ("all have won and all shall have prizes"). Reviewing the research literature 40 years later, Luborsky, Singer, and Luborsky (1975) came to the same conclusion, and more recently, Wampold (2001), after examining a much larger number of studies and formal meta-analyses, again concluded that the data strongly support a dodo bird verdict.

Paradoxically, the absence of differences between procedures based on entirely different theories provides an important clue as to the most effective ingredients in psychological treatments. If success depends on factors common to all methods, the effectiveness of therapy must depend on "nonspecific" or "common" factors. (These factors are only called nonspecific because we do not quite know how to specify them.)

Frank and Frank (1991) proposed an influential explanation of how the common factors in therapy actually work. Patients come to therapy hopeless and demoralized, but treatment remobilizes inner resources. Thus, therapists' theories are less important than their capacity to establish an alliance and make patients regain hope.

Third, some patients do better in therapy than others. The most consistent findings are that severity of symptoms, as well as lower functional levels in work and relationships, are correlated with a poorer outcome for psychotherapy (Clarkin & Levy, 2004).

Fourth, the importance of common factors points to the role of therapist skill. However, differences among therapists do not seem to be a function of experience or of the ability to apply specific techniques; those who are empathic and good at promoting a strong therapeutic alliance usually get better results (Beutler et al., 2004).

Fifth, both patient and therapist factors affect the quality of the therapeutic alliance, which is one of the best predictors of outcome (Orlinsky, Ronnestad, & Willutski, 2004). However, it is the patient's subjective experience of the alliance (not that of the therapist) that predicts results.

Orlinsky et al. (2004) proposed a "generic model" of psychotherapy describing the common factors in all methods, from psychoanalysis to behavior therapy. The most important elements of successful treatment are establishing a well-defined contract, creating a strong alliance, encouraging openness in the patient, and maintaining a focus on current life problems and relationships.

These principles are largely derived from research on brief therapies. But there is no reason to assume they do not apply to treatments of greater length. The more important question is whether longer treatment produces better results.

Long courses of therapy have become less common, and there is less demand for open-ended therapy as potential patients seek out briefer therapies and/or psychopharmacological interventions (Paris, 2005a). Moreover, in the United States, therapists have had to adjust their practice to the demands and the scrutiny of third-party payers. Insurers tend to be skeptical about extended periods of treatment.

Actually, there is good evidence that briefer therapies can be effective for most patients. In a classical study, Howard,

Kopta, Krause, and Orlinsky (1986) found that one half of all patients improve within 8 weeks, and that three quarters improve with 26 weeks of therapy. In contrast, we have almost no data concerning the value of open-ended psychological treatments. Although long-term psychotherapy is often prescribed (especially for patients with personality disorders), there is no supporting research at all for treatments lasting more than 12 months.

To what extent can these conclusions be applied to chronically suicidal patients? The general principles suggest that we can expect psychotherapy to work; well-conducted therapy, whatever its theoretical basis, can be effective. Patients who have more areas of healthy functioning will usually do better than those who are dysfunctional in every area of their lives. Therapist skill will make a difference, especially in forming and maintaining an alliance. The main area of uncertainty concerns the length of therapy. This chapter suggests that continuous therapy is not always the best choice and that therapists should consider an intermittent course of treatment for chronically suicidal patients.

Psychoanalytic Psychotherapy and Borderline Personality Disorder

Patients with chronic suicidality are likely to meet criteria for a personality disorder, particularly borderline personality (Forman, Berk, Henriques, Brown, & Beck, 2004). Stern (1938) introduced the term *borderline* based on the idea that this form of pathology falls between neurosis and psychosis. After almost 70 years, Stern's original article still presents a vivid and accurate clinical picture. He described borderline patients as suffering from "psychic bleeding," a chronically dysphoric state that defies all attempts at help or comfort. Stern also wrote his article to explain why these patients are unsuitable for psychoanalysis. Stern's observation was that these patients failed to improve, or even got worse, with this form of treatment. Most subsequent writers on BPD have agreed with that judgment.

Gunderson and Singer (1975) noted that some of the phenomena seen in borderline patients relate to the lack of inner psychological structures. Even in an initial interview, they appear to be sicker if the clinician asks few questions and just allows them to talk but seem healthier when the interview is structured with specific questions. This observation suggests that these patients may require highly structured treatment. In fact, the most successful psychotherapies for BPD have had strong structural components.

In this context, it should be no surprise that classical psychoanalytic therapy does not work well in this population. As we will see, the adaptations of psychoanalysis used for this population differ from classical methods in important ways. Free association leaves patients adrift, because it does not provide them with the sense of connection and predictability they need to develop a therapeutic alliance, without which therapy cannot proceed. The fragility of that alliance in BPD has been documented (Frank, 1992). Therapists cannot simply assume they have an alliance with these patients but have to hope that it will emerge in the course of treatment (Adler, 1979).

Given these problems, it is surprising that even today, classical psychoanalytic therapy continues to be recommended for borderline patients. This might be explained by the fact that for many years, psychodynamic psychotherapy was the only game in town. It was generally recognized, however, that chronically suicidal patients with BPD need modified methods, in which the therapist provides structure through greater activity (Gabbard, 2004; Kernberg, 1984).

There may be as many as 100 books about how to treat BPD, most written by psychoanalysts. Many have sold well, because therapists are eager to learn about how to manage their most difficult patients. (For the same reason, conferences and courses about treating BPD patients are well attended.) However, until recently, all these books were exclusively based on the clinical experience of their authors. They provided no empirical evidence whatsoever that the therapeutic methods they recommended were effective.

If anything, we have some reason to believe that long-term dynamic therapy in BPD is often unsuccessful. Fonagy and Bateman (2006) even suggested that inappropriate psychotherapy has been one reason for slow recovery from this disorder. Several studies have documented high dropout rates among patients offered open-ended treatment (Gunderson et al., 1989; Skodol, Buckley, & Charles, 1983; Waldinger & Gunderson, 1984), affecting as many as two out of three cases. Whatever these patients need, it must be something different—if they vote with their feet. One also wonders, if psychodynamic methods were consistently helpful in BPD, why so many therapists have had bad experiences using it, often to the point that they end up avoiding these cases. The idea that one needs unusual levels of skill (or must first master one's counter-transference) to treat this population may be nothing but a series of excuses.

However, in recent years, adaptations of psychoanalytic therapy for BPD have been subjected to RCTs. The first RCT was reported by Bateman and Fonagy in England, testing a method they called "mentalization-based treatment" (MBT; Bateman & Fonagy, 2004). MBT is based on the idea that patients with BPD lack a "theory of mind;" that is, their mental states and actions reflect a lack of understanding of the feelings, thoughts, and actions of other people (as well as their own feelings, thoughts, and actions). The emphasis on impaired empathy and self-observation resembles an older idea: that borderline patients need to develop an "observing ego" (Frieswyk, Colson, & Allen, 1984), an ability that is essential for developing a therapeutic alliance. MBT also uses concepts developed in cognitive behavioral therapy, in that the treatment encourages patients to see their relationships in a different light by applying cognitive principles such as reframing and reappraisal (Beck & Freeman, 2002).

MBT may also be different from previous methods of analytic therapy in that it is not primarily concerned with reviewing childhood events or with transference phenomena. Moreover, even though childhood experiences can shed light on adult behavioral patterns, there is no empirical evidence showing that detailed exploration of a patient's childhood is an essential element of therapy (Paris, 2000, 2005a). In fact, effective therapy usually maintains a focus on the resolution of current problems (Orlinsky et al., 2004). Also, research has shown that in patients with fragile egos and a limited capacity for self-reflection, transference interpretations can be counterproductive (Piper et al., 1991). In this context, it makes sense for MBT to focus on developing a greater ability in patients to observe their own emotions as well as those of other people.

In this respect, MBT might even be considered a form of cognitive therapy. In fact, one can note several overall commonalities between psychodynamic and cognitive therapies; in both types of treatment, patients have to unlearn dysfunctional behavior patterns and learn more functional ones. A form of CBT called "schema therapy" (Young, 1999), includes a psychodynamic element, in that therapists focus on the effects of childhood experiences on the patients' view of their world and try to modify these schemas. The main difference between these methods is that psychodynamic methods traditionally focuses on "working through" problems in the relationship with a therapist, whereas for cognitive therapists, most of the work leading to change occurs with other people outside the therapy room.

Thus far, the results of trials for MBT have been promising. Patients receiving MBT in a year of day treatment have shown definite improvement in an RCT (Bateman & Fonagy, 1999), and these results remained stable on 1-year follow-up (Bateman & Fonagy, 2001). Although it was not clear whether it was MBT or a well-structured day treatment that made the difference, MBT is currently being tested in an outpatient setting, and preliminary results have found it to be effective (Fonagy, 2004).

A number of outstanding questions remain about the efficacy of MBT. Patients with BPD are chronically ill, and we do not know the long-term outcome of treatment or whether short-term improvements are sufficient to say that a remission has taken place. There is also a practical problem in that this treatment has been developed in a tertiary care center and is highly resource intensive; we do not know if it can be modified for use in ordinary clinical settings.

Another psychodynamic therapy for BPD that has recently been subjected to a clinical trial is transference-focused psychotherapy (TFP; Yeomans, Clarkin, & Kernberg, 2002) and deriving from the work of Kernberg (1984), which places an emphasis on interpreting transferential problems in the relationship with the therapist. Unlike MBT, TFP is much more traditionally psychodynamic. But this method has one unusual twist: Patients have to contract to stop acting out with overdoses and self-cutting, and if they do not, they are discharged. We do not know whether this kind of limit setting actually reduces suicidality or whether it only reduces the sample being treated to more manageable patients.

Results from an RCT of TFP, comparing its effectiveness to dialectical behavior therapy, were recently reported by Levy (2004), but they have not yet been published. The findings were similar to those previously reported for MBT, in that treatment led to a decrease in suicidal behavior as well as improved functioning after a year of therapy. As with MBT, we do not know whether TFP has long-term effects on chronic suicidality.

Good results for TFP might seem to contradict my earlier statement that transference is not an essential element of good therapy. However, it is not clear how central this kind of intervention is in practice. Although the model behind TFP derives from the work of Kernberg (1984), TFP might be more eclectic in the real world than in theory. Also, studies of this kind cannot tell you whether the way the theory behind the treatment, or the way the treatment was conducted, was crucial in producing results. It is possible that any well-structured approach, conducted in a way that promotes an alliance with the patient and deals with real life problems, would be successful. (If you were to ask patients what worked, they might not focus on transference interpretations at all.) This conclusion would be consistent with the common factors described earlier in the chapter, as well as with general theories of psychotherapy.

In summary, recent studies of psychoanalytic therapy for BPD are promising. We can no longer reply on clinical experience and charisma. No one will accept any longer (nor will insurance companies support) the efficacy of psychodynamic therapy without clinical trials. The future may bring a better understanding of the common factors shared between these approaches and the cognitive-behavioral methods to be discussed below.

Dialectical Behavioral Therapy and Other Forms of CBT for BPD

Dialectical behavior therapy (DBT; Linehan, 1993) was developed specifically for chronically parasuicidal patients. (Linehan, trained in cognitive-behavioral therapy and in suicide research, discovered only later that all the patients she was treating had a diagnosis of BPD.)

DBT is an adaptation of cognitive-behavioral therapy (CBT) for a chronically suicidal patient population; in addition to "classical" CBT, it adds an eclectic mix of methods common to other approaches. DBT was most specifically designed to target the mood instability seen in BPD but also addresses impulsive behaviors, which are seen as attempts to cope with emotional dysregulation. Applying behavioral analysis to incidents leading to self-injury and overdoses (i.e., a reconstruction of what led up to the event), DBT helps patients to observe how their emotions are dysregulated in response to stressors, and it encourages them to find better ways of dealing with these painful feelings. DBT also places emphasis on how the therapist responds empathically to emotions. As with many forms of psychoanalysis, DBT emphasizes empathy because it provides validation for inner experiences.

Linehan, Armstrong, Suarez, Allmon, and Heard's (1991) original report was the first RCT of any psychotherapy for BPD. The data showed that DBT was superior to "treatment as usual" (TAU), that is, outpatient therapy in the community. After a year, the group receiving DBT was found to be less likely to make suicide gestures and to have spent less time in the hospital. Although the results showed a narrower gap between the samples at 2-year follow-up (with no significant difference in the frequency of parasuicide), patients treated with DBT still attained a higher functional level than those in the comparison group (Linehan, Heard, & Armstrong, 1993).

More than 90% of the patients treated with DBT in this study stayed in therapy for the full year. This was a remarkable finding in a patient population known for a lack of treatment compliance. However, it should be noted that the patients received free treatment, whereas the cohort in TAU did not. Also, studies of DBT in other centers (Verheul et al., 2003) have noted higher rates of attrition (up to one third of cases).

This observation raises the question whether DBT is as effective outside of its original research center, with all the enthusiasm that such an environment can create. But the results of the first study have been replicated in other samples (Koerner & Linehan, 2000), and several independent studies outside Linehan's university have also yielded similar findings (Bohus et al., 2004; Katz, Cox, Gunasekara, & Miller, 2004; van den Bosch, Verheul, Schippers, & van den Brink, 2002; Verheul et al., 2003). It has also been shown that DBT is effective in BPD patients with substance abuse (Linehan et al., 2002). The main difference is that patient dropouts have been much higher outside Linehan's setting (e.g., Verheul et al., 2003).

One can also question whether TAU provides a fair comparison to assess a well-structured treatment like BPD. Ordinary clinical management can be slipshod or even messy (Westen, Novotny, & Thompson-Brenner, 2004). However, a second study by Linehan (in press) found that DBT remained superior to "treatment by experts" (TBE), in which experts with a special interest in BPD conducted psychodynamic or client-centered therapies. In this research, differences were less striking than they were in the comparison with TAU. The main finding after 1 year was a reduction in overdoses and subsequent hospitalizations, although again the comparison group tended to catch up at 1-year follow-up. As in the original study comparing DBT with TAU, fewer patients dropped out of DBT than out of TBE. However, there was no difference between the treatment conditions in reduction of self-mutilation, which was accomplished equally well by both types of therapy. Both conditions also were successful in reducing suicidal ideation and improving quality of life. Thus, although DBT remained superior to TBE, there were fewer differences than were seen in the comparison to TAU.

Several questions about DBT remain outstanding. The first concerns its claim to specific efficacy. The comparison with treatment by community experts (Linehan et al., 2006) shows that similar results can be obtained in other ways, even if improvement is somewhat slower. Also, DBT has not often been compared directly with other methods supported by controlled trials.

The second question concerns generalizability. We lack replication studies of the efficacy of BPD in larger samples. Although research on this population is difficult, many established treatments in psychiatry have been subjected to multiple-center clinical trials. Moreover, selection biases in clinical research can affect outcome (Westen et al., 2004). Not every BPD patient will follow through with DBT, and we do not know whether the treatment can be applied to the larger clinical population (Scheel, 2000).

The third question concerns the long-term outcome of patients who receive DBT. Linehan (1993) suggested that a full course of treatment could take several years, but only the first stage (in which parasuicidal behaviors are targeted and brought under control) has been tested. It would also be interesting to see if treated samples maintain their gains and whether they continue to improve or experience new symptoms. The original cohort studied by Linehan et al. (1991) received therapy 15 years ago but unfortunately has never been followed up.

The fourth question concerns practicality. DBT, like MBT, is resource intensive and expensive. For this reason, more than a decade after its introduction, its implementation has been spotty. Even where DBT is available, long waiting lists are common, an inevitable situation for a treatment that takes at least a year. It would be useful to see if DBT can be dismantled and streamlined to allow for greater clinical impact.

Some authors have suggested different cognitive-behavioral strategies for BPD. Young (1999) developed a method he calls "schema therapy," which includes some psychodynamic elements in that there is detailed exploration of the patient's childhood experiences. This approach is currently undergoing clinical trials in the Netherlands, with a comparison between schema therapy and TFP, but the results have not yet been published (A. Arntz, personal communication March, 2006). Beck and Freeman (2003) have offered their own approach to CBT in borderline patients, although that method has not undergone any clinical trials. It is possible that some of these approaches might have the same success as that already documented for DBT.

The main conclusion that emerges from the research summarized here is that psychotherapy for chronically suicidal patients needs to be highly structured and active. Although several methods have now been exposed to trials confirming their efficacy, it is not known whether the specific techniques presented in the handbooks describing these methods are in fact the most important. Again, the common ("nonspecific") effects of therapy (Lambert, 2004) involve establishing a good therapeutic alliance, providing empathy and validation, and taking a practical problem-solving approach. These principles help explain the success of DBT but are common to all methods.

In addition to these common factors, chronically suicidal patients may benefit from specific interventions. Both DBT and MBT work to help patients identify their emotions and to understand the links between emotions and impulsive actions. Both methods consistently validate the patient's emotions and encourage patients to reappraise their responses by becoming more aware of other people's feelings. The approach to treatment presented in chapter 9 is consistent with these principles.

Intermittent Therapy and Chronic Suicidality

Long-term continuous psychotherapy should not be the only option for chronically suicidal patients. Recent follow-up studies of BPD (Skodol et al., 2005; Zanarini, Frankenburg, Khera, & Bleichmar, 2003) have confirmed earlier findings (see review in Paris, 2003) showing that these patients have a waxing and waning course, with eventual recovery in most cases. In other words, not all chronically suicidal patients are suicidal all the time; patients can have crises yet function well between them.

This observation raises the possibility that chronically suicidal patients can be managed *intermittently*. This approach was suggested some years ago by McGlashan (1993), one of the authors of a major long-term follow-up study of patients with BPD, and I have also written in support of the option (Paris, 2003).

The approach to therapy depends on three strands of evidence. First, BPD patients recover gradually over time (see chap. 4) and often function better between crises. For this reason, it may not be cost-effective to see them continuously for years. Second, intermittent therapy allows patients to avoid unnecessary dependence and regression, allowing them to master life skills on their own. In this approach, patients can focus on their own development while retaining the option of returning to therapy if and when they hit a snag. Third, many patients have difficulty managing long-term therapy relationships, both in life and with mental health professionals. This is another reason why it may be helpful for them to take breaks in therapy.

In order to carry out intermittent therapy, one needs to let patients go when they are ready for a break but to remain available and to be in a position to take them back whenever they need to be seen. This also means that therapists who have rigid schedules probably cannot do this kind of work.

Nonetheless, there will always be patients who require long periods of regular therapy to obtain enough life satisfaction to separate, albeit temporarily, without feeling abandoned. These are patients who challenge us by remaining chronically suicidal for long periods. Chapter 8 examines how therapists can learn to tolerate that situation.

(7)

Pharmacotherapy and Chronic Suicidality

～

Psychotherapy is a well-documented way to treat patients with chronic suicidality. But this form of treatment has been overshadowed in recent years by pharmacological interventions. This chapter reviews the empirical evidence for the use of drugs in these patients. I show that although these agents are highly effective for a variety of mental disorders, they are only of limited value for chronic suicidality.

Pharmacotherapy and Contemporary Psychiatry

Whereas in the past, the zeitgeist of mental health practice favored an almost exclusive focus on psychotherapy, the pendulum has swung strongly in favor of pharmacotherapy. This is the result of discoveries of drugs for mental disorders that are dramatically effective for a wide variety of symptoms. We have agents that largely reverse psychotic symptoms, that stabilize mood, and that prevent recurrences of manic episodes. We also have agents that effectively control depression and anxiety, which are the most common symptoms therapists see. The problem is that many patients with complex problems do not respond well to any of these agents. (Indeed, if that were not the case, this book might be unnecessary!)

Life would be simpler if we could treat every difficult case with expert pharmacology. But in patients with personality disorders, the value of these agents has been vastly overrated (see review in Paris, 2003). I have tried to understand why psychiatrists have so much faith in prescribing drugs for chronically suicidal patients. I can only conclude that my discipline, having just emerged from its long infatuation with psychoanalysis, is in the grip of a new set of myths and has taken on a quasi-religious belief in the value of pharmacological methods.

Moreover, many patients accept these beliefs. Instead of wanting to be "completely analyzed," patients now want to correct their "chemical imbalances." People sometimes come into clinics asking for a practitioner with special expertise in psychopharmacology. They have come to believe that they need to have their medications adjusted, and adjusted repeatedly. No doubt the psychiatrists who do this kind of work believe in what they are doing. Like psychoanalysts, they act on the basis of theories rather than on evidence drawn from rigorous clinical trials.

In many of these patients, medication works for a short period of time and then mysteriously stops working. This phenomenon suggests that we are seeing powerful placebo effects. Are patients benefiting from medication "adjustments" because their neurotransmitters are better balanced? Or do they improve because they are being seen frequently and receiving tender loving care under the guise of psychopharmacology?

Psychotherapists who would prefer to manage these patients without drugs have been made to feel insecure. Even therapists who believe in their methods feel a need to be "covered" by psychiatric consultations to determine whether patients also require pharmacological interventions. The predictable result is that every patient ends up receiving one or more drugs. There is a large literature supporting the efficacy of the combination of psychotherapy and pharmacology in many mental disorders (Lambert, 2004). But the data do not show that *every* patient needs pharmacotherapy. Yet today, who is willing to say that a patient can manage on psychotherapy alone? It is difficult, if not impossible, to find such a consultant.

The Pharmacological Mismanagement of Chronic Suicidality

I am usually inclined to defend my own profession from its many critics. But when it comes to chronic suicidality, psychiatrists sometimes do more harm than good.

The problem arises from several sources. The first is a change in psychiatry itself. At one time, we were considered experts in psychotherapy who were frequently consulted by nonmedical therapists for advice about the optimal psychological management of patients. Then, in a single generation, the discipline of psychiatry underwent a paradigm shift, rejecting psychotherapy as its primary base in favor of biological interventions (Paris, 2005a). At the same time, psychologists, particularly practitioners of cognitive-behavioral therapy, have taken over leadership in studying and applying "talking therapies." Psychiatrists have retreated from that field, concentrating on their expertise in psychopharmacology. When consulted by colleagues, the question they are asked usually concerns medication.

Arguably, this model of psychiatry makes some sense for the treatment of chronically psychotic patients with schizophrenia or bipolar disorder. (The problem is that these patients also need psychotherapy.) But a purely biological approach is particularly unhelpful for chronically suicidal patients with personality disorders. Medication has only marginal effects in this group, many of whom who are likely to benefit from psychotherapy. Once patients get to psychiatrists, these patients often end up on a "polypharmacy" regime of dubious value.

How does this happen? When a distressed patient sees a doctor, the interaction creates an expectation that something needs to be done. (This is one of the reasons why medical patients often receive unnecessary antibiotics.) For the psychiatrist, "doing something" has come to mean writing a prescription. Because suicidal patients usually meet the fuzzy DSM-IV criteria for depression, they are prescribed antidepressants. But what happens if the medication does not work (as it often doesn't)?

One option is to continually adjust the dose. I have seen a number of patients in consultation who have been in treatment with psychiatrists who describe themselves as specialists in psychopharmacology. When patients experience increased distress, they are given more medication (or an "adjunctive" agent believed to increase the potency of antidepressants). This procedure, developed for patients with severe depression, has no basis in evidence from clinical trials in cases of milder or chronic depression. Even so, many patients will feel better after a medication adjustment, probably due to a placebo effect. Unfortunately, improvements are usually quite temporary.

Another option involves adding on another group of drugs. Although the same results can be obtained using antidepressants, neuroleptics or mood stabilizers may be added. The addition of a second or a third medication occurs when the first one has yielded little or no effect. Again, because placebo effects occur, one seems to see a temporary response. But the patient has not been taken off the original antidepressant, out of fear of a "relapse." Then, when the second drug has not removed symptoms, a fourth or a fifth is added, possibly an antianxiety agent or a second antidepressant.

This is how polypharmacy happens. Unfortunately, it is bad medicine and has no basis in evidence. No one has ever carried out clinical trials on drug combinations, even though we see patients taking them every day. For this reason, outpatient clinics in hospitals and the private offices of psychiatrists can be as toxic for chronically suicidal patients as inpatient wards.

Therapists treating this population should therefore be careful about requesting medical consultations, even in a crisis situation. It is tempting to believe that patients who are out of control will do better on medication, particularly when therapy alone is not containing their symptoms and the medication they are already on seems insufficient. There is a role for pharmacotherapy in these patients, but a single agent (usually a specific serotonin reuptake inhibitor [SSRI] antidepressant) will yield as much therapeutic effect as one can hope for, and it is usually best to stop there and get on with one's job.

Similarly, in a crisis where patients threaten suicide, nonmedical therapists may feel required to send their patients to an emergency room. In some cases, professional organizations have published guidelines insisting that this procedure is necessary. For example, referral to an emergency room is supported by the American Psychiatric Association (2003) guidelines for suicidal patients. Psychologists and social workers have been given similar guidelines. The problem is that once patients enter the medical system, they step on to a treadmill of repetitive hospital admissions and polypharmacy, so that the original purpose of treatment is almost forgotten.

Moreover, chronically suicidal patients who go to the emergency room are particularly likely to end up being "psychiatrized." By this I mean a process in which they are frequently admitted to wards and treated with multiple drugs. Patients will eventually accommodate their psychopathology to a system that reinforces it so strongly. In the name of medicine, psychiatrists end up mismanaging many chronically suicidal patients.

Today we hardly ever see patients who are not taking some psychopharmacological agent. It has become the received wisdom that suicidal patients cannot be properly treated without medication. And when patients are not doing well, psychiatrists are unlikely to see them without suggesting a new agent that has not yet been tried.

But psychiatrists are not the only cause of the problem. Because nonmedical therapists cannot prescribe these drugs, they tend to overvalue them. At the same time, therapists may want someone to share the burden and responsibility if something goes wrong.

Although it is often useful for clinicians of any professional background carrying difficult cases to get a second opinion, the consultant need not be a psychiatrist; one might just as easily choose an experienced nonmedical psychotherapist. Another received wisdom is that physicians are uniquely qualified to assess suicide risk. This is probably because the medical profession is used to making life-and-death decisions. Paradoxically, the only basis on which I have felt uniquely qualified as a psychiatrist to treat this population is that as a physician, I am in a better position to know the limits of my armamentarium and to treat patients more conservatively.

Research on Pharmacotherapy in Personality Disorders

I next support arguments presented here by critically examining evidence for the effectiveness of medication in personality disorders, most particularly BPD, which are associated with chronic suicidality.

Neuroleptics

Although neuroleptics were developed for the treatment of psychosis, it has long been known that low doses can reduce impulsive symptoms in patients with personality disorders (Soloff, 2000). Mood may not necessarily improve, but the tendency to act on suicidal ideation can be ameliorated. Yet in view of their side effects, psychiatrists have been rightly cautious about prescribing these agents. Neuroleptics were developed with another purpose in mind; their use in personality disorders is a rough-and-ready application that has a minimal theoretical basis.

For example, haloperidol, a neuroleptic widely used until a few years ago, has marginal effects on the symptoms of BPD, producing a general calming effect that reduces anger and aggression (Soloff, 2000). In one systematic follow-up (Soloff et al., 1993), patients tended to stop taking this drug, and short-term effects were not maintained at 6 months. The main problem was the side effects of this agent, which produces serious extrapyramidal effects (restlessness, shaking, and the facial appearance of Parkinson's disease).

In recent years, atypical neuroleptics such as risperidal and olanzapine, with milder side effect profiles, have replaced older drugs like haloperidol. In a controlled trial of olanzapine in BPD (Zanarini et al., 2001), the results suggested that these agents can be used in the same way as other neuroleptics. However, these newer drugs have their own side effects, most particularly, obesity associated with the long-term use of olanzapine.

Antidepressants

Chronically suicidal patients are depressed, but they do not respond to antidepressants in the same way as those with acute episodes of depression (Gunderson & Phillips, 1991). We should therefore be cautious in prescribing these agents. We no longer use tricylic antidepressants in highly suicidal patients, because it is too easy to kill oneself with these drugs—a week's supply can be fatal. Similar problems afflict monoamine oxidase inhibitors (Soloff, 2000).

Specific serotonin reuptake inhibitors (SSRIs) have been widely used for depression and are commonly prescribed in BPD, usually targeting depressive symptoms. But controlled trials have documented only modest improvements in mood in this population; the results fail to match the dramatic effects of antidepressants in melancholic depression (see reviews in Soloff, 2000; Paris, 2003).

Instead, SSRIs may actually be more effective for impulsive symptoms in personality disorders (Coccaro & Kavoussi, 1997). High doses (e.g., 60–80 mg of fluoxetine) have a specific effect that reduces self-mutilation (Markovitz, 1995), paralleling the use of these doses for other impulsive disorders such as bulimia nervosa. However, patients may have difficulty tolerating such levels, due to side effects such as akithisia, a form of motor restlessness that can actually increase suicidality (Healy, 1997).

When we prescribe the usual doses of SSRIs, the clinical results are equivocal. Most of the literature has suggested that mood in BPD is not consistently affected but that impulsive aggression is reduced (Coccaro & Kavoussi, 1997, also see reviews in Soloff, 2000; Paris, 2003). Only one study (Rinne, van den Brink, Wouters, & van Dyck, 2002) found that an SSRI (fluvoxamine) improved mood rather than impulsivity. Non-SSRI antidepressants such as venlflaxine and buproprion have not been formally tested in patients with BPD.

It is unusual today to see a patient with a personality disorder who is not on an antidepressant. Yet this practice is based more on clinical lore than on evidence from controlled trials. My own experience has been that antidepressants "take the edge off" the symptoms but do not have strong effects on underlying pathology.

Mood Stabilizers

The evidence for the use of mood stabilizers in personality disorders is also equivocal. Again, these drugs were developed for another category of patient, those with bipolar disorder. Today they are used widely for patients with BPD, on the assumption that they must be effective for mood swings, whether mood instability is associated with a mood disorder or a personality disorder. They are also prescribed on the assumption that patients with BPD "really" have a mood disorder, particularly bipolar II (Paris, 2004a).

However, empirical studies have not supported this practice. The only controlled study of lithium in BPD (Links, Steiner, Boiago, & Irwin, 1990) yielded marginal results, and few clinicians would wish to use a drug that is so dangerous on overdose. Results for other mood stabilizers (carbamazepine, valproate, lamotrigine) have also been inconsistent and equivocal. Carbamazepine was of some value in reducing impulsivity, albeit in one very small study (Cowdry & Gardner 1988). A controlled study of valproate (Hollander et al., 2001) found only marginal effectiveness in BPD; moreover, most patients dropped out of the trial. Later reports by the same group, with larger samples at multiple sites (Hollander et al., 2003; Hollander, Swann, Coccaro, Jiang, & Smith, 2005), found that valproate reduces impulsive aggression but is less effective for affective instability. Similarly, an uncontrolled trial of valproate (Kavoussi & Coccaro, 1998) observed anti-impulsive (but weak antidepressant) effects. The main exception to the rule is a study in which better results for valproate (for both unstable mood and impulsivity) were reported in a controlled trial by Frankenburg and Zanarini (2001). However, the sample in this study was limited to patients comorbid for bipolar II disorder (i.e., with clear-cut hypomanic episodes). Similar observations have been reported for other mood stabilizers. Both topiramate (Nickel et al., 2004) and lamotrigine (Tritt et al., 2005) are mainly effective for aggression and anger and do not reduce mood swings.

Thus, like neuroleptics and SSRIs, mood stabilizers seem to be more helpful for impulsivity than for mood instability itself (Kavoussi & Coccaro, 1998). For example, valproate is somewhat effective in impulsive children with conduct disorder (Fava, 1997). The problem is that when clinicians see mood swings, they respond with a knee-jerk request for this group of drugs. Once again, theory trumps evidence.

To understand why these drugs are not as effective as we wish, we need to consider the nature of affective instability. This is a key feature of BPD that distinguishes it from bipolar disorder as well as from other personality disorders (Koenigsberg et al., 2002; Paris, 2004a). The emotional dysregulation we see in chronically suicidal patients with personality disorders is a different phenomenon from the clinical picture of bipolar spectrum disorders (Paris, 2004a). Instead of mood that remains high or low for weeks on end, one sees changes that can occur over several hours, driven by the patient's sensitivity to life events and interpersonal stressors. In short, it is not that surprising that mood stabilizers have only marginal effects in chronically suicidal patients with BPD if this phenomenon may turn out to have an entirely different basis in neurobiology from the disorders for which they were designed. At this point, we know little about the mechanisms behind affective instability. However, the suggestion that personality disorders are nothing but bipolar variants (Akiskal, 2002) is backed up by little evidence beyond diagnostic overlap. Thus, it should not be surprising that mood stabilizers fail to produce the dramatic effects that are seen in classical bipolar disorders.

In this context, it is worth noting that many medications used in psychiatry show a much broader spectrum of action on psychopathology than would be suggested by their traditional names. Antidepressants are also effective for a variety of anxiety disorders and, as we have seen, have a strong anti-impulsive effect. Neuroleptics can be used to calm patients who have no psychotic illness. Similarly, mood stabilizers are effective against impulsivity and do not always reduce fluctuations in mood.

Anxiolytics

No matter what other drugs patients are receiving, they are often prescribed a benzodiazepine. These agents are usually offered as sleeping pills, because most patients with severe mental disorders suffer from insomnia.

However, there have been no clinical trials to determine whether suicidal patients with personality disorders derive benefit from these agents. Moreover, benzodiazepines are addictive, and one should be cautious in prescribing them for patients who already have substance abuse.

Other Agents

Because BPD is so difficult to treat, almost everything current in pharmacology seemed to have been tried at one point or another. For example, Zanarini and Frankenburg (2003) reported that omega-3 fatty acids may be an effective dietary supplement for BPD symptoms (at least in the small sample of patients they examined). This finding is consistent with evidence that omega-3s reduce violence in prisoners and may be useful in some cases of depression (Freeman, 2000). However, a single study does not provide sufficient evidence to recommend this treatment for this clinical population. Again, it was interesting to note that the supplement was more effective for impulsivity than for mood symptoms.

Overview

Although I am skeptical about the necessity of prescribing drugs for chronically suicidal patients, the evidence reviewed here shows that these drugs have some useful effects. The problem is that all the drugs that have been tried do much the same thing! Thus, neuroleptics, antidepressants, and mood stabilizers all make people less impulsive. This is useful, but patients taking these medications are usually as dysphoric and miserable as they were at the start. In this respect, pharmacotherapy should be seen as providing temporary symptomatic relief while psychotherapy, which aims for a more substantive improvement, is being conducted. Drugs should not be seen as definitive treatments, based on the mistaken assumption that these patients suffer from "treat-ment-resistant" mood disorders.

To be fair, psychotherapy is also more effective for impulsivity than for the deep psychic pain that characterizes these patients. Linehan (1993) found that the main effect of dialectical behavior therapy (DBT) was to reduce parasuicide and that patients remained dysphoric. This is consistent with research on the long-term outcome of patients with BPD (Paris, 2003), showing that impulsivity declines much more over time than does affective instability. Evidently, the easiest thing to help these patients with is impulsivity, which can often be reduced effectively in a short time. Emotional regulation and affective stability change much more slowly, and both psychotherapy and pharmacotherapy have a long way to go before they can demonstrate that they are effective for dysphoria.

Implications of Research for Practice

The data on both psychological and pharmacological treatments for patients with personality disorders are far from definitive. Yet they define the current state of empirical knowledge about the treatment of chronically suicidal patients. How can we apply these findings in practice?

Psychotherapy remains the mode of treatment with the most clearly proven effectiveness. If this is the case, why is it not used more extensively? There are three reasons. First, talking therapies take time, something that clinicians do not always have. Second, not everyone does well in therapy, and this is a population that may require special skills. Third, successful therapies can be resource-intensive, leading to waiting lists and unavailability. These problems affect all the methods that have been studied: DBT, MBT, and TFP.

Psychopharmacology, although it has produced miracles for many patients with severe depression, has been a major disappointment in chronically suicidal populations. Again, although these agents do provide some degree of symptomatic relief, most drugs do more or less the same thing. For this reason, it makes sense to prefer agents that have the least side effects (such as antidepressants).

The problem is that clinicians have been convinced that different drugs must have different actions. Thus, treatment-resistant patients who do not respond to a single agent receive drugs from several groups. It is not unusual today to see patents receiving a package of four or five drugs including SSRIs, non-SSRIs, mood stabilizers, neuroleptics, and benzodiazepines (Zanarini et al., 2001). And because none of these agents produces a remission, these patients are virtually guaranteed to experience troublesome side effects.

Again, if all you have is a hammer, everything looks like a nail. Thus, if most of what you do for patients is medicate them, you are almost bound to fall into the trap of polypharmacy.

I believe the evidence supports very different conclusions. First, if all drugs have the same effects, one should be enough. Second, you should choose a drug with the least troublesome side effects, most probably an SSRI. Finally, if the patient has not had a fair trial of psychotherapy, he or she should be offered that form of treatment. Finally, difficult as chronically suicidal patients are, they do not necessarily have to be referred to specialized treatment centers. The next two chapters suggest practical ways to manage these problems in ordinary clinical practice.

8

Tolerating Chronic Suicidality

∽

Chronically suicidal patients are a unique population, and they require unique interventions. One cannot apply protocols developed to manage suicidal ideas and actions in depressed patients with acute suicidality to patients with personality disorders who are chronically suicidal.

In fact, treating chronically suicidal patients as if they were acutely depressed is likely to lead not to management but to mismanagement. When we treat every suicidal threat as if it were a separate incident that must be managed for "safety," treatment becomes locked into a dead end of repeated (and unhelpful) hospital admissions. Because safety is an illusion in patients who are chronically suicidal, and attempts to prevent completion are usually futile and counterproductive, we need a better way to proceed.

What is the best way to deal with a patient's option for suicide? In psychotic or melancholic patients, we rightly see the choice of death as irrational. But in chronically suicidal patients, therapists may need to tolerate and accept the option of suicide.

This approach may seem paradoxical. However, acceptance and respect for a patient's autonomy helps therapists to focus on two important goals. First, tolerating suicidality prevents us from being distracted from our job by anxiety. It allows us to devote our energies to treating the problems that have made patients consider ending their lives in the first place. If we cannot, in any case, prevent suicide in these patients, we should do what we can do rather than what we cannot do.

Moreover, as follow-up studies have shown, chronically suicidal patients do not usually kill themselves in the midst of treatment. If they die, it will be after everything has been tried and has failed. In this context, we can lower our level of anxiety and concentrate on therapeutic tasks. This means working to alter the life circumstances that lead patients to be "half in love with death."

Second, tolerating suicidality acknowledges the communication of distress while respecting choice. As discussed in chapter 2, chronically suicidal patients have a unique inner world in which suicidality becomes not an alien state but part of their personality and identity. Failure to respect autonomy can be counterproductive, in that the therapist is seen as just one more person in the patient's life imposing an agenda. The most empathic position for therapists is to let the patient know that although we disagree that suicide is necessary, and hope that it will eventually become unnecessary, we understand that for the present, it needs to be retained as an option.

Reflection Versus Action

Empathic responses are of particular importance in the management of chronically suicidal patients. Although accurate empathy is an essential element of all therapies, empathic responses model reflection over action. By understanding (rather than panicking), therapists can model this preference. In contrast, when we move directly to action (e.g., by rushing the patient to an emergency room or a hospital), we implicitly agree with the patient that emotional distress cannot be tolerated. If we agree that action on our part is necessary (to prevent action on their part), therapy moves in the wrong direction.

Of course, it is the patient who is pressing the therapist to act. Yet this is often the same way that these clients deal with the outside world. Therapists see coping in a different way. We teach our patients to observe emotions and control impulses. Our primary tools are reflection and empathy, and we believe that patients need to learn the same skills.

Let us consider a scenario that every therapist who has worked with this population will recognize. A patient threatens to commit suicide and does not seem willing to consider alternatives. Threats (or attempts) escalate as a way of forcing the therapist's hand. One feels caught in a game of "chicken" that no one can win.

Clearly, patients with chronic suicidal ideation can put therapists in a difficult, if not impossible, position. The patient threatens to die and may even suggest that the therapist will be at fault for his or her death. Therapists may also be accused of not caring if they do not act in the way the patient expects. Appeals to the therapeutic alliance go unheard. Patients may make disturbing statements such as "Don't talk to me about next week; I won't be here," or more angrily, "You'll read about it in the newspapers."

In this scenario, patients expect us to respond by hospitalizing them—even when they overtly protest against admission. Context is all-important here. Suicidality is not being communicated in a vacuum but to a professional who is expected to provide relief from distress. Therapists may be sorely tempted to accept the patient's implicit or explicit request. Admission seems to be the only way to make sure the patient knows we are listening.

Actually there are other important reasons, aside from suicidal intent, why our patients may want to stay in a hospital. In many cases, admission for suicidality has been a pattern in previous treatments with other therapists. Not responding in the same way can be perceived as not caring.

Often, the most important reason why patients request admission is that they actually *like* to be on a hospital ward (even if that environment is not good for them!). These patients have problematical lives from which they wish respite. Suicidal patients are generally lonely. On a ward, they at least have nurses to talk to. They may also meet other patients with similar problems (even if such contacts provide a context for social contagion of suicidal behaviors).

Taking into account the practical impossibility of preventing suicide completion, I recommend avoiding hospitalization for chronically suicidal patients under almost all circumstances. I have listed exceptions to this rule in chapter 5: near-fatal attempts and psychotic episodes. I have also suggested that when therapy is out of control, day hospital provides a better and less regressive alternative to full admission.

Clinical Example

Georgina was a 26-year-old student who had been admitted from a university mental health service to a hospital for chronic suicidality, self-mutilation, and micropsychotic symptoms. Her therapist had been particularly concerned that Georgina was hearing voices telling her to kill herself, accompanied by a disturbing feeling that strangers were talking about her and commenting on her behavior.

Georgina was admitted to a schizophrenia unit and stayed there for 6 months. Because of this putative diagnosis, Georgina received large doses of several types of neuroleptic drugs, none of which had any perceptible effect on her condition. Following a review of the case, and a rediagnosis of psychotic depression, Georgina was moved to a mood disorders unit. She remained there for another 6 months, while being prescribed selective serotonin reuptake inhibitors (SSRIs), monoamine oxidase (MAO) inhibitors, and various "augmenting" agents. When this course of treatment failed,

Georgina's parents had her discharged and transferred to a less specialized hospital closer to home.

However, this new environment was equally unhelpful. Now diagnosed with "complex post-traumatic stress disorder," Georgina received another 6 months of treatment in hospitals, this time focusing on psychological treatment to help her "recover" traumatic memories. The result was that Georgina regressed and continued to cut herself daily (despite all restrictions), while being placed on constant nursing observation.

When I was called to consult on Georgina's treatment, my main recommendation was that she be immediately discharged and transferred to a day hospital. This was done, and although her stay there was stormy, Georgina was able to move back to her home. Although Georgina did not return to school, she was now able to find a job and avoid being readmitted.

This example illustrates the "comedy of errors" that can sometimes emerge from certain practices of modern psychiatry, with its propensity to adopt diagnostic and treatment fads. No one recognized that Georgina had a fairly typical case of BPD (personality disorders being almost never diagnosed on any of the units she was admitted to). As a result, Georgina suffered from pharmacological and psychological interventions that made her worse. Moreover, a series of long hospital stays cut her off from her social and educational environment, to which she never returned. Georgina was "psychiatrized" by the system, and became a "chronic case," albeit as an outpatient. Although the outcome could have been the same with more conservative treatment, Georgina would not have lost almost 2 years of her life.

The Vicious Cycle of Repeated Hospitalization

Let us now consider the consequences of multiple hospitalizations in more detail. Therapy is suspended, if not derailed, every time we admit patients to a ward. One can hardly help someone to deal with life problems when their life consists of taking medication, attending occupational therapy, and watching TV on a ward. Moreover, to be in and out of hospitals for suicidal threats and actions usually means that patients cannot hold a job and have to give up any serious opportunity to develop meaningful relationships.

When this sequence goes on for long enough, the mental health system becomes the main source of interpersonal satisfaction for the patient. We see this outcome in patients who remain in treatment over decades in psychiatric clinics. These psychiatrized patients have lost contact with their social milieu, and their lives have come to center on their role as patient and on the response (or lack of response) of professionals to their needs. This is a process that can eventually become irreversible.

The more frequently patients are admitted, the more likely is this grim scenario. Yet many clinicians are still reluctant to refuse hospitalization in these situations. In discussing this contentious issue with colleagues, I have often heard the riposte "one cannot do therapy on a dead patient." Yet as previous chapters have shown, this argument, however rhetorically effective it may be, does not correspond to the facts. Patients rarely commit suicide under circumstances in which they are actively threatening or angrily confronting the therapist. The scenario for suicide is much more likely to be one of hopelessness and disconnection. We often think we should have known how to prevent a suicide—once it has already occurred. And when patients do commit suicide, we cannot know whether admitting them to a hospital would have made a difference.

Some colleagues have expressed the concern that refusing to act on suicidal threats can be seen as invalidating the patient's emotions. I do not agree with this view. When we do not hospitalize chronically suicidal patients, we are not in any way dismissing or devaluing them. In some ways, we are actually providing them with more validation. The message to a

patient should, of course, never be "you are just trying to ma-
nipulate me, and I won't let you." That is not therapy but a
power struggle. Rather, the message should be, "You must be
feeling terrible to be thinking about suicide, but we need to
understand what your problems are, and work on them. And I
believe you are capable of doing that." Therapists always have
to have confidence in their patients and connect to their
healthy side.

Clinical Example

Lydia was a 22-year-old woman completing a university degree
who was in long-term psychodynamic therapy for chronic
suicidality. Over the course of this treatment, her therapist was
frequently alarmed by Lydia's suicidality. In addition to taking
several overdoses of pills, Lydia threatened to hang herself (stat-
ing she had only been interrupted from carrying out this intention by a phone call). Lydia was also a chronic cutter.

   Each time Lydia made a suicide attempt (or threatened to),
the therapist responded by suggesting she would be "safer" in
a hospital. The result was that Lydia was admitted two to
three times a year. These episodes usually followed the failure
of an intimate relationship. Typically, the behavior only consisted of a wrist cut or a small overdose, but Lydia had a way of
making her threats frightening, for example, informing her
therapist that she had written a will and that she had already
arranged all the details of her funeral.

   In this example, therapy was derailed by responses to
suicidality; hospitalization provided consistent reinforcement
for the patient's pathology. Eventually Lydia, who was fairly
bright, managed to graduate university. But her pattern, now
reinforced by the system, continued for years thereafter, inter-
fering with her ability to establish meaningful commitments
in life.

Regression and Chronic Suicidality

Therapists must be careful about giving patients the message that extreme dependency is legitimate. No matter how "regressed" a patient seems to be, we need to believe that he or she is capable of functioning at a higher level. We communicate an important message of hope by expressing confidence in the patient's eventual ability to recover.

I have discussed the negative effects of hospitalization and the futility of treating patients with multiple forms of medication. But there are many roads to regression, not all of which arise from medical interventions. Some of these complications come from the way therapy is conducted. Chronically suicidal patients with personality disorders may take a role in which they define themselves as helpless and needy. Psychotherapists sometimes do things that only reinforce this perception.

Encouraging regression has been associated with the psychoanalytic model, as well with other forms of therapy in which patients are seen as needing some form of "reparenting" (Greben, 1985). Although every patient needs to depend *healthily* to receive meaningful help, the therapeutic relationship is collaborative, not parental. We have only one chance in life to be a child, and there is no going back. In general, recovery comes from cutting one's losses and moving on. If the focus of therapy is on childhood, and the therapist becomes the good parent the patient never had, regression is a predictable outcome.

Similarly, psychotherapy must not be allowed to turn into a life-or-death struggle, in which the love and approval of the therapist count for everything. This is exactly what tends to happen with other intimate relationships in the life of chronically suicidal patients. Instead, the consistent message of the treatment has to be, " I understand your needs, but they cannot be satisfied here in therapy. Instead I can help you find ways to find more satisfaction in your life outside, even if that process will take time."

Another concept that promotes regression, also derived from the psychoanalytic model, is transference. In a classical Freudian approach, therapists expected a cure to take place in "the crucible of the transference" (Greben, 1985), that is, by reliving problems with a therapist and understanding them in a new way. Psychotherapy can sometimes produce a "corrective emotional experience" (Alexander & French, 1946), in the sense that a therapist takes a respectful approach that counters certain past experiences for the patient. But treatment that uses regression deliberately, in an attempt to provide reparenting, is dangerous. It has never been shown to be effective, even for better functioning patients, and may carry particular risks for patients with chronic suicidality.

A strong belief in transference interpretation as the *sine qua non* of good therapy has led to misuse of this kind of intervention. Research shows that transference interpretations are counterproductive in patients with poorer functioning (Piper et al., 1991). In people with interpersonal impairments, constant harping on the way they feel about the therapists, as opposed to problems in their outside life, only drives patients deeper into unhelpful dependency.

A related issue concerns the regressive effects of seeing patients too often. Sometimes we are tempted to see suicidal patients two or three times a week, on the grounds that they need that frequency to avoid falling apart between sessions. But seeing people so often carries an implicitly regressive message. We are telling them they cannot manage without us, rather than encouraging them to wait for their sessions and work on better coping. We need to avoid being "caring" therapists who go along with patients' belief that they cannot survive until the next session.

In contrast, once-a-week therapy gives the message that the real work required for recovery has to be done outside the therapy room and will not be magically provided by treatment. Similarly, focusing too much on therapist vacations and absences works against the goals of treatment (with the exception that one may need to provide a substitute when the therapist is absent for prolonged periods). Again, do we want to tell patients they are helpless without us or give their healthy side a vote of confidence?

Finally, psychoanalytic therapists have traditionally believed that exploring the past is a crucial element of effective psychotherapy. Yet there is no empirical evidence that this is true (Paris, 2000, 2005a). As documented in chapter 6, therapy works mostly due to common factors, and most change takes place by dealing with current issues, not by working through past traumas. Moreover, focusing too much on childhood traumas can become another source of regression. Some patients will become more and more mired in the past, particularly if they are encouraged to feel like victims. This approach rarely leads to change in the present, where it is most needed.

Although I was trained to use a psychodynamic model, I have learned to apply that approach sparingly with chronically suicidal patients. I make sure that I know about the past, and I do show patients, when appropriate, that they are repeating patterns or misperceiving people in the light of previous experiences. But I do not spend most of the time of therapy on these issues. For many patients, the traumas of childhood need not be dwelled on. There are times in life when people must move on and give up brooding on the past. As patients often remind us, knowing is not the same as changing.

Not every form of therapy focuses on the past. The main difference between psychoanalytic and cognitive models is that cognitive-behavioral therapy (CBT) maintains a consistent orientation to the present and is more interested in current problems than earlier experience. Although some cognitive therapists (e.g., Young, 1999) also focus on the effects of childhood experiences (which can produce cognitive "schema") in therapy, they still spend most of their efforts developing practical strategies to improve the quality of adult life.

In summary, to avoid mismanaging chronically suicidal patients, we have to believe that they can get better. When we psychiatrize patients, prescribing excessive medication and unnecessary hospital admissions, while encouraging helplessness and dependence, we can only be working regressively, not progressively. Patience—rather than panic—is called for. And as we have seen, most chronically suicidal patients do get better with time, so therapists can feel some degree of confidence that their efforts will be successful.

Unfortunately, some patients have been sufficiently treated (or mistreated) by the system that they fall into an irreversible regression. We have all seen patients who end up on welfare, losing all meaningful relationships over time. This is most likely to happen in patients who are in and out of hospitals over many years. The tragic truth is that it is difficult to reverse this process once it has been allowed to happen. When developmental milestones have been missed, life does not necessarily give us a second chance.

Responding Empathically to Suicidality

A therapist who focuses on understanding patients without actively intervening in a crisis is working on a knife-edge. Yet this scenario also provides an opportunity for therapists to get their message across.

First, maintaining an empathic stance models something important for patients. Treatment supports the benefits of reflection over action. We can let chronically suicidal patients know that they need to learn how to tolerate painful emotions, and that although feelings may be very painful, action is not required to suppress them.

At the same time, an empathic stance shows that the therapist understands the implicit communication behind suicidal threats. The message is that the therapists understand how exquisite the suffering of patients must be if they are considering death as a way of escape.

In summary, therapists need to stand their ground, even in the face of suicidal threats, but to do so without giving the impression that suicidality is not being taken seriously. On the contrary, we need to say, "I take your feelings very seriously indeed." Any suggestion that suicide threats or attempts are viewed as attention-getting maneuvers has to be scrupulously avoided. The therapist communicates genuine concern but works to have the patient join in an exploration of what lies behind suicidality.

And if hospitalization is not offered, the patient deserves an explanation. The therapist can state clearly the pros and cons of a hospital stay. Moreover, if, as is often the case, the patient has had previous admissions, one can review the extent to which they were or were not helpful.

Gunderson (2001) described an interesting take on this kind of situation. He tells patients he will hospitalize them if they insist but explains why he does not recommend doing so. This strategy aims to avoid a power struggle and give the patient more control. The main problem with this suggestion is that if the patient still chooses to go to the hospital, the therapist has to agree.

Linehan (1993) finesses the problem in a rather different way. She does not herself send patients to the hospital but tells them they can, if they wish, present to an emergency room, where an overnight hold might be offered by another clinician. Thus Linehan herself takes no responsibility for arranging admissions that she does not believe in. At the same time, she makes it clear that taking up this option works against the overall goals of therapy, which are to help patients cope with current life situations. Giving this message might even be one of the factors behind the success of dialectical behavior therapy (DBT) in reducing hospitalizations.

My own approach is not to bring up the hospital as an option. If the patient raises the issue, I explain why I do not think this course of action will be helpful. If the patient still threatens to commit suicide before the next session, I will respond by saying, "You have been thinking about suicide for a long time, and you will probably continue to think about it. You and I both know that we cannot prevent you from dying. But I want to keep working with you and can see your life eventually getting better. So although I realize how upset you are feeling now, I have to continue on the assumption that you will come to see me next week."

Even when patients avoid entering the hospital, the subsequent course of treatment is not necessarily going to be easy. The therapist may face weeks to months during which a patient is continuously threatening suicide. Sessions may end in uncertainty as to whether therapist and patient will ever see each other again. Yet as frightening as this situation can be, it is a rare scenario for completed suicide. Paradoxically, chronic suicidality can become a bonding force between therapist and patient. Both are locked into a life-and-death struggle in which neither can let go without a resolution.

Clinical Example

Julia was a 32-year-old woman who had difficulties since adolescence (with serious substance abuse) and who had been chronically suicidal for 4 years. Currently she was living with a man and working as a publicist.

In her previous long-term therapy, Julia had been hospitalized on multiple occasions, with the result that she had stopped working and gone on long-term disability. At the same time, her relationship with her partner deteriorated to the point that he announced he would be leaving within the next few months. Following an overdose, she had still another admission and a period of 3 months in day hospital. At this point, Julia was referred to a specialized personality disorder program.

Although Julia talked about suicide in every session, the therapist noted that she looked inquiringly at him when communicating these thoughts, searching for a response. Each time this happened, the therapist let the patient know that he understood how bad her life must be for her to be thinking along these lines. The patient would then say, "Aren't you worried enough to do something about it?"

The therapist would respond by saying that suicide was ultimately Julia's choice and that there was nothing he could do to prevent it if she were to embrace that option. At the same time, he pointed out to Julia that she had not always felt this way, because that there had been happier times in her life, showing that she was not doomed to live in constant despair.

Finally, the therapist suggested that losing her boyfriend would be terrible and that it would take some time to get over that loss. On the other hand, given the present state of that relationship (which made Julia feel even more inadequate), ending it would not necessarily be the end of the world. Finally, he emphasized the importance of getting back to work, where competence had given her some degree of worth.

Julia did not respond immediately to these interventions. In fact, she tested the therapist by taking a small overdose early on in the treatment. Nevertheless, within a few months she accepted the separation from her partner, while reconciling herself with family and obtaining increased support from her sister and parents. At the same time, Julia made plans to return to her previous job.

Protecting the Therapist

Patients with chronic suicidality can be difficult and frightening. One can therefore understand how a certain degree of irrationality on the therapist's part can affect treatment. Chapter 10 focuses on how fear of litigation influences practice. At this point, I focus on the emotional drain of treating chronically suicidal patients.

The clinical literature in this area has described the toll that these patients can impose on therapists. More than 30 years ago, in an eloquent article, Maltsberger and Buie (1974) described the reactions of therapists to chronically suicidal patients as "counter-transference hate." In other words, the pressure that patients put therapists under can make them wish that their patients would actually commit suicide, removing the burden produced by repeated threats. Although such reactions may not come out in any overt way, Maltsberger and Buie suggested that this situation can lead to a subtle withdrawal of empathy that leaves patients feeling emotionally abandoned.

Yet although such "counter-transference" feelings certainly occur, I do not agree that recognizing and mastering them are the key to success in treatment. Instead, I suggest that therapists need to protect themselves from an onslaught long before their personal reactions reach a boiling point.

To accomplish that goal, therapists need to have a perspective on what therapy can and cannot do. As recommended by many writers on the subject (Gunderson, 2001; Kernberg, 1987; Maltsberger, 1994a), therapists should understand that, as much as they favor life over death, they are not usually able to prevent patients from committing suicide. Standing our ground about what we can actually offer, we are better protected from hating our patients.

Therapists also need to share the burden. One cannot expect to manage patients like this without consultation. Linehan's (1993) DBT has a built-in consultative process for all treating personnel. In practice, every active therapist needs colleagues to talk to, preferably those who know this kind of patient. Moreover, consultation reduces the fear of (and the danger of) litigation (see chapter 10). Finally, as chapter 9 suggests, the patient's family should be brought in as allies (and not as adversaries).

Hope and Recovery From Chronic Suicidality

Tolerating chronic suicidality also implies that we need to accept a wide range of outcomes after treatment. As discussed in chapter 6, most people can eventually be expected to recover from this state of mind. But when we treat people over extended periods, it is difficult to know what has actually helped. Would the patient have gotten better over time? Does our main function consist of supporting people through difficult times? Are there specific things we can do that make a difference?

Most likely, the answer to all these questions is "yes." As people mature, their emotions become less volatile and they are less likely to act impulsively. Therapy helps reduce the frequency and the consequences of dysfunctional behavior. There is also evidence that specific interventions targeting emotional dysregulation and impulsive actions make this process work faster.

Some patients who begin therapy with a picture of chronic suicidality make a complete recovery. These are the cases we like to talk about with our colleagues! Others only show partial improvement. As documented in long-term follow-up studies of BPD, most patients will succeed in finding a niche in life, but not all will attain stable intimacy. (But keep in mind that this is more or less true for many people in today's world.)

Therapists must be comfortable with partial results. They need not continue treating patients for life, hoping for changes that are unlikely to take place. (Interminable psychotherapy is one of the more problematic legacies of psychoanalysis.) When some degree of recovery is obtained, most patients can be discharged. The main point to keep in mind for this population is that there is no such thing as "finishing" therapy. Patients must be allowed (or even encouraged) to return for further sessions when they are in a crisis or if they simply want to touch base with the therapist.

Finally, it must be acknowledged that some chronically suicidal patients do not do well, even with the best therapy. Treatment failures go with the territory of mental health practice, because patients with more severe disorders have a more chronic course (Paris, 2003). And some of these patients never enter therapy; they are seen in emergency rooms and crisis centers but never quite connect with anyone. Thus, the people who enter treatment are already somewhat preselected for motivation.

There will always be patients we cannot help and can only maintain or support. We have a great deal to offer most of the patients we see, but we need to be humble about what we can and cannot do.

9

Managing Chronic Suicidality

∽

This chapter outlines, in broad strokes, a practical approach for the management of chronic suicidality. I will adapt some overall evidence-based principles of psychotherapy to the unique characteristics of these patients. But since this book is not a treatment manual, I do not try to describe every aspect of psychotherapy in systematic detail. Instead, this chapter suggests overall guidelines for dealing with suicidal threats and attempts, as illustrated by clinical examples.

Other disclaimers are in order. I am not proposing a unique method or technique of therapy. My approach draws on the work of many other writers and is in line with the ideas of leading researchers on personality disorders (Gunderson, 2001; Linehan, 1993; Livesley, 2003). I also have no intention of describing a new type of therapy labeled with an acronym (the field already has too many of these!). Finally, although I have not conducted clinical trials on my approach, it is consistent with empirical data on the treatment of chronically suicidal patients with personality disorders (see chapter 6).

I begin by addressing three practical issues that define some of the structures of treatment: alliance building, the handling

of suicidal crises, and the use of telephone contact. I then propose three general principles to guide therapeutic interventions in chronically suicidal patients: helping patients regulate
intense emotions, helping them learn to curb impulsivity, and
helping them find a way to "get a life."

Alliance Building and Help Rejection

The first step in any therapy always involves establishing an alliance. Once both parties agree on what needs to be done and
how to go about doing it, therapy will be off to a good start.

The interventions shown by research to be the key elements
of success in all forms of psychological treatment consist of
empathy, a working alliance, and a focus on current life problems (Lambert, 2004). These general principles have been described as common factors that apply to therapy with all types
of patients, each of which is more important than any specific
technique (Wampold, 2001). Common factors may even be of
even greater importance for people who do not expect to be
understood or validated, who have serious problems with
trust, and who have almost given up hope for solving life's
challenges.

Understanding the inner world of chronically suicidal patients is not simple. Although empathy is a crucial element of
all therapy, it is only useful if the patient actually *feels* understood. Similarly, one can only work on building trust and addressing life problems if the patient agrees. This is why the
impact of any specific intervention must be framed in the context of a strong alliance.

The therapeutic alliance in chronically suicidal patients has
been found to be, at best, fragile, particularly among those diagnosed with personality disorders (Frank, 1992). To be
chronically suicidal implies a point of view: No one can be
trusted, so that the patient needs to maintain control over her
or his own death "for dear life." In this sense, suicidality im-

plicitly carries the message, "I don't really think you can help me, even if we are sitting here together. And I reserve the right to kill myself if my assumption turns out to be right."

Many years ago, Adler (1979) suggested that for these patients, developing a working alliance should be seen as the endpoint of therapy, rather than its precondition. Adler archly pointed out that patients with BPD may not even share the concept of "we." (That is what therapists take for granted when they talk about common goals). Adler emphasized that in this population, trust in others is at best tenuous, and patients cannot be expected to maintain a consistent therapeutic alliance until they are much better.

Adler's observations make good clinical sense. These are patients whose participation in therapy is often hard to assess. I have had the experience of having to face withering criticism, even when I believed I was trying my very best to be therapeutic. I have also thought I had a good therapy session, only to discover that the patient found it unhelpful. Understanding the reasons for these discrepancies helped me to learn how to work with this population. In some cases, I had been pleased to explore issues that I thought were important, but these issues were perceived as irrelevant by patients, who were more preoccupied with hopelessness. In other cases, patients thought that if I was pleased with the session, this only proved that I was working on some agenda of my own while discounting their inner despair.

In this respect, chronically suicidal patients are often afraid that pleasing others, including therapists, can only occur at their own expense. At the same time, their fear of abandonment may be so great that any statement by the therapist that things are going well (or even a nonverbal expression of pleasure) can be perceived as abandonment. One of the reasons why these patients are half in love with death is that their suicidality binds others and makes them care.

Chronically suicidal patients have a fragile connection to therapists but tend to move in and out of a therapeutic alliance over time. Thus, even when patients are most help-rejecting, therapists need to keep in touch with the part of them that wants to get better. In fact, therapists need to tolerate rejection in the same way as they tolerate chronic suicidality itself.

When patients are hostile and devaluing, one begins by simply acknowledging the situation. The therapist can let the patient know that although, at least for the moment, they are not working together, the situation can change.

Clinicians who have worked with this population will recognize the experience of feeling rejected despite experiencing real concern and care. One can be trying one's best to be empathic and then be brushed aside, with comments like, "It doesn't really matter any more," or "You have to say that, since that's what you're paid for." In this state of mind, any reasonable suggestions to move into a problem-solving mode will be dismissed with contempt. But this is a situation that does not usually last. No matter how negative and upsetting a therapy session, there is another chance for both parties to do better.

Handling Suicidal Crises

Suicidal crises usually emerge from problems with relationships. Something or someone has touched on the patient's sensitivity, most often a rejection by a person playing a significant role in the patient's life. Anger and abandonment then fuel the idea of suicide. In the patient's mind, the world, which has so cruelly rejected her, will be better off without her presence. There can be a bitter feeling that no one has ever cared or ever will care. Yet bubbling just below the surface is the idea that those responsible for these rejections should end up paying, by suffering regret after the patient's death.

How can therapy manage this kind of situation? The first principle is not to panic and to continue focusing on the task at hand. Even in patients who always retain the option of suicide, the therapist can examine reasons for changes in the level of suicidal ideas. One can carry out this exploration while maintaining a consistent frame and structure.

Thus, suicidal ideas and actions must always be considered as workable. For example, after being rejected in an intimate relationship, patients may feel that they cannot go on living. But the therapist, while understanding and reflecting on how crushing such a loss can be, will approach the situation as a psychological problem that has a solution. Thus, however distressing the situation, it can be of benefit in teaching the patient how to handle distress. We need to tell our patients that this is our goal. We can suggest to patients that however tempting it may be to act out impulsively rather than "suffer in silence," they have an opportunity to learn other ways of coping.

A second principle is that therapists need to draw on the common factors of psychotherapy when they face a crisis. Patients go out of control because, unlike other people, they feel totally isolated and uncared for. To the extent that suicidality reflects a feeling of being unheard and misunderstood, therapy provides empathic understanding that tends to contain dysphoric emotions.

Difficult as it is, we must imagine in our own minds the inner world of these patients and communicate our concern and empathy for their pain. To the extent that suicidality reflects hopelessness, the consistently positive attitude of the therapist, supporting long-term hopefulness, provides a corrective. To the extent that suicidality is based on impulsivity, therapists offer an approach that favors reflection over action. To the extent that suicidality represents a way of establishing control of a life that feels out of control, therapy respects this need while anticipating a time when better ways of coping will be found.

When we apply these principles, a session that deals with a suicidal crisis need not be very different from any other. A threat of suicide should not bring the normal procedures of treatment to a halt. As discussed in chapter 8, one need not respond with hospitalization, because doing so has not been shown to prevent suicide and is as likely to make things worse as better. Similarly, as discussed in chapter 6, there are no magical interventions (such as interpretations) that are likely to make a difference in this situation. However, suicidal threats correspond to implicit breaches in the alliance. Thus, when patients are in crisis, therapists must be prepared to see their most empathic comments rejected or dismissed. Finally, as discussed in chapter 7, there is no evidence that reassessing or changing a medication regime is likely to be effective in a suicidal crisis.

Some things that therapists do when patients threaten suicide can actually be counterproductive. One of the most common responses to a suicidal crisis is to see the patient more frequently. There is no evidence that doing so is effective. Some research exists on the length of psychotherapy (see Lambert, 2004), yet surprisingly, no one has ever conducted a study on whether frequency makes a difference. If there is not a stitch of evidence that seeing patients twice a week is better than seeing them once a week in any form of therapy, we should think twice before assuming that more is better. And no one has ever studied whether increasing sessions makes a difference in a crisis. Most patients come to therapy once a week. In the absence of research evidence demonstrating that a higher frequency makes any difference, this can be considered the default condition.

Moreover, increasing the frequency of sessions has a potential to be counterproductive. First, seeing the therapist more often provides an implicit reward for being suicidal. From a purely behavioral point of view, this kind of reinforcement makes repetition in the future more likely. Second, increasing frequency may not even succeed in calming the patient. Third, by stirring up powerful emotional needs in the therapeutic relationship, increasing frequency can lead to further regression.

One aspect concerns boundary problems, which are particularly likely to occur in suicidal patients with personality disorders (Gutheil & Gabbard, 1993). If you see a patient several days a week, he or she is more likely to imagine having a relationship with you outside the therapy room.

Malignant regressions, in both inpatient and outpatient treatment, are equally common in this population (Dawson & MacMillan, 1993). The more frequently a patient is seen, the more suicidal behaviors are elicited, because they have become a ticket to obtaining care and connection.

If seeing patients twice a week is not enough, the process can become unstoppable—patients may end up being seen three times a week, or even daily. When that happens, treatment is not on a path toward health but is moving rapidly toward regression and pathological dependency.

Thus, even if patients threaten suicide or insist that they cannot wait a week for another session, the therapist is best advised to stand firm. Although following these recommendations requires a thick skin, doing so is important for maintaining the frame of therapy. Such situations are frightening (and can lead to lost sleep for the therapist), but we must always remember that ultimately the choice between life and death does not lie in our hands. Keeping this principle in mind makes it easier to remain consistent and maintain a focus on our task: to find solutions to the problems that led the patient to have a suicidal crisis in the first place.

Finally, we need not fall into the trap of agreeing with patients that they are helpless in the grip of suicidal ideas. This is another way in which treatment can come to lie on a knife-edge of regression. Therapy works best when it addresses itself to the healthiest part of the person, not the sickest. Thus, patients should be expected to keep working on their problems, even if they cannot solve them in the short run. Both therapist and patient must keep in mind that treatment requires both time and hope.

Telephone Contact: Pros and Cons

In addition to offering extra sessions, many therapists treating suicidal patients follow the practice of offering patients telephone contact in a crisis. Fortunately, many (if not most) patients are reassured by these offers and never call. But if they do call, what should therapists actually say to patients threatening suicide? It is not usually possible to conduct a psychotherapy session on the telephone. At best we might take the opportunity to offer an extra session, although it is not clear whether doing so will help. And if the only advice we give is to go to a hospital, then the telephone call may not have even been necessary.

Linehan's (1993) dialectical behavior therapy (DBT) takes a different approach to these thorny issues. Her method provides coaching on the telephone to support techniques that the patient has already learned to reduce suicidal ideation. This telephone strategy is one of the unique aspects of DBT. Patients are actually encouraged to call, as long as they remain in distress but do not act out impulsively. The aim of the call is to break the links between emotions and actions by helping patients to develop positive coping strategies when stressed to the point of having suicidal thoughts. It is not designed for support in a crisis but to reinforce the use of previously taught skills.

DBT also provides negative reinforcements (temporary loss of sessions) if the patient actually goes on to overdose or cut. Telephone contacts are brief (usually no more than 10 minutes). Moreover, every DBT therapist has a pager with an answering machine, so that patients are expected to wait until they are called back (usually on the same day). Even this relatively brief wait gives out the message that reflection is better than action. And therapists are protected from being awakened in the middle of the night.

Even so, not every therapist is willing to have personal time interrupted by a telephone call. In fact, calls out of hours are probably one of the main reasons why therapists are reluctant to treat chronically suicidal patients. Mental health work is hard, and we need time for ourselves and for our families. For this reason, some clinicians find treating this population too stressful and exclude them from their practice. It is unfortunate that these patients, who find it difficult to engage in therapy under the best of circumstances, have trouble locating a clinician willing to treat their problems. Reluctant therapists, if told that they cannot treat these patients without a pager, might become even more likely to refuse such cases.

In this era of cell phones, patients may use communication technology impulsively, expecting immediate responses from significant others to their every concern and desire. I have treated people who hardly ever let their cell phone text messager out of their hand and feel indignant about messages that are not returned. Certainly few therapists would want to give out a cell phone number to patients. Silk and Yager (2003) suggested using the "cooler" medium of e-mail to bridge gaps between sessions. But no one has determined whether that approach is effective.

We do not know whether the telephone strategy is a necessary element of DBT. As discussed in chapter 6, Linehan's method is an eclectic mix of techniques that has not been "dismantled" to determine its most effective ingredients. And no one has carried out any direct studies on whether telephone availability reduces suicidal actions. Recent data (see review in Paris, 2005c) comparing several methods applied to patients with BPD raise the question of whether therapies that use minimal or no telephone contact may be as effective as those that do. For example, in transference-focused therapy (Clarkin, Levy, Lenzenweger, & Kernberg, 2004; Yeomans, Clarkin, & Kernberg, 2002), patients are only allowed to phone to change a session or to report on serious accidents or illnesses.

In the absence of solid research data, I can only state my own experience with telephone contact between sessions. Over time, I have come to believe that these interventions are not necessary. I must admit that I used to have a very different opinion. For many years, I freely provided my phone number to patients I was concerned about. Although most people never used this option, a few did, and I found these calls troubling. I was never sure what I could say that could be useful in such circumstances. In addition, some patients would experience crises at times of the night when I am fast asleep. Having spent many years covering a hospital emergency room as part of my duties as a psychiatrist, I am sensitive to having my sleep disrupted. Like most physicians, I have had enough pager calls to last a lifetime. (And I am not getting any younger!) Although it is possible that my experience could have been different if I had been trained in DBT, I remain to be convinced of the necessity of talking to patients between sessions.

Also, like extra sessions, telephone contact can be used counterproductively in a way that promotes regression and dependency. Some years ago, I treated Alice, a patient who had received extensive therapy from four senior psychiatrists in my community. Although she had not really benefited from any of these treatments, having been in and out of the hospital for years, all her previous therapists had allowed her to call when she felt the need. But Alice called frequently, and she was always in a panic. This was probably one of the reasons why every therapist who saw her ended up burning out.

My compromise when taking on Alice's care was to propose that she be allowed to call me only once a week and to keep the contact brief. But early on in the therapy, Alice called me a second time in the same week, immediately saying, "Dr. Paris, I'm going to kill myself." My response was, "Alice, we'll talk about that on Tuesday." After this limit-setting intervention, Alice did not call again. She also never killed herself (and eventually recovered).

The question of how to use the telephone arose again a few years ago. I was involved in the opening of a hospital specialty clinic for patients with BPD. Thus far, our team has treated about 150 BPD patients, most presenting with chronic

suicidality. Before starting the clinic, our group had long dis-
cussions about whether to offer telephone contact to these patients. We did not actually believe that being available by
phone would prevent suicide. However, we were concerned
that if we did not provide availability, patients would present
themselves in the emergency room, making demands on already harassed psychiatrists, while complaining about our
unresponsiveness.

In the end, we came to the conclusion that accepting calls
between sessions could only give patients the wrong message.
We were running a program offering cognitive group therapy
(supplemented by individual sessions) designed to teach patients how to control impulsivity and how not to act on their
emotions. Because we were asking patients to learn how to delay responses to distress, waiting for the next session had to be
part of that learning process.

As it turned out, over 5 years, only 3% of our patients went
to the emergency room or took overdoses during the course of
treatment. The others, despite having had previous patterns
of suicidal actions, worked with our nonreinforcement of
suicidality. We have not seen any suicides in the course of
treatment.

Clinical experience does not constitute a research study, and
I am not suggesting that anyone should rely on mine. But I
would suggest that the burden of proof lies with those who believe that telephone contact, which can be burdensome for
therapists, is truly necessary. It is one of many interventions
whose efficacy has not yet been firmly demonstrated.

Boundary Maintenance and Suicidality

The management of chronic suicidality provides a specific example of the problem of boundary maintenance in therapy. Suicide attempts, like other impulsive actions, disrupt treatment,
and therapists need to set some kind of limit on these activities.

It is easier to state a principle than to carry it out. After all, patients are coming for treatment of symptomatic behavioral patterns. How can stopping them be a precondition for conducting therapy?

Researchers and clinicians who have written about the management of suicidality in patients with personality disorders have approached this problem in contrasting ways. In DBT, Linehan (1993) asks patients to commit themselves to stopping suicidal behaviors (and self-mutilation), but instead of asking for an immediate halt, she uses reinforcement contingencies to control pathological behaviors (positive responses to calling before acting, and session cancellations in response to actually carrying out suicidal acts). TFP (Yeomans et al., 2002) also asks the patient to stop cutting or overdosing, but this method builds in a much more severe contingency: If the patient continues to act out despite therapy, the treatment is discontinued.

My own approach to this problem owes something to the concept of "motivational interviewing," developed for the treatment of substance abuse (Miller & Rolnick, 2002). Giving up suicidal acts is not that dissimilar to giving up drinking, in that the patient must learn to tolerate painful feelings without resorting to self-destructive actions. Doing so takes time, and one cannot assume that patients are ready to change simply because they are in treatment. As Alcoholics Anonymous has long preached, recovery occurs one day at a time.

Thus, I do not see it as reasonable to stop treatment when patients continue, despite therapeutic interventions, to act out with overdoses and cutting. When therapists agree to treat such patients, they must accept that suicidality goes with the territory. Although therapists should not remove care when these actions occur, they should be careful not to reinforce suicidal behaviors by seeing patients more often or accepting repeated telephone calls.

This having been said, there are situations in which a patient can make outpatient treatment impossible. For example, one can do little for patients who repeatedly fail to show up for sessions. Also, when substance abuse is out of control, this symptom may have to be managed before any other problem can be dealt with. These "therapy-interfering behaviors" (Linehan, 1993) can sometimes be modified through specific interventions. However, there are times when the patient is simply not ready to embark on treatment and has to be let go. There are also times when the patient stops therapy, disappears for a while, and then reappears at a later time with better motivation.

To illustrate this point, a chronically suicidal young woman I treated attended sessions irregularly for about a year and then disappeared entirely for about 6 months. Then she showed up at my office at her old time (and was actually surprised that I had not kept the slot for her). We went on to embark on a second course of therapy, lasting for 9 months, which she attended regularly and which was more productive. Tolerating and working one's way around interruptions are consistent with the intermittent model of therapy discussed in chapter 6.

Emotion Regulation: Tolerating, Decentering, Reappraising

The treatment of chronically suicidal patients can be guided by identifying personality traits that are used in maladaptive ways. Therapy targets these dysfunctional traits, with the aim of modulating them. Treatment aims to make patients' personality work for them rather than against them (Paris, 1998, 2003).

Research on borderline personality suggests that two personality trait dimensions underlie the disorder: affective instability and impulsivity (Siever & Davis, 1991). A combination of unstable mood and the tendency to act on impulse leads to a clinical picture characterized by rapid mood swings and impulsive actions. These are also the major target areas for treating patients with chronic suicidality.

The key concept for managing affective instability is *emotion regulation*. Research on emotion has recently been an important area of theoretical development and empirical investigation in psychology (Campos, Frankel, & Camras, 2004). Many of the researchers in this area have had a background in cognitive psychology, and Linehan (1993) has applied these concepts to clinical issues.

My approach to managing affective instability has been greatly influenced by Linehan's work; I have no wish to reinvent her wheel! Yet the database for treating chronically suicidal patients is not yet broad enough, nor are the effects of DBT specific enough, to exclude other approaches based on different principles. As Leichsenring and Leibing (2003) demonstrated in a meta-analysis, more than one method of psychotherapy is effective for patients with severe personality disorders. And, as more evidence has come in (Paris, 2005d), it has become clear that approaches based on different theories can obtain similar results.

I have one area of disagreement with Linehan: She sees emotional dysregulation as the primary temperamental factor behind the suicidality seen in BPD, whereas I believe that chronic suicidality is equally rooted in impulsive traits. Impulsivity is a separate dimension of personality that is only partly dependent on emotional dysregulation (as explained in chapter 4). Therefore, my approach focuses as much on controlling impulses as on managing dysphoric emotions.

Since opening a clinic for patients with BPD, I have been influenced by Deborah Sookman, a psychologist trained in cognitive–behavioral methods (and the leader of our groups). Although our team has not conducted any clinical trials, we have been pleasantly surprised with the results we have obtained, primarily through CBT conducted in a group setting. Although the formal program lasts only 12 weeks, we have helped the majority of our patients. (This may seem a bit surprising, but it is consistent with the intermittent approach to therapy.) When I call patients for follow-up a year later, most patients remember the strategies they have been taught, even when they have forgotten all other details of the treatment.

Dr. Sookman has proposed the following sequence of interventions to promote emotion regulation and impulse control.

The first step in managing any emotion is to *tolerate* it. We can teach our patients to do that by labeling and recognizing feelings, no matter how intense. Once one recognizes an emotion, one is in a better position to observe it rather than becoming overwhelmed. The second step involves *decentering*, that is, standing outside one's feelings and observing them. The third step involves *reappraisal,* which is a key cognitive component. This involves thinking about feelings in a way that "defangs" them by seeing them in a new way. Let us examine these steps in a bit more detail.

Tolerating feelings helps us to avoid acting on them and to refrain from attempts at immediate emotional relief (often associated with self-destructive behaviors). For example, a patient who feels intensely sad because of the end of an intimate relationship can learn to accept those feelings as a way of not being flooded by them.

Decentering (distancing oneself from feelings) is equally necessary, however intensely emotions are experienced. To stand outside oneself and observe that one is having a feeling makes it easier to avoid feeling flooded by emotion. Decentering is followed by strategies to recognize, label, and modulate feelings. In many cases, simple labeling can be helpful: In the previous example, in which a patient feels sadness after a breakup, the therapist can encourage the patient to take note of the feeling and understand its relationship to the event. Simply observing an emotional response helps patients not to be flooded.

Reappraisal introduces a cognitive component in which dysfunctional thoughts are identified. In this stage, strategies are taught to identify dysfunctional emotional responses and to generate more adaptive alternates. This leads to the modulation of emotions, which reduces affective instability and impulsivity. Patients also need to avoid "emotional reasoning," in which strong feelings are seen as realistic responses to events. Instead these reactions must be understood as subjective experiences that can be reappraised on reflection. To return to the same example, a patient might feel that an interpersonal rejection proves that she is unlovable and unwanted. Reappraisal can help to place life events in context while avoiding a rush to hopelessness. Returning to the same example, a patient may be encouraged to consider that specific rejections do not imply universal rejection.

Thus, although patients have to consider, at a later point, what they contributed to the failure of a relationship, they can reappraise their failures without succumbing to hopelessness. Progress comes one step at a time, often two steps forward and one back. Or, in the famous phrase popularized by Alcoholics Anonymous, recovery comes "one day at a time."

In summary, when emotions are modulated, they become less intense and easier to get past. At the same time, therapists must modulate their own reactions to be effective with highly emotional patients. Whether or not one uses the term *countertransference,* intense emotions can be contagious. Therapists need to know how to retain their cool if they have any hope of showing patients how to do the same thing.

Linehan (1993) described a similar procedure by which therapists teach patients how to control intense and unstable affects. In *behavioral analysis,* the therapist works to understand the distress behind a threat or an action and to help the patient develop more effective strategies to manage the life issues behind that distress. In this way, therapy validates dysphoric feelings and identifies the problems leading to dysphoria. Once the causes of suicidality are established, therapy moves into a problem-solving mode and works toward developing alternative solutions and strategies to deal with life problems.

Case Example

Miriam was a 32-year-old administrative assistant. As an adolescent, Miriam had serious problems with alcohol and drugs and had made a number of suicidal threats. As an adult, she managed to hold a steady job for many years but could only enter into superficial and passing relationships. Her live-in boyfriend, George, was the first person Miriam had really become close to. The main crisis in her current life concerned this relationship, which had been disintegrating. As she became more angry at George, Miriam found him increasingly withdrawn and unresponsive. A series of suicide attempts by overdose were associated with unemployment and put Miriam in and out of the hospital over the next 2 years.

Miriam learned in therapy to break this pattern by developing a different way of handling emotions. She realized that she would often not realize she was angry until she was in a rage. Once that happened, Miriam's emotions would turn quickly to hopelessness, and the only way out seemed to be to take pills. Miriam learned that she could tolerate these feelings and then put herself outside them (decentering). Miriam was also able to reappraise her emotions, seeing them as reactions to a specific situation rather than the end of the world. Once this was accomplished, Miriam was able to manage the end of her relationship with George and to prepare for a return to work.

Managing Impulsivity: Slowing Down and Thinking Things Over

Impulsivity is a risk factor for many forms of psychopathology (Moeller et al., 2001). As discussed in chapter 4, this dimension of personality describes a tendency to act without thinking or to use action as a way of dealing with feelings.

Most research has taken a purely biological perspective on this trait, leading to the idea that medication could be used to manage impulsivity. Although this scenario might become true sometime in the future, these tools are currently not that effective. As discussed in chapter 7, a wide variety of drugs reduce impulsivity, but we have no specific agent for this trait. Surprisingly, few articles have been published on psychological methods to promote impulse regulation. In the absence of a psychological literature on impulsivity to parallel that on emotion regulation, the database for developing interventions is thin.

It is also very difficult to separate the problem of impulsivity from that of emotional dysregulation. For example, some impulsive actions, especially self-mutilation, tend to develop an addictive quality, because cutting can be regularly used to deal with dysphoria. But because actions take feelings away (or successfully distract people from them), actions eventually become partially independent of emotions. Patients with poor self-reflection are more likely to develop these automatic responses.

An absence of reflection with a tendency toward action is particularly characteristic of patients with substance abuse (Dougherty, Mathias, March, Moeller, & Swann, 2004) and with antisocial personality disorder (Lykken, 1995). In these conditions, impulsivity is a central feature, whereas affective instability is not prominent. At the same time, many patients who are emotionally dysregulated (e.g., suffering from chronic anxiety, chronic depression, or both) are not impulsive. Although it is always tempting to make complex issues simple, these are probably two separate aspects of personality that are linked in patients with chronic suicidality.

Another important link between emotion and action concerns anger. In BPD, emotional instability is often characterized by shifts from depression to anger (Koenigsberg et al., 2002). In some patients, anger is the most prominent (and problematic) emotion they experience. By and large, therapists, who usually work with anxiety or depression, are more comfortable with sadness and hopelessness than with angry explosions.

One of the cognitive techniques for dealing with this problem is anger management (Edmondson & Conger, 1996). Although the evidence base for the method is not very solid, the concept behind it makes sense. We need to help patients recognize angry feelings and prevent escalation to a point when actions can no longer be con   trolled. Thus, anger management defines specific steps to observe impulses and then helps patients to slow down and think things over. Similar concepts have been used for many decades by self-help organizations for addictions, such as Alcoholics Anonymous. We can probably apply the same principles to impulsive actions such as cutting or overdosing.

Case Example

Mariel was a 28-year-old clerical worker who had a psychiatric history dating back to adolescence. The focus of her current difficulties consisted of several impulsive actions: self-cutting and overdosing, or physical attacks after quarrels with a boyfriend. On one occasion, Mariel seriously assaulted her mother after a disagreement as to whether she needed therapy (or, as the mother claimed, whether Mariel was simply a bad person). Mariel would also drive dangerously when angry, leading to a series of accidents.

Mariel worked in therapy on developing increased reflective capacity. In the past, when her boyfriend insulted her verbally, she would develop an almost knee-jerk reaction of rage, leading directly to action. (Her parents had also been verbally abusive.) Mariel learned to recognize the triggers that led to impulsive actions as well as to tolerate, decenter, and reappraise the emotions that provoked them. When she no longer responded to her boyfriend in the same way, she was in a better position to examine what was good and bad in the relationship (which eventually led her to end it).

Getting a Life

Patients do not recover from chronic suicidality because they finally understand what went wrong in their childhood or because they find a way to increase their self-esteem. Nor do they necessarily recover after learning to control their emotions and their impulses. None of these accomplishments means much without a life.

Commitments to work and relationships are the primary context of psychological treatment. Attending therapy without getting a life is like going to school without doing any homework. Therapy is a protected environment that provides a space where psychological work can be done. At the same time, staying too long in treatment can sometimes be a danger. Some patients remain in therapy for years, avoiding the rough ride of outside reality, while failing to make any real attempt to improve their quality of life.

But in order to get a life, one first has to decide to live. This means giving up something important: the comforting and strangely empowering option of suicide. Patients who are chronically suicidal are attached to this state of mind. To give this up, they must believe they can find meaningful sources of satisfaction in life.

That this is possible is shown by follow-up studies of patients with BPD, which have documented a strong trajectory toward health (Paris, 2003). These findings show that many chronically suicidal patients eventually re-enter the work force. These findings also suggest that even if patients do not find one stable intimate relationship, they can establish a circle of friends and links to the community that provide an important sense of connection.

In some ways, the change process in chronically suicidal patients resembles recovery from an addiction. Suicidality, like a substance, can function as a universal solvent for all kinds of problems in life. It is not only self-mutilation that is addictive; the same principles apply to suicidal actions—and even to suicidal ideas. Like substance abusers, patients must break all connections with their old way of life to enter a healthier world.

Thinking of the chronically suicidal patient in this way underlines the need to modify standard methods of psychotherapy for them. We know from research on addictions and other behavioral disturbances (Galanter & Kleber, 1999) that therapeutic strategies designed for internalizing disorders, such as depression and anxiety, often fail when applied to externalizing disorders.

One of the most interesting approaches to the problem of addiction has come from Miller and Rolnick (2002), with their method of "motivational interviewing." This approach combines Rogerian principles (designed to maximize empathy) with cognitive–behavioral methods (that encourage changes in behavior). Motivational interviewing was first developed for a clientele who are highly resistant to giving up their own preferred ways of dealing with their problems. Miller and Rolnick emphasize that therapists have to work gradually to create motivation for change and avoid unproductive confrontations. The approach has a number of similarities to DBT, in which empathy and paradoxical interventions, which Linehan (1993) called "radical acceptance," are used simultaneously (dialectically) to promote the therapeutic process.

Getting a life requires a meaningful goal. For some, this will involve a commitment to work. It has been my experience that patients rarely do well if they remain permanently unemployed. Without the broad connections and social recognition that work provides, patients remain inevitably marginal.

In some cases, getting a life involves finding an intimate relationship. In such cases, a permanent attachment to a supportive partner can be the key to recovery. Even so, one must still account for what makes such an outcome possible—internal change usually precedes external change. I have often had the experience that patients meet someone suitable shortly after emerging from an extended state of hopelessness.

Meaning in life can also come from having children. Although parenting is a difficult task, it has been my experience that most patients will give up suicidality out of a feeling of responsibility for someone who is totally dependent on them. Those who cannot give up their suicidality often end up being involved with child protection services and may even lose the care of their children.

However, not everyone is happier in an intimate relationship, and not everyone enjoys being a parent. For some patients, recovery involves a meaningful but less intimate link with a larger community. Some of the subjects in my own follow-up study started doing well after becoming involved in religious communities that provided them with a strong sense of connection.

None of these ways of getting a life is a panacea. Work can be unstable or unfulfilling. Relationships may fail. Children may rebel or develop symptoms of their own. People with strong emotional needs may have trouble maintaining connections to the larger community. But even an imperfect life is better than no life at all.

Case Example

Dorothy was a student, first seen at age 22 and then followed intermittently over the next 10 years. Dorothy had been chronically suicidal since childhood. Her mother, a single woman with a good education but no employment, who probably suffered from BPD, had often talked to Dorothy, her only child, about the "existential" problem of suicide, and even suggested they have a pact to end their lives together if conditions became too difficult. When Dorothy eventually left her mother, she often worried that she would one day receive a phone call that she was dead. (In fact, this never happened.)

Dorothy had a long series of unsuccessful relationships with men, and when they ended she would immediately think of killing herself. Yet even though Dorothy took several overdoses during the course of treatment, she still managed to do well in school. Dorothy had the manner of a 19th-century romantic and would describe to her therapist how beautiful she would look as a corpse in the morgue. She often compared herself with a character in a popular science fiction film: an android who was hopelessly in love with a man but could never achieve human status.

Dorothy was only able to give up on suicidality when she found something to live for. Her intimate relationships continued to be difficult, and by the age of 30 she was divorced. Dorothy had a reasonably successful professional career, but this did not provide her with deep satisfaction. What gave meaning to her life were the two daughters she had with her ex-husband. Dorothy may have wondered if she could handle the needs of her children but was determined to ensure that they did not have the same experience she had with her own mother. In that context, suicidality was no longer an option.

Working With the Families of Chronically Suicidal Patients

Most models of psychotherapy focus on individuals. Yet most of the patients we see have families with whom they are involved and who are deeply involved with them. Of course, family members can also create conflicts that increase problems. But in most cases, they are engaged in caring for the pain and suffering that patients experience.

It goes without saying that patients who consider and attempt suicide are a source of intense distress for those who love them. Yet the literature is largely silent on this subject. Therapists have a long history of excluding families, of seeing them as part of the problem, not part of the solution. But we need not automatically agree with patients who blame loved ones for their difficulties; such perceptions are biased by current levels of distress and by the tendency of patients (particularly those with personality disorders) to externalize their problems. Gunderson (2001) is one of the few psychiatrists who have developed a program for supporting families. Hoffman et al. (2005) recently described a formal approach to working with the families of patients with BPD.

I recommend that therapists meet routinely with family members of chronically suicidal patients. This should be done at the beginning of treatment and periodically thereafter. Families deserve, at the very least, to be informed of the patient's condition. They should also be asked to understand and accept sharing the burden of staying with a patient who remains chronically suicidal over time. Packman and Harris (1998) recommended that therapists inform any suicidal patient early in treatment that the family will be contacted if the patient seems to be in danger. Kernberg (1987) made similar recommendations. I believe that not seeing families can be a mistake and that there are several other benefits to involving them in treatment.

Ethics and confidentiality usually require that patients agree to family meetings (unless we believe their life is in danger). Sometimes it takes some convincing to get patients to agree to a family meeting, but most patients will accept the idea if it is explained properly. At a minimum, we can tell patients that meeting their family will provide information that will be of assistance in working on their problems. At the same time, we can explain that family members are understandably concerned about their condition and that meeting the therapist may help them to play a more constructive role.

Sometimes patients portray their family members as dangerous or destructive, making us reluctant to talk to them. But this is the patient's perception; it may not be fully accurate. Many patients with personality disorders will have had conflictual or dependent relationships with their families. Some will attempt to prevent therapists from having any relationships with their relatives. At other times, the family of the patient may be over-involved and banging at our doors every day asking what is going on in treatment.

Leaving families out of the loop loses an opportunity to warn them of the risk and to join with them in sharing the burden. Chronic suicidality is not a scenario in which therapists should promise patients that we will never talk to anyone else about them, no matter what the circumstances. Moreover, therapists who treat chronically suicidal patients have some degree of responsibility to their families. Involving the family should be seen as a necessary parameter of treatment that need not involve a breach of confidentiality. (One might note a parallel with the relationships therapist have with the families of psychotic patients.)

Thus, therapists can set three goals for family meetings: (a) to obtain independent information on the patient, (b) to demystify the process of treatment for the patient's family, and (c) to share the burden of chronic suicidality with the family. The therapist can take the opportunity to explain the rationale behind the management plan and to obtain cooperation with therapy.

The main challenge for the therapist at such meetings is to be respectful to the patient and to the family, who will often have different agendas. Also, one needs to conduct these meetings in a way that avoids unnecessary and stressful arguments and wrangling; this involves maintaining the structure and placing the emphasis on practical issues.

In the following example, the main value of meeting the family was to obtain more information about family relationships as well as to demystify the treatment for the parents of a chronically suicidal patient.

Clinical Example

Marcia was a 20-year-old nursing student in treatment after taking a large overdose of pills. She had been considering suicide for some time and attributed her problems to having been misunderstood by her parents. The image Marcia presented to the therapist of her family was as at best hurtful and at worst malevolent.

A family meeting early in the course of therapy helped clarify the nature of these interactions. This was a military family with four children, and everyone had been expected to cope with multiple moves. Marcia, the third child, was unusually sensitive and needy but got lost in the shuffle. Marcia's father described her as an extremist—correctly noting that she used extreme means to obtain responses but not realizing that Marcia's feelings of neglect were at least partially based in reality. Marcia's mother, chronically depressed, did not have the emotional equipment to manage a large family and tended to withdraw in puzzlement when anything went wrong.

Despite these limitations, Marcia's family was reassured when told that their daughter would need therapy and that they should not expect her suicidality to rapidly disappear. The therapist encouraged Marcia to keep her problems away from her family and, because they lived in another city, to maintain relationships on a low-key and reasonably positive level. As Marcia began to get a life, through career and intimacy, she was able to forgive her parents and enjoy seeing them while presenting a more balanced image of her family to the therapist.

Planning for the Long Haul

One might think that patients who are chronically suicidal must need long-term treatment. Yet although this is sometimes the case, extended courses of therapy are not always required.

Chapter 6 introduced the concept that intermittent psychotherapy may be suitable for chronically suicidal patients. McGlashan (1993) suggested that this kind of structure is particularly appropriate for patients with BPD, who recover with time but who may need periodic "retreads." At the same time, intermittent therapy can be considered as a general frame for psychotherapy practice.

Many decades ago, Alexander and French (1946) suggested that regular therapy sessions over many years have an addictive quality that can work against the goals of treatment. These authors proposed that therapy should normally include planned interruptions, in which patients stop regular therapy for a period of time and practice what they have learned in real life. In this model, patients would also be encouraged to return to therapy for additional periods of work to review the results of their efforts.

This model of treatment fits well with the emphasis I have placed on getting a life. But can one prescribe planned interruptions for patients who are chronically suicidal and who are continually in crisis? Obviously, things have to settle down a bit before one can consider taking a break. However, only a few patients remain in a crisis mode for years on end. A more common scenario is for some degree of improvement to appear, even though the option of suicide may be retained for some time. It is at this stage, which may take a year or more to reach, that one can consider making treatment intermittent. Most patients will buy into the plan if they know they can return without delay when they need to. As research has suggested (Waldinger & Gunderson, 1984), therapists may be more likely to resist this idea than patients.

One obvious exception is that one cannot continue to be available if either the therapist or the patient relocates. But in my experience, practicing in the same city for several decades, I have found it both fascinating and gratifying to monitor the development of patients over time, even when they move away. They may drop in for a follow-up, come for a bit more therapy, or just send a card, but patients who have been through such an intense experience in treatment may always keep some degree of attachment to their therapist.

Thinking Differently About Chronically Suicidal Patients

Managing chronic suicidality is one of the most complex tasks for any clinician, no matter how experienced she or he is. The saving principle is to always address our therapeutic efforts to the healthy part of the patient. By treating people as if they were helpless and unable to function, we make chronic and irreversible impairment more likely. In contrast, treating suicidality, like any other symptom, as a marker of distress that can be reduced by practical life changes can tip the balance toward recovery and health.

Why are these ideas controversial? I have often presented them in conferences and clinical rounds and have found that although therapists are often sympathetic to my approach, they are skeptical about whether it can be put into practice. The sticking point concerns the danger of suicide completion and the responsibility of clinicians to prevent such an outcome. These ideas have been drilled into every therapist, and few have stopped to ask whether these ideas are based on evidence.

The recommendations in this chapter do not correspond to standard clinical guidelines to managing suicidality (e.g., American Psychiatric Association, 2003) or to official guidelines for managing suicidality in patients with personality disorders (Oldham et al., 2001). The reason for the discrepancy is that I believe these guidelines are wrong and must eventually be changed.

First, as I have emphasized, general guidelines for suicide prevention have been designed for acute but not chronic suicidality. Second, even in acute situations, the standard approach has a weak evidence base. The bitter truth is that most of what has been written about suicide prevention is scientifically weak. Again and again, experts are willing to ignore the problems of base rates and false positives. They present guidelines for suicide completion as if risk factors can be used to create an algorithm for prevention. Although these ideas can only be described as spurious, they fill a need, because clinicians are (understandably) frightened of suicide and often grasp at any straw.

I have argued throughout the book that following published guidelines for suicide prevention will lead to treatment failure in patients with chronic suicidality. In the meantime, I advise therapists to do what is right for patients rather than be ruled by fear of litigation or of disapproval by their colleagues. (Chapter 10 deals with the medico-legal issues raised by this approach.)

Much of the received wisdom about chronic suicidality takes us down the wrong path. If prevention is a myth, we need to focus on what we can do rather than what we cannot do. This requires a hard-headed practical approach to thorny clinical problems. We also need to believe that our patients, however much they seem to be in love with death, can eventually find a way to live.

(10)

Suicidality and Litigation

～

Fear of litigation after completed suicide is a worry for therapists. When I present my position on management of chronically suicidal patients to colleagues, I can count on being asked, "What if I am sued?"

This concern is the main source of resistance to the ideas presented in this book, even among those who agree with me in principle. Thus, although many clinicians are aware of the limited value of hospitalization, they can feel compelled to admit a patient who threatens suicide if they believe they may face litigation if the patient carries out the threat. Clearly, the recommendations presented in this book will not be followed if its readers believe that doing so will lead to a lawsuit.

In this chapter I try to counter that perception. I show that lawsuits following chronic suicidality are not likely to occur under normal conditions of practice. I also show that there are practical ways to prevent litigation.

Suicide as a Normative Risk of Mental Health Practice

In the practice of any mental health professional, suicide is always a possibility. Many of us have had to endure the death of a patient (and those who have been spared are sure to know of cases from our colleagues).

Surveys have shown the suicide occurs at least once in the careers of 50% of psychiatrists (Chemtob, Hamada, Bauer, Kinney, & Torigoe, 1988a) as well as in the careers of 20% of psychologists (Chemtob, Hamada, Bauer, Kinney, & Torigoe, 1988b). These overall numbers mask the relationship between prevalence and clinical setting. A therapist with an office practice might avoid having any completed suicides, particularly if she or he sees a clientele restricted to relatively healthy people. On the other hand, in hospitals and community clinics, it is hard to find a practitioner who has never lost a patient to suicide.

Let us begin by accepting a general principle: No one can practice psychotherapy without accepting at least some risk of suicide (Hendin, Lipschitz, Maltsberger, Haas, & Wynecoop, 2000). Physicians have been trained to accept that patients can die when under our care; psychologists and social workers may be more sensitive to life-and-death issues. At the same time, the extent to which clinicians of any professional background are comfortable with working with that risk may depend on personality. Some therapists are activists: They feel responsible for patients' lives and tend to favor intervention over watchful waiting. Other therapists take a more contemplative position: They believe a patient is ultimately responsible for her own life and do not necessarily feel a need to be active in the face of suicidal threats. Each of us tends to gravitate toward one pole or another. Perhaps the ideal therapist should be capable of taking both points of view (depending on the clinical situation). But when suicides cannot be prevented, therapists should lean toward respecting autonomy rather than intervention.

Treating people with mental disorders is rarely easy. Although most of us find our work challenging and exciting, we have to admit that therapy is not always successful. Sometimes we help patients dramatically—even a few experiences of this kind can keep us going in the face of other frustrations. Most of the time we help our patients to some extent, but they continue to have difficulties. This kind of result should be both respectable and satisfying.

The most difficult part of our work comes when we fail to help patients at all and have to live with failure. Most cases of this kind would probably not have done any better with another therapist—even if we imagine that to be the case. We are caring therapists, and when a patient commits suicide, we feel at least partly responsible. Although such experiences test us, we must bear them and move on.

Unfortunately, most therapists have difficulty being philosophical about suicide (Hendin et al., 2000). We entered our profession to help people, not to see them die. The problem that this book has emphasized is that attempts to prevent suicide at all costs are often futile. Fear of having to defend ourselves in a court of law can paralyze and disorient us.

Under What Conditions Are Therapists Sued After a Suicide?

Therapists sometimes face litigation after losing a patient to suicide. Completed suicide is the leading cause of lawsuits against mental health professionals, accounting for 20% of all cases (Kelley, 1996).

On the other hand, data drawn from various jurisdictions around the United States (Gutheil, 1992; Packman & Harris, 1998) show that only a very small fraction of suicide completions lead to litigation. Moreover, only a minority (about 20%) of these lawsuits will eventually be upheld.

Thus, although many therapists will experience a suicide, most will never have to endure litigation as a consequence, and those who do have to endure it can expect a decision in their favor. Yet even with these facts in mind, no one wants to undergo a process that is bound to cause enormous stress. We only need to talk to anyone who has gone through the ordeal of being accused of malpractice.

To put the problem in perspective, let us consider factors that can influence the frequency and outcome of malpractice suits. First, litigation is more likely to occur in some clinical scenarios than in others. The vast majority of cases brought to the courts involve inpatients treated for major Axis I conditions such as psychoses and melancholic depressions; cases involving chronically suicidal patients with personality disorders are much more rare (Kelly, 1996). One reason may be that acutely ill patients have an illness that is out of character, and families, who have been hopeful for their recovery, are more likely to consider that a mistake has been made if a suicide occurs. In contrast, chronically suicidal patients have been ill for a long time and have often exhausted their family supports, so that death may not come as a surprise.

Second, we need to consider the setting in which patients are treated. Most lawsuits focus on issues relevant to the circumstances of a hospital admission for acute suicidality, that is, whether patients were discharged too early; the outcome more rarely turns on whether patients should have been hospitalized in the first place (Kelly, 1996).

Third, lawsuits after suicide focus on whether patients were managed properly. The crucial point is that when clinicians are found liable, the outcome is almost never based on the fact of suicide alone (Gutheil, 1992, 2004). Thus therapists who conduct their practice within the guidelines of normal professional practice—and can show that they have done so—are rarely held responsible. Most courts know that suicide cannot always be prevented (in this respect they are more reasonable than we are!). The legal system does not routinely find clinicians at fault when suicide happens and may also recognize that chronic suicidality is a unique situation (Sansone, 2004). Although all of these points can require the arguments of a good advocate to convince a jury, experience has shown that they are valid.

Malpractice suits can only be successful when therapists, who have taken on a duty to the patient to provide reasonable care, are deemed to be negligent. This means that care has fallen short of a reasonable standard, set by the larger community of clinicians. Moreover, malpractice requires proof that any failure of care is the actual cause of a suicidal outcome. Thus, therapists can only be held liable if it can be shown that the suicide would not have occurred if the care had been more adequate.

There are several ways in which liability depends on a failure to meet professional standards of care (Gutheil, 1992). There can sometimes be gross clinical misjudgments (such as an incorrect diagnosis or an obviously aberrant treatment method). But the most important factor is the failure to assess patients carefully and to document such assessments.

Making Litigation Less Likely

Documentation is the most important thing therapists need to do to prevent lawsuits. We must keep careful notes about mental states, describe in detail the results of re-evaluations when patients threaten suicide, and discuss our rationale for avoiding hospitalization.

In chronically suicidal patients, there is a palpable risk if one fails to maintain adequate records that could justify a management plan. Thus, whatever you do with a chronically suicidal patient, you need to write it down. There is no substitute for complete notes that describe what you have seen and explain why are you are doing what you do. Specifically, if you decide to accept suicidal risk (in order to treat patients effectively), you need to write a detailed clinical note to explain your reasoning. If you have a specific rationale for taking a calculated risk (such as the failure of previous hospitalizations to help the patient), your position must be documented. The chronic nature of suicidality should be noted and its implications discussed. If a chronically suicidal patient threatens to make an immediate attempt, and if hospitalization is not carried out, the therapist needs to write a note describing what the patient said, how the threat fits into a long-term pattern, and the reasons for adhering to a long-term plan of care.

In a related scenario, patients sometimes present therapists with "a date with death" (Gutheil & Schetsky, 1998). In these cases, patients threaten suicide at some future time (e.g., "if things don't get better by Christmas, that will be the end"). Although this kind of communication can have a chilling effect, such statements need to be carefully documented in the clinical notes, along with the therapist's response.

Gutheil (2004) recommended that therapists also document any explicit or implicit contract. For example, it can be agreed in advance that whatever the crisis situation, the patient accepts a long-term plan for therapy and is competent to accept the plan. Sometimes a plan can explicitly state that because the risk of suicide is chronic, both therapist and patient agree to work together in outpatient therapy and avoid hospitalization. Some therapists have experimented with no-suicide contracts; Gutheil pointed out that although there is no evidence that any agreement of this sort can actually prevent fatal outcomes, it is important to have written proof that the patient understands what the therapist is doing and agrees to work within those parameters.

Gutheil (2004) also recommended a procedure that should be standard for chronically suicidal patients: The therapist should routinely obtain a consultation from a trusted colleague. Whatever you do with a patient, you are always protected if a colleague agrees with you and says so in writing. It is surprising that consultation is not routine, but it should be, no matter how experienced the therapist.

When clinicians do all these things, they can make themselves much less vulnerable. There will always be bad lawyers and bad juries, but we can do much to protect ourselves.

Families and Litigation

The climate following a completed suicide works against cool reason. The family may be guilty about the outcome, leading them to seek out someone else to blame. At the same time, most therapists tend to feel guilty about a suicide. The issue is how to handle that emotion. One common (but unfortunate) result of guilt is that therapists may avoid the patient's family instead of talking with them openly. The first hours and days after a suicide are particularly crucial. Gutheil (2004) suggested that many lawsuits after suicide occur when therapists fail to return phone calls and meet with family members to comfort them.

If therapists have not been in prior contact with the family, the situation after a suicide will be more risky. (This will not happen if the recommendations in chapter 9 are followed.) Agreeing to a patient's request to exclude family members can come back to haunt us if the patient does commit suicide.

Moreover, family members, who have often had to endure a patient's suicidality without having anyone to help them, will feel supported by being brought into an alliance. And if a suicide still ensues, they will have less reason to feel angry and excluded. For this reason, involving the family is one of the most important ways to reduce the risk of litigation.

Case Example

Robert was a businessman who had been a social activist in his youth. However, although he married and made a living, he had not been able to make a commitment to his adult roles. Failing to give up his "1960s" habits, Robert suffered from polysubstance abuse. Unwilling to give up uppers and downers (ranging from cocaine and amphetamine to sedatives), he gradually lost everything.

The first thing to go was Robert's marriage. One day Robert came home and found that all the locks on the house had been changed and his wife wanted nothing more to do with him. Robert lacked a social network and made little effort to find another relationship. He went back to live with his elderly and widowed mother. The only other family Robert had was a younger brother who was married with children and had little interest in helping him.

Robert tried to immerse himself in his work, but it provided little compensation for an empty life. Gradually clients stopped coming to see him, and he often spent days at his office with little to do. It was at this point that he began to consider suicide, and the idea never left his mind.

Over the next 3 years, Robert made five serious suicide attempts by overdose, leading to admissions to intensive care units and then to psychiatric wards. He had never followed through on recommendations for psychotherapy but agreed to see a psychiatrist after the fifth admission. These sessions were not fruitful, and there was no evidence that a therapeutic alliance was developing. Most of the discussion concerned the emptiness of Robert's current life, although there were no overt suicidal threats. Antidepressant medication was prescribed but was not notably effective. The psychiatrist also met with Robert's mother, who was able to provide a more detailed history but who felt helpless to reverse the course of her son's decline.

After several months of weekly sessions, Robert's mother called the psychiatrist early one morning. She informed him that she had found her son dead in his bed. An empty bottle of a strong painkiller medication was on his night table. The psychiatrist went immediately to the house, confirmed that Robert was dead, and waited with the mother for the police to come. Several hours later, Robert's brother arrived and met his brother's physician for the first time. He was upset and angry, commenting to the psychiatrist that the family should have been more involved. However, the brother also acknowledged that Robert's death had long been on the horizon. In fact, this was the last contact between the psychiatrist and the family.

Even with reasonable care, some of our patients will commit suicide. This example illustrates how the management of relationships with the patient's family can make a difference. As discussed earlier, a lawsuit is unlikely when a patient is chronically suicidal, because the family is already primed to expect that death may be the outcome of illness. This is a possibility that had been openly acknowledged by Robert's family, and it may not therefore be an accident that they never considered suing the psychiatrist.

On the other hand, the therapist might be criticized for focusing his efforts on building an alliance with Robert while only collecting historical data from the mother. He also failed to contact the brother, an important player in the story. It would have been better for everyone concerned if he had called for a family meeting that would have included all parties involved in Robert's illness.

Summary

Litigation is a nightmare for all therapists who work with people who consider suicide. However, it is relatively rare for such cases to end up in court. The risk can be reduced by keeping careful documentation, consulting with colleagues, and establishing an alliance with family members.

The attitude of therapists toward suicidal patients should be characterized by care and concern, accompanied by respect for a patient's autonomy. Although we always try to practice in the best way we can, we should not feel too guilty about our outcomes. Guilt does not help patients and it certainly does not help therapists. When progress is slow, we need to remember that we are treating someone who is severely ill. If death ensues, we need not feel responsible and expect to be punished. Most important, the fear of such an outcome need not paralyze us.

As this book has repeatedly suggested, therapists need to work with patients on their problems and not conduct a defensive practice. In the words of one writer on suicide (S. Rachlin, 1984), "We cannot afford to be so afraid of litigation as to deny our patients the right to learn to live" (p. 306).

Summary:
Guidelines for
Therapists
⮂

I will now summarize the theoretical and research perspectives discussed in this book and describe their most important clinical implications.

- Suicide is a real and serious problem in public health. However, research evidence has failed to show that we know how to prevent it. In chronic suicidality, attempts at prevention tend to be particularly counterproductive.
- Therapists must distinguish between the different types of suicidality. Suicidal ideation is common, so that one cannot assume that, by itself, the presence of suicidal ideas indicates a high risk. Suicidal attempts should elicit greater concern (depending on their lethality), but most attempters never complete suicide. Self-mutilation does not usually have a suicidal intent.
- Chronically suicidal patients can think about or attempt suicide over the course of many years. Problems often begin in childhood, but the clinical picture of suicidal ideas and attempts presents clinically in adolescence.

- Chronic suicidality carries out psychological functions, particularly the relief of dysphoria and communication of distress. Instead of being a temporary phenomenon related to depression, suicidality becomes part of a patient's personality structure.
- The management of chronic suicidality is based on a different set of principles than those developed for acute suicidality. Admission to a hospital has never been shown to be helpful, but there is evidence for the value of day hospitals.
- Chronically suicidal patients often meet criteria for a personality disorder. This population is difficult to treat. Pharmacotherapy has some value but mainly acts to reduce impulsivity. The main form of treatment is psychotherapy, and several methods have been supported by clinical trials.
- One of the key elements in treating chronically suicidal patients is to tolerate and accept risk. The more we attempt to prevent suicide, the more likely it is that treatment will be derailed.
- Chronically suicidal patients recover when their quality of life improves. This usually takes time, but it may be accelerated by a strategy in which patients learn how to regulate intense emotions, to curb impulsivity, and to "get a life."
- Chronically suicidal patients usually do not necessarily need to work through childhood traumas in therapy. Instead, therapy needs to be a springboard for making meaningful investments in work and relationships.
- One cannot treat chronically suicidal patients in a climate of fear. The problems of therapy in this population are significant but can be addressed.
- Research tells us that most chronically suicidal patients get better. We can therefore remain optimistic and positive, even in the face of frightening suicidal threats.
- Suicide completion will probably occur at least once in the lives of many, if not most, therapists and has to be considered a normative risk of practice.
- Therapists can minimize the risk of litigation if a suicide does occur, so that fear of legal action is not the driving force behind treatment plans.

Research Directions

What kind of research could answer the questions raised in this book? This is definitely an area where the future will bring more knowledge. I can make three general suggestions as to where investigations might go.

First and foremost, we need more studies on the causes, both proximal and distal, of suicide and suicidality. Only then will we be in a position to think about evidence-based methods of prevention. Correlation studies of risk have not provided an answer: We still need to understand why a minority of suicidal patients eventually kill themselves.

Second, we need to carry out systematic studies to determine whether there is any value in hospitalizing patients with chronic suicidality. Although this book has taken an extremely doubtful view, I would change my mind if it could be shown that admission reduces suicidality, either in the short term or the long term.

Third, we need data on effective treatment methods for chronically suicidal patients. Research could eventually show which specific interventions, either psychotherapeutic or psychopharmacological, are most efficacious for specific subgroups of patients. As with any other clinical problem, progress in treatment will only come with empirical data.

Some Final Comments

It has been a challenge to write a book on a clinical problem that is unusually difficult for therapists but about which there are few solid data. As a researcher, I have been trained to hold off on making judgments without empirical support. But as a clinician, I know that therapists cannot wait another generation for data, and that patients need help in the present. And even in our current state of painfully limited knowledge, we can still manage most of these cases effectively. Finally, until we know more, we should avoid making problems worse by trying to do the impossible.

Feelings are infectious, and the hopelessness associated with suicidality can sometimes draw us in. Therapists must maintain a consistent focus on long-term goals. Although we understand the depths of human suffering, the work of a therapist is always rooted in a reasonable and practical optimism. Unlike chronically suicidal patients, who try to close the door to hope, we know that death is not the only solution to emptiness and pain and that life brings many surprises.

References

Aaron, R., Joseph, A., Abraham, S., Muliyil, J., George, K., Prasad, J., et al. (2004). Suicides in young people in rural southern India. *Lancet, 363,* 1117–1118.

Achenbach, T. M., & McConaughy S. H. (1997). *Empirically based assessment of child and adolescent psychopathology: Practical applications* (2nd ed.). Thousand Oaks, CA: Sage.

Adler, G. (1979). The myth of the alliance with borderline patients. *American Journal of Psychiatry, 136,* 642–645.

Adler, G., & Buie, D. H., Jr. (1979). Aloneness and borderline psychopathology: The possible relevance of child development issues. *International Journal of Psycho-Analysis, 60,* 83–96.

Akiskal, H. S. (2002). The bipolar spectrum: The shaping of a new paradigm in psychiatry. *Current Psychiatry Reports, 4,* 1–3.

Akiskal, H. S., Chen, S. E., & Davis, G. C. (1985). Borderline: An adjective in search of a noun. *Journal of Clinical Psychiatry, 46,* 41–48.

Alexander, F., & French, T. (1946): *Psychoanalytic therapy.* New York: Ronald.

Alvarez, A. (1971). *The savage god: A study of suicide.* New York: Random House.

American Association of Suicidology. (2006). United States suicide statistics. Retrieved April 20, 2006, from http://www.suicidology.org

American Psychiatric Association. (2000). *Diagnostic and statistical manual of mental disorder* (4th ed., text rev.). Washington, DC: American Psychiatric Press.

American Psychiatric Association. (2003). Practice guideline for the assessment and treatment of patients with suicidal behaviors. *American Journal of Psychiatry, 160*(Suppl. 11), 1–60.

Barratt, E. (1985). Impulsive subtraits: Arousal and information processing. In J. T. Spence & C. E. Izard (Eds.), *Motivation, emotion, and personality* (pp. 137–146). New York: Elsevier.

Bateman, A., & Fonagy, P. (1999). Effectiveness of partial hospitalization in the treatment of borderline personality disorder: A randomized controlled trial. *American Journal of Psychiatry, 156,* 1563–1569.

Bateman, A., & Fonagy, P. (2001). Treatment of borderline personality disorder with psychoanalytically oriented partial hospitalization: An 18-month follow up. *American Journal of Psychiatry, 158,* 36–42.

Bateman, A., & Fonagy, P. (2004). *Psychotherapy for borderline personality disorder: Mentalization based treatment.* Oxford, England: Oxford University Press.

Beautrais, A. L. (2001): Suicides and serious suicide attempts: Two populations or one? *Psychological Medicine, 31,* 837–845.

Beautrais, A. L. (2003). Subsequent mortality in medically serious suicide attempts: A 5-year follow-up. *Australian & New Zealand Journal of Psychiatry, 37,* 595–599.

Beck, A. T., Resnik, L., & Lettieri, D. J. (1974). *The prediction of suicide.* Bowie, MD: Charles Press.

Beck, A. T., & Freeman, A. (2002). *Cognitive therapy of personality disorders* (2nd ed.). New York: Guilford.

Beutler, L. E., Malik, M., Alimohamed, S., Harwood, M., Talchi, H., Noble, S., et al. (2004). Therapist variables. In M. J. Lambert (Ed.), *Bergin and Garfield's handbook of psychotherapy and behavior change* (pp. 227–306). New York: Wiley.

Bland, R. C., Dyck, R. J., Newman, S. C., & Orn, H. (1998). Attempted suicide in Edmonton. In A. A. Leenaars, S. Wenckstern, I. Sakinofsky, R. J. Dyck, M. J. Kral, & R. C. Bland (Eds.), *Suicide in Canada* (pp. 136–150). Toronto: University of Toronto Press.

Bohus, M., Haaf, B., Simms, T., Limberger, M. F., Schmahl, C., Unckel, C., et al. (2004). Effectiveness of inpatient dialectical behavioral therapy for borderline personality disorder: A controlled trial. *Behaviour Research & Therapy, 42,* 487–999.

Brent, D. A. (2001). Assessment and treatment of the youthful suicidal patient. *Annals of the New York Academy of Sciences, 932,* 106–128.

Brent, D. A., Oquendo, M., Birmaher, B., Greenhill, L., Kolko, D., Stanley, B., et al. (2002). Familial pathways to early-onset suicide attempt: Risk for suicidal behavior in offspring of mood-disordered suicide attempters. *Archives of General Psychiatry, 59,* 801–807.

Brent, D. A., Oquendo, M., Birmaher, B., Greenhill, L., Kolko, D., Stanley, B., et al. (2003). Peripubertal suicide attempts in offspring of suicide attempters with siblings concordant for suicidal behavior. *American Journal of Psychiatry, 160,* 1486–1493.

Brent, D. A., Perper, J. A., Moritz, G., Baugher, M., Roth, C., Balach, L., et al. (1993). Stressful life events, psychopathology, and adolescent suicide: A case control study. *Suicide & Life-Threatening Behavior, 23,* 179–187.

Brezo, J., Paris, J., Tremblay, R., Vitaro, F., Hébert, M., Zoccolillo, M., et al. (in press). Personality traits as correlates of suicidal attempts and ideation in young adults. *Psychological Medicine.*

Brezo, J., Paris, J., Turecki, G., Zoccolillo, M., Vitaro, F., Hébert, M., et al. (2005, March). *Personality factors and childhood behavioral patterns in relation to suicidal behaviors in a longitudinally followed cohort of young adults.* Poster presented at the meeting of the American Psychopathological Association, New York.

Brown, J., Cohen, P., Johnson, J. G., & Smailes, E. M. (1999). Childhood abuse and neglect: Specificity of effects on adolescent and young adult depression and suicidality. *Journal of the American Academy of Child & Adolescent Psychiatry, 38,* 1490–1496.

Brown, M. Z., Comtois, K. A., & Linehan, M. M. (2002). Reasons for suicide attempts and nonsuicidal self-injury in women with borderline personality disorder. *Journal of Abnormal Psychology, 111,* 198–202.

Campos, J. J., Frankel, C. B., & Camras, L. (2004). On the nature of emotion regulation. *Child Development, 75,* 377–394.

Carter, G., Reith, D. M., Whyte, I. M., & McPherson, M. (2005). Repeated self-poisoning: Increasing severity of self-harm as a predictor of subsequent suicide. *British Journal of Psychiatry, 186,* 253–257.

Caspi, A., McClay, J., Moffitt, T. E., Mill, J., Martin, J., Craig, I. W., et al. (2002). Role of genotype in the cycle of violence in maltreated children. *Science, 297,* 851–854.

Caspi, A., Moffitt, T. E., Newman, D. L., & Silva, P. A. (1996). Behavioral observations at age three predict adult psychiatric disorders: Longitudinal evidence from a birth cohort. *Archives of General Psychiatry, 53,* 1033–1039.

Caspi, A., Sugden, K., Moffitt, T. E., Taylor, A., Craig, I. W., Harrington, H., et al. (2003). Influence of life stress on depression: Moderation by a polymorphism in the 5-HTT gene. *Science, 301,* 386–389.

Cavanagh, J. T., Carson, A. J., Sharpe, M., & Lawrie, S. M. (2003). Psychological autopsy studies of suicide: A systematic review. *Psychological Medicine, 33,* 395–405.

Chemtob, C. M., Hamada, R. S., Bauer, G. B., Kinney, B., & Torigoe, R. Y. (1988a). Patient suicide: Frequency and impact on psychiatrists. *American Journal of Psychiatry, 145,* 224–228.

Chemtob, C. M., Hamada, R. S., Bauer, G. B., Kinney, B., & Torigoe, R. Y. (1988b). Patient suicide: Frequency and impact on psychologists. *Professional Psychology: Research and Practice, 19,* 416–420.

Cipriani, C., Pretty, H., Hawton, K., & Geddes, J. R. (2005). Lithium in the prevention of suicidal behavior and all-cause mortality in patients with mood disorders: A systematic review of randomized trials. *American Journal of Psychiatry, 162,* 1805–1819.

Clarke, R. V., & Lester, D. (1989). *Suicide: Closing the exits.* New York: Springer.

Clarkin, J., & Levy, K. L. (2004). The influence of client variables on psychotherapy. In M. J. Lambert (Ed.), *Bergin and Garfield's handbook of psychotherapy and behavior change* (pp. 227–308). New York: Wiley.

Clarkin, J. F., Levy, K. L., Lenzenweger, M. F., & Kernberg, O. F. (2004). The Personality Disorders Institute/Borderline Personality Disorder Research Foundation randomized control trial for borderline personality disorder: Rationale, methods, and patient characteristics. *Journal of Personality Disorders, 18,* 52–72.

Cloninger, C. R., Svrakic, D. M., & Pryzbeck, T. R. (1993). A psychobiological model of temperament and character. *Archives of General Psychiatry, 50,* 975–990.

Coccaro, E. F., & Kavoussi, R. J. (1997). Fluoxetine and impulsive aggressive behavior in personality-disordered subjects. *Archives of General Psychiatry, 54,* 1081–1088.

Coccaro, E. F., Siever, L. J., Klar, H. M., Maurer, G., Cochrane, K., Cooper, T. B., et al. (1989). Serotonergic studies in patients with affective and personality disorders. *Archives of General Psychiatry, 46,* 587–599.

Comtois, K. A. (2002). A review of interventions to reduce the prevalence of parasuicide. *Psychiatric Services, 53,* 1138–1144.

Conners, C. (1994). *Continuous Performance Test Computer Program* (CPT). San Antonio, TX: Psychological Corporation.

Cooper, J., Kapur, N., Webb, R., Lawlor, M., Guthrie, E., Mackway-Jones, K., et al. (2005). Suicide after deliberate self-harm: A 4-year cohort study. *American Journal of Psychiatry, 162,* 297–303.

Costa, P. T., & Widiger, T. A. (Eds.). (2001). *Personality disorders and the five factor model of personality* (2nd ed.). Washington, DC: American Psychological Association.

Coté, S., Tremblay, R. E., Nagin, D., Zoccolillo, M., & Vitaro, F. (2002). The development of impulsivity, fearfulness, and helpfulness during childhood: Patterns of consistency and change in the trajectories of boys and girls. *Journal of Child Psychology & Psychiatry & Allied Disciplines, 43,* 609–618.

Cowdry, R. W., & Gardner, D. L. (1988). Pharmacotherapy of borderline personality disorder: Alprazolam, carbamazepine, trifluoperazine, and tranylcypromine. *Archives of General Psychiatry, 45,* 111–119.

Crawford, T. N., Cohen, P., & Brook, J. S. (2001a). Dramatic-erratic personality disorder symptoms: I. Continuity from early adolescence to adulthood. *Journal of Personality Disorders, 15,* 319–335.

Crawford, T. N., Cohen, P., & Brook, J. S. (2001b). Dramatic-erratic personality disorder symptoms: II. Developmental pathways from early adolescence to adulthood. *Journal of Personality Disorders, 15,* 336–350.

Crawley, J. N., Sutton, M. E., & Pickar, D. (1985). Animal models of self destructive behavior and suicide. *Psychiatric Clinics of North America, 8,* 299–310.

Dawson, D., & MacMillan, H. L. (1993). *Relationship management of the borderline patient: From understanding to treatment.* New York: Brunner/Mazel.

Dougherty, D. M., Mathias, C. W., Marsh, D. M., Moeller, F. G., & Swann, A. C. (2004). Suicidal behaviors and drug abuse: Impulsivity and its assessment. *Drug & Alcohol Dependence, 76*(Suppl. 7), S93–S105.

Eddleston, M., & Gunnell, D. (2006). Why suicide rates are high in China. *Science, 311*(5768), 1711–1713.

Edmondson, C. B., & Conger, J. C. (1996). A review of treatment efficacy for individuals with anger problems: Conceptual, assessment and methodological issues. *Clinical Psychology Review, 16,* 251–275.

Esposito-Smythers, C., & Spirito, A. (2004). Adolescent substance use and suicidal behavior: A review with implications for treatment research. *Alcoholism: Clinical & Experimental Research*, 28(Suppl. 5), 77S–88S.

Ettlinger, R. (1975). Evaluation of suicide prevention after attempted suicide. *Acta Psychiatrica Scandinavica Supplement, 260,* 1–135.

Fava, M. (1997). Psychopharmacologic treatment of pathologic aggression. *Psychiatry Clinics of North America, 20,* 427–451.

Favazza, A. R. (1996). *Bodies under siege: Self-mutilation and body modification in culture and psychiatry* (2nd ed.). Baltimore: Johns Hopkins University Press.

Fergusson, D. M., Woodward, L. J., & Horwood, L. J. (2000). Risk factors and life processes associated with the onset of suicidal behaviour during adolescence and early adulthood. *Psychological Medicine, 30,* 23–39.

Fergusson, D. M., Horwood, L. J., Ridder, E. M., & Beautrais, A. L. (2005). Suicidal behaviour in adolescence and subsequent mental health outcomes in young adulthood. *Psychological Medicine, 35,* 983–993.

Fine, M. A., & Sansone, R. A. (1990). Dilemmas in the management of suicidal behavior in individuals with borderline personality disorder. *American Journal of Psychotherapy, 44,* 160–171.

Fombonne, E., Worstear, G., Cooper, V. Harrington, R., & Rutter, M. (2001). The Maudsley long-term follow-up of depressed adolescents. *British Journal of Psychiatry, 179,* 210–217.

Fonagy, P., & Bateman, A. (2006). Progress in the treatment of borderline personality disorder. *British Journal of Psychiatry, 188,* 1–3.

Forman, E. M., Berk, M. S., Henriques, G. R., Brown, G. K., & Beck, A. T. (2004). History of multiple suicide attempts as a behavioral marker of severe psychopathology. *American Journal of Psychiatry, 161,* 437–443.

Frank, A. F. (1992). The therapeutic alliances of borderline patients. In J. F. Clarkin, E. Marziali, & H. Munroe-Blum (Eds.), *Borderline personality disorder: Clinical and empirical perspectives* (pp. 220–247). New York: Guilford.

Frank, J. D., & Frank, J. B. (1991). *Persuasion and healing* (3rd ed.). Baltimore: Johns Hopkins University Press.

Frankenburg, F. R., & Zanarini, M. C. (2002). Divalproex sodium treatment of women with borderline personality disorder and bipolar II disorder: A double-blind, placebo controlled pilot study. *Journal of Clinical Psychiatry, 63,* 442–446.

Freeman, M. P. (2000). Omega-3 fatty acids in psychiatry: A review. *Annals of Clinical Psychiatry, 12,* 159–165.

Frieswyk, S. H., Colson, D. B., & Allen, J. G. (1984). Conceptualizing the therapeutic alliance from a psychoanalytic perspective. *Psychotherapy: Theory, Research, Practice, Training, 21,* 460–464.

Fu, Q., Heath, A. C., Bucholz, K. K., Nelson, E. C., Glowinski, A. L., Goldberg, J., et al. (2002). A twin study of genetic and environmental influences on suicidality in men. *Psychological Medicine, 32,* 11–24.

Gabbard, G. O. (2004). *Long-term psychodynamic psychotherapy: A basic text.* Washington, DC: American Psychiatric Press.

Galanter, M., & Kleber, H. D. (1999). *Textbook of substance abuse treatment* (3rd ed.). Washington, DC: American Psychiatric Press.

Gaynes, B. N., West, S. L., Ford, C. A., Frame, P., Klein, J., & Lohr, K. (2004). Screening for suicide risk in adults: A summary of the evidence for the U.S. Preventive Services Task Force. *Annals of Internal Medicine, 140,* 822–835.

Gerson, J., & Stanley, B. (2002). Suicidal and self-injurious behavior in personality disorder: Controversies and treatment directions. *Current Psychiatry Reports, 4,* 30–38.

Goldney, R. D. (2000). Prediction of suicide and attempted suicide. In K. Hawton & K. van Heeringen (Eds.), *The international handbook of suicide and attempted suicide* (pp. 585–596). New York: Wiley.

Goldstein, R. B., Black, D. W., Nasrallah, A., & Winokur, G. (1991). The prediction of suicide. *Archives of General Psychiatry, 48,* 418–422.

Goodwin, F. K., Fireman, B., Simon, G. E., Hunkeler, E. M., Lee, J., & Revicki, D. (2003). Suicide risk in bipolar disorder during treatment with lithium and divalproex. *Journal of the American Medical Association, 290,* 1467–1473.

Gould, M. S., Greenberg, T., Velting, D. M., & Shaffer, D. (2003). Youth suicide risk and preventive interventions: A review of the past 10 years. *Journal of the American Academy of Child & Adolescent Psychiatry, 42,* 386–405.

Grant, B. F., Hasin, D. S., Stinson, F. S., Dawson, D. A., Chou, S. P., Ruan, W. J., et al. (2004). Prevalence, correlates, and disability of personality disorders in the United States: Results from the national epidemiologic survey on alcohol and related conditions. *Journal of Clinical Psychiatry, 65,* 948–958.

Greben, S. E. (1985). *Love's labor: The experience and practice of psychotherapy.* New York: New American Library.

Grilo, C. M., McGlashan, T. H., & Skodol, A. E. (2000). Stability and course of personality disorders. *Psychiatric Quarterly, 71,* 291–307.

Grunbaum, J. A., Kann, L., Kinchen, S., Ross, J., Hawkins, J., Lowry, R., et al. (2004). Youth risk behavior surveillance—United States. *Morbidity & Mortality Weekly Report. Surveillance Summaries/CDC, 53,* 1–96.

Grunebaum, M. F., Ellis, S. P., Li, S., Oquendo, M. A., & Mann, J. J. (2004). Antidepressants and suicide risk in the United States, 1985–1999. *Journal of Clinical Psychiatry, 65,* 1456–1462.

Gunderson, J. G. (2001). *Borderline personality disorder: A clinical guide.* Washington, DC: American Psychiatric Press.

Gunderson, J. G., Bender, D., Sanislow, C., Yen, S., Rettew, J. B., Dolan-Sewell, R., et al. (2003). Plausibility and possible determinants of sudden "remissions" in borderline patients. *Psychiatry, 66,* 111–992.

Gunderson, J. G., Frank, A. F., Ronningstam, E. F., Wahter, S., Lynch, V. J., & Wolf, P. J. (1989). Early discontinuance of borderline patients from psychotherapy. *Journal of Nervous and Mental Diseases, 177,* 38–42.

Gunderson, J. G., & Phillips, K. A. (1991). A current view of the interface between borderline personality disorder and depression. *American Journal of Psychiatry, 48,* 967–975.

Gunderson, J. G., & Singer, M. T. (1975). Defining borderline patients: An overview. *American Journal of Psychiatry, 132,* 1–9.

Gunnell, D., & Ashby, D. (2004). Antidepressants and suicide: What is the balance of benefit and harm? *British Medical Journal, 329,* 34–38.

Gutheil, T. G. (1992). Suicide and suit: Liability after self-destruction. In D. Jacobs (Ed.), *Suicide and clinical practice* (pp. 147–167). Washington, DC: American Psychiatric Press.

Gutheil, T. G. (2004). Suicide, suicide litigation, and borderline personality disorder. *Journal of Personality Disorders, 18,* 248–256.

Gutheil, T. G., & Gabbard, G. O. (1993). The concept of boundaries in clinical practice. *American Journal of Psychiatry, 150,* 188–196.

Gutheil, T. G., & Schetsky, D. (1998). A date with death: Management of time-based and contingent suicidal intent. *American Journal of Psychiatry, 155,* 1502–1507.

Guzder, J., Paris, J., Zelkowitz, P., & Feldman, R. (1999). Psychological risk factors for borderline pathology in school-aged children. *Journal of the American Academy of Child and Adolescent Psychiatry, 38,* 206–212.

Guzder, J., Paris, J., Zelkowitz, P., & Marchessault, K. (1996). Risk factors for borderline pathology in children. *Journal of the American Academy of Child and Adolescent Psychiatry, 35,* 26–33.

Harris, J. R. (1998). *The nurture assumption.* New York: The Free Press.

Harriss, L., Hawton, K., & Zahl, D. (2005). Value of measuring suicidal intent in the assessment of people attending hospital following self-poisoning or self-injury. *British Journal of Psychiatry, 186,* 60–66.

Haw, C., Hawton, K., Houston, K., & Townsend, E. (2001). Psychiatric and personality disorders in deliberate self-harm patients. *British Journal of Psychiatry, 178,* 48–54.

Hawton, K., Fagg, J., Simkin, S., Bale, E., & Bond, A. (1997). Trends in deliberate self-harm in Oxford, 1985–1995. Implications for clinical services and the prevention of suicide. *British Journal of Psychiatry, 171,* 556–560.

Hawton, K., Harriss, L., Hall, S., Simkin, S., Bale, E., & Bond, A. (2003). Deliberate self-harm in Oxford, 1990–2000: A time of change in patient characteristics. *Psychological Medicine, 33,* 987–995.

Hawton, K., Harriss, L., Simkin, S., Bale, E., & Bond, A. (2001). Social class and suicidal behaviour: The associations between social class and the characteristics of deliberate self-harm patients and the treatment they are offered. *Social Psychiatry & Psychiatric Epidemiology, 36,* 437–443.

Hawton, K., Houston, K., & Shepperd, R. (1999). Suicide in young people. Study of 174 cases, aged under 25 years, based on coroners' and medical records. *British Journal of Psychiatry, 175,* 271–276.

Hawton, K., Townsend, E., Arensman, E., Gunnell, D., Hazell, P., House, A., et al. (1999). Psychosocial and pharmacological treatments for deliberate self harm. *The Cochrane Database of Systematic Reviews, 4,* CD001764. DOI: 10.1002/14651858.CD001764.

Hawton, K., & van Heeringen, K. (Eds.). (2000). *The international handbook of suicide and attempted suicide.* New York: Wiley.

Hawton, K., Zahl, D., & Weatherall, R. (2003). Suicide following deliberate self-harm: Long-term follow-up of patients who presented to a general hospital. *British Journal of Psychiatry, 182,* 537–542.

Healy, D. (1997). *The antidepressant era.* Cambridge, MA: Harvard University Press

Hendin, H. (1981). Psychotherapy and suicide. *American Journal of Psychotherapy, 35,* 469–480.

Hendin, H., Lipschitz, A., Maltsberger, J. T., Haas, A. P., & Wynecoop, S. (2000). Therapists' reactions to patients' suicides. *American Journal of Psychiatry, 157,* 2022–2027.

Hepp, U., Wittmann, L., Schnyder, U., & Michel, K. (2004). Psychological and psychosocial interventions after attempted suicide: An overview of treatment studies. *Crisis: Journal of Crisis Intervention & Suicide, 25,* 108–117.

Herpertz, S. (1995). Self-injurious behaviour. Psychopathological and nosological characteristics in subtypes of self-injurers. *Acta Psychiatrica Scandinavica, 91,* 57–68.

Herpertz, S. C., Kunert, H. J., Schwenger, U. B., & Sass, H. (1999). Affective responsiveness in borderline personality disorder: A psychophysiological approach. American Journal of Psychiatry, 156, 1550–1556.

Hills, A. L., Cox, B., McWilliams, L. A., & Sareen, J. (2005). Suicide attempts and externalizing psychopathology in a nationally representative sample. *Comprehensive Psychiatry, 46,* 334–339.

Hirschfeld, R. M. (1999). Personality disorders and depression: Comorbidity. *Depression & Anxiety, 10,* 142–146.

Hendin, H. (1981). Psychotherapy and suicide. *American Journal of Psychotherapy, 35,* 469–480.

Hoffman, P. D., Fruzzetti, A. E., Buteau, E., Neiditch, E. R., Penney, D., Bruce, M. L., et al. (2005). Family connections: A program for relatives of persons with borderline personality disorder. *Family Process, 44,* 217–225.

Hollander, E., Allen, A., Lopez, R. P., Bienstock, C. A., Grossman, R., Siever, L. J., et al. (2001). A preliminary double-blind, placebo-controlled trial of divalproex sodium in borderline personality disorder. *Journal of Clinical Psychiatry, 62,* 199–203.

Hollander, E., Swann, A. C., Coccaro, E. F., Jiang, P., & Smith, T. B. (2005). Impact of trait impulsivity and state aggression on divalproex versus placebo response in borderline personality disorder. *American Journal of Psychiatry, 162,* 621–624.

Hollander, E., Tracy, K. A., Swann, A. C., Coccaro, E. F., McElroy, S. L., Wozniak, P., et al. (2003). Divalproex in the treatment of impulsive aggression: Efficacy in cluster B personality disorders. *Neuropsychopharmacology, 28,* 1186–1197.

Horwitz, A. V. (2002). *Creating mental illness.* Chicago: University of Chicago Press.

Horwitz, A. V., Widom, C. S., McLaughlin, J., & White, H. R. (2001). The impact of childhood abuse and neglect on adult mental health: A prospective study. *Journal of Health & Social Behavior, 42,* 184–201.

Howard, K. I., Kopta, A. M., Krause, M. S., & Orlinsky, D. E. (1986). The dose–effect relationship to psychotherapy. *American Psychologist, 41,* 159–164.

Hufford, M. R. (2001). Alcohol and suicidal behavior. *Clinical Psychology Review, 21,* 797–811.

Hull, J. W., Yeomans, F., Clarkin, J., Li, C., & Goodman, G. (1996). Factors associated with multiple hospitalizations of patients with borderline personality disorder. *Psychiatric Services, 47,* 638–641.

Hwu, H. G., Yeh, E. K., & Change, L. Y. (1989). Prevalence of psychiatric disorders in Taiwan defined by the Chinese Diagnostic Interview Schedule. *Acta Psychiartica Scandinavica, 79,* 136–147.

Inskip, H. M., Harris, E. C., & Barraclough, B. (1998). Lifetime risk of suicide for affective disorder, alcoholism and schizophrenia. *British Journal of Psychiatry, 172,* 35–37.

Isacsson, G. (2000). Suicide prevention—A medical breakthrough? *Acta Psychiatrica Scandinavica, 102,* 113–117.

Isacsson, G., Bergman, U., & Rich, C. L. (1996). Epidemiological data suggest antidepressants reduce suicide risk among depressives. *Journal of Affective Disorders, 41,* 1–8.

Isacsson, G., Holmgren, P., Druid, H., & Bergman, U. (1997). The utilization of antidepressants—A key issue in the prevention of suicide: An analysis of 5,281 suicides in Sweden during the period 1992–1994. *Acta Psychiatrica Scandinavica, 96,* 94–100.

Isometsa, E. T., Henriksson, M. M., Heikkinen, M. E., Aro, H. M., Marttunen, M. J., Kuoppasalmi, K. I., et al. (1996). Suicide among subjects with personality disorders. *American Journal of Psychiatry, 153,* 667–673.

Isometsa, E. T., & Lonnqvist, J. K. (1998). Suicide attempts preceding completed suicide. *British Journal of Psychiatry, 173,* 531–535.

Jang, K. L., Livesley, W. J., Vernon, P. A., & Jackson, D. N. (1996). Heritability of personality traits: A twin study. *Acta Psychiatrica Scandinavica, 94,* 438–444.

Jenkins, R., & Singh, B. (2000). General population strategies of suicide prevention. In K. Hawton & K. van Heeringen (Eds.), *The international handbook of suicide and attempted suicide* (pp. 597–615). New York: Wiley.

Jennings, C., Barraclough, B. M., & Moss, J. R. (1978). Have the Samaritans lowered the suicide rate? A controlled study. *Psychological Medicine, 8,* 413–422.

Ji, J., Kleinman, A., & Becker, A. E.(2001). Suicide in contemporary China: A review of China's distinctive suicide demographics in their sociocultural context. *Harvard Review of Psychiatry, 9,* 1–12.

Johnson, J. G., Cohen, P., Brown, J., Smailes, E. M., & Bernstein, D. P. (1999a). Childhood maltreatment increases risk for personality disorders during early adulthood. *Archives of General Psychiatry, 56,* 600–606.

Johnson, J. G., Cohen, P., Skodol, A. E., Oldham, J. M., Kasen, S., & Brook, J. S. (1999b). Personality disorders in adolescence and risk of major mental disorders and suicidality during adulthood. *Archives of General Psychiatry, 56,* 805–811.

Johnson, J. G., First, M. B., Cohen, P., Skodol, A. E., Kasen, S., & Brook, J. S. (2005). Adverse outcomes associated with personality disorder not otherwise specified in a community sample. *American Journal of Psychiatry, 162,* 1926–1932.

Joiner, T. E., Jr. (2002). The trajectory of suicidal behavior over time. *Suicide & Life-Threatening Behavior, 32,* 33–41.

Joiner, T. E., Jr., Brown, J. S., & Wingate, L. R. (2005). The psychology and neurobiology of suicidal behavior. *Annual Review of Psychology, 56,* 287–314.

Kahn, A. A., Jacobson, C. O., Gardner, C. A., & Kendler, K. S. (2005). Personality and comorbidity of common psychiatric disorders. *British Journal of Psychiatry, 186,* 190–196.

Kasen, S., Cohen, P., Skodol, A. E., Johnson, J. G., Smailes, E., & Brook J. S. (2001). Childhood depression and adult personality disorder: Alternative pathways of continuity. *Archives of General Psychiatry, 58,* 231–236.

Kavoussi, R. J., & Coccaro, E. F. (1998). Divalproex sodium for impulsive aggressive behavior in patients with personality disorder. *Journal of Clinical Psychiatry, 59,* 676–680.

Kelley, J. T. (1996). *Psychiatric malpractice.* New Brunswick, NJ: Rutgers University Press.

Kernberg, O. F. (1984). *Severe personality disorders: Psychotherapeutic strategies.* New Haven, CT: Yale University Press.

Kernberg, O. F. (1987a). Diagnosis and clinical management of suicidal potential in borderline patients. In J. S. Grotstein & M. F. Solomon (Eds.), *The borderline patient: Emerging concepts in diagnosis, psychodynamics and treatment* (pp. 69–80). New York: Psychoanalytic Inquiry Book Series.

Kernberg, P. F., Weiner, A. S., & Bardenstein, K. K. (2000). *Personality disorders in children and adolescents.* New York: Basic Books.

Kessing, L. V., Vedel, L. Søndergård, L., Kvist, K., & Andersen, P. K. (2005). Suicide risk in patients treated with lithium. *Archives of General Psychiatry, 62,* 860–866.

Kessler, R. C., Berglund, P., Borges, G., Nock, M., & Wang, P. S. (2005). Trends in suicide ideation, plans, gestures, and attempts in the United States, 1990–1992 to 2001–2003. *Journal of the American Medical Association, 293,* 2487–2495.

Kessler, R. C., Berglund, P., Demler, O., Jin, R., Merikangas, K. R., & Walters, E. E. (2005). Lifetime prevalence and age-of-onset distributions of DSM–IV disorders in the National Comorbidity Survey Replication. *Archives of General Psychiatry, 62,* 593–602.

Kessler, R. C., McGonagle, K. A., Nelson, C. B., Hughes, M., Eshelman, S., Wittchen, H. U., et al. (1994). Lifetime and 12-month prevalence of DSM–III–R psychiatric disorders in the United States. *Archives of General Psychiatry, 51,* 8–19.

Kirmayer, L. J., Brass, G. M., & Tait, C. L. (2000). The mental health of Aboriginal peoples: Transformations of identity and community. *Canadian Journal of Psychiatry, 45,* 607–616.

Klonsky, E. D., Oltmanns, T. F., & Turkheimer, E. (2003). Deliberate self-harm in a nonclinical population: Prevalence and psychological correlates. *American Journal of Psychiatry, 160,* 1501–1508.

Knox, K. L., Litts, D. A., Talcott, G. W., Feig, J. C., & Caine, E. D. (2003). Risk of suicide and related adverse outcomes after exposure to a suicide prevention programme in the US Air Force: Cohort study. *British Medical Journal, 327,* 1376–1381.

Koenigsberg, H. W., Harvey, P. D., Mitropoulou, V., Schmeidler, J., New A. S., Goodman, M., et al. (2002). Characterizing affective instability in borderline personality disorder. *American Journal of Psychiatry, 159,* 784–788.

Koerner, K., & Linehan, M. M. (2000). Research on dialectical behavior therapy for patients with borderline personality disorder. *Psychiatric Clinics of North America, 23,* 151–167.

Kreitman, N., Carstairs, V., & Duffy, J. J. (1991). Association of age and social class with suicide among men in Great Britain. *Journal of Epidemiology and Community Health, 45,* 195–202.

Kreitman, N., & Casey, P. (1988). Repetition of parasuicide: An epidemiological and clinical study. *British Journal of Psychiatry, 153,* 792–800.

Krueger, R. F. (1999). The structure of common mental disorders. *Archives of General Psychiatry, 56,* 921–926.

Kullgren, G. (1988). Factors associated with completed suicide in borderline personality disorder. *Journal of Nervous and Mental Disease, 176,* 40–44.

Lambert, M. (Ed.). (2004). *Bergin and Garfield's handbook of psychotherapy and behavior change.* New York: Wiley.

Lapierre, Y. D. (2003). Suicidality with selective serotonin reuptake inhibitors: Valid claim? *Journal of Psychiatry & Neuroscience, 28,* 340–347.

Leibenluft, E., Gardner, D. L., & Cowdry, R. W. (1987). The inner experience of the borderline self-mutilator. *Journal of Personality Disorders, 1,* 317–324.

Leichsenring, F. (2004). Quality of depressive experiences in borderline personality disorders: Differences between patients with borderline personality disorder and patients with higher levels of personality organization. *Bulletin of the Menninger Clinic, 68,* 9–22.

Leichsenring, F., & Leibing, E. (2003). The effectiveness of psychodynamic therapy and cognitive behavior therapy in the treatment of personality disorders: A meta-analysis. *American Journal of Psychiatry, 160,* 1223–1232.

Lerner, D. (1958). *The passing of traditional society.* New York: The Free Press.

Lesage, A. D., Boyer, R., Grunberg, F., Morisette, R., Vanier, C., Morrisette, R., et al. (1994). Suicide and mental disorders: A case control study of young men. *American Journal of Psychiatry, 151,* 1063–1068.

Levy, K. N. (2004, October). *Past research, current findings, and future directions in borderline personality disorder research.* Paper presented at the National Educational Association for Borderline Personality Disorder Conference, Hamilton, ON.

Lewinsohn, P. M., Rohde, P., & Seeley, J. R. (1995). Adolescent psychopathology: III. The clinical consequences of comorbidity. *Journal of the American Academy of Child & Adolescent Psychiatry, 34,* 510–519.

Leyton, M., Okazawa, H., Diksic, M., Paris, J., Rosa, P., Mzengeza, S., et al. (2001). Brain regional rate a-methyl {11} trapping in impulsive subjects with borderline personality disorder. *American Journal of Psychiatry, 158,* 775–782.

Linehan, M. M. (1993). *Dialectical behavioral therapy of borderline personality disorder.* New York: Guilford.

Linehan, M. M., Armstrong, H. E., Suarez, A., Allmon, D., & Heard, H. (1991). Cognitive behavioral treatment of chronically parasuicidal borderline patients. *Archives of General Psychiatry, 48,* 1060–1064.

Linehan, M. M., Comtois, K. A., Murray, A. M., Brown, M. Z., Gallop, R. L., Heard, H. L., et al. (in press). Two-year randomized trial + follow-up of dialectical behavior therapy vs. therapy by experts for suicidal behaviors and borderline personality disorder. *Archives of General Psychiatry.*

Linehan, M. M., Dimeff, L. A., Reynolds, S. K., Comtois, K A., Welch, S. S., Heagerty, P., et al. (2002). Dialectical behavior therapy versus comprehensive validation therapy plus 12-step for the treatment of opioid dependent women meeting criteria for borderline personality disorder. *Drug & Alcohol Dependence, 67,* 13–26.

Linehan, M. M., Goodstein, J. L., Nielsen, S. L., & Chiles, J. A. (1983). Reasons for staying alive when you are thinking of killing yourself: The Reasons for Living Inventory. *Journal of Consulting & Clinical Psychology, 51,* 276–286.

Linehan, M. M., Heard, H. L., & Armstrong, H. E. (1993): Naturalistic follow-up of a behavioral treatment for chronically parasuicidal borderline patients. *Archives of General Psychiatry, 50,* 971–974.

Linehan, M., Rizvi, S. L., Welch, S. S., & Page, B. (2000). Psychiatric aspects of suicidal behavior: Personality disorders. In K. Hawton & K. van Heeringen (Eds.), *The international handbook of suicide and attempted suicide* (pp. 147–178). New York: Wiley.

Links, P. S., Gould, B., & Ratnayake, R. (2003). Assessing suicidal youth with antisocial, borderline, or narcissistic personality disorder. *Canadian Journal of Psychiatry, 48,* 301–310.

Links, P. S., Heslegrave, R., & van Reekum, R. (1999). Impulsivity, core aspect of borderline personality disorder. *Journal of Personality Disorders, 13,* 131–139.

Links, P. S., & Kolla, N. (2005). Assessing and managing suicide risk. In J. Oldham, A. E. Skodol, & D. Bender (Eds.), *American Psychiatric Publishing textbook of personality disorders* (pp. 449–462). Washington DC: American Psychiatric Publishing.

Links, P. S., Steiner, M., Boiago, I., & Irwin, D. (1990). Lithium therapy for borderline patients: Preliminary findings. *Journal of Personality Disorders, 4,* 173–181.

Livesley, W. J. (2003). *The practical management of personality disorder.* New York: Guilford.

Livesley, W. J., Jang, K. L., & Vernon, P. A. (1998). Phenotypic and genetic structure of traits delineating personality disorder. *Archives of General Psychiatry, 55,* 941–948.

Lofgren, D. P., Bemporad, J., King, J., Lindem, K., & O'Driscoll, G. (1991). A prospective follow-up study of so-called borderline children. *American Journal of Psychiatry, 148,* 1541–1545.

Luborsky, L., Singer, B., & Luborsky, L. (1975). Comparative studies of psychotherapy: Is it true that "everyone has won and all shall have prizes"? *Archives of General Psychiatry, 41,* 165–180.

Lykken, D. (1995). *The antisocial personalities.* Hillsdale, NJ: Lawrence Erlbaum Associates.

Lynch, J., Smith, G. D., Harper, S., & Hillemeier, M. (2004). Is income inequality a determinant of population health? Part 2. U.S. national and regional trends in income inequality and age- and cause-specific mortality. *Milbank Quarterly, 82,* 355–400.

Maltsberger, J. T. (1994a). Calculated risk taking in the treatment of suicidal patients: Ethical and legal problems. *Death Studies, 18,* 439–452.

Maltsberger, J. T. (1994b). Calculated risk in the treatment of intractably suicidal patients. *Psychiatry, 57,* 199–212.

Maltsberger, J. T., & Buie, D. H. (1974). Countertransference hate in the treatment of suicidal patients. *Archives of General Psychiatry, 30,* 625–633.

Mann, J. J. (1998). The neurobiology of suicide. *Nature Medicine, 4,* 25–30.

Mann, J. J. (2003). Neurobiology of suicidal behaviour. *Nature Reviews Neuroscience, 4,* 819–828.

Mann, J. J., Apter, A., Bertolote, J., Beautrais, J., Currier, D., Haas, A., et al. (2005). Suicide prevention strategies: A systematic review. *Journal of the American Medical Association, 294,* 2064–2074.

Mann, J. J., Brent, D. A., & Arango, V. (2001). The neurobiology and genetics of suicide and attempted suicide: A focus on the serotonergic system. *Neuropsychopharmacology, 24,* 467–477.

Maris, R. (1981). *Pathways to suicide.* Baltimore: Johns Hopkins University Press.

Maris, R. W., Berman, A. L., & Silverman, M. M. (2000). *Comprehensive textbook of suicidology.* New York: Guilford.

Markovitz, P. J. (1995). Pharmacotherapy of impulsivity, aggression, and related disorders. In E. Hollander & D. J. Stein (Eds.), *Impulsivity and aggression* (pp. 263–286). New York: Wiley.

Marttunen, M. J., Aro, H. M., Henriksson, M. M., & Lonnqvist, J. K. (1991). Mental disorders in adolescent suicide. DSM–III–R axes I and II diagnoses in suicides among 13- to 19-year-olds in Finland. *Archives of General Psychiatry, 48,* 834–839.

Maughan, B., & Rutter, M. (1997). Retrospective reporting of childhood adversity. *Journal of Personality Disorders, 11,* 4–18.

McDowall, D., & Loftin, C. (2005). Are U.S. crime rate trends historically contingent? *Journal of Research in Crime and Delinquency, 42,* 359–383.

McGlashan, T. H. (1986). The Chestnut Lodge follow-up study III: Long-term outcome of borderline personalities. *Archives of General Psychiatry, 43,* 2–30.

McGlashan, T. H. (1993). Implications of outcome research for the treatment of borderline personality disorder. In J. Paris (Ed.), *Borderline personality disorder: Etiology and treatment* (pp. 235–260). Washington DC: American Psychiatric Press.

McGlashan, T. H. (2002). The borderline personality disorder practice guidelines: The good, the bad, and the realistic. *Journal of Personality Disorders, 16,* 119–121.

McIntyre, R. S., & O'Donovan, C. (2004). The human cost of not achieving full remission in depression. *Canadian Journal of Psychiatry, 49*(Suppl. 1), 10S–16S.

Meltzer, H., & Okayli, G. (1995). Reduction of suicidality during clozapine treatment of treatment-resistant schizophrenia. *American Journal of Psychiatry, 152,* 183–190.

Miller, W. R., & Rollnick, S. (2002). *Motivational interviewing* (2nd ed.). New York: Guilford.

Millon, T. (1993). Borderline personality disorder: A psychosocial epidemic. In J. Paris (Ed.), *Borderline personality disorder: Etiology and treatment* (pp. 197–210). Washington DC: American Psychiatric Press.

Moeller, F. G., Barratt, E. S., Dougherty, D. M., Schmitz, J. M., & Swann, A. C. (2001). Psychiatric aspects of impulsivity. *American Journal of Psychiatry, 158,* 1783–1793.

Moffitt, T. E., Caspi, A., Rutter, M. M., & Silva, P. A. (2001). *Sex differences in antisocial behavior.* New York: Cambridge University Press.

Mohino, J. S., Ortega-Monasterio, L., Planchat-Teruel, L. M., Cuquerella-Fuentes, A., Talon-Navarro, T., et al. (2004). Discriminating deliberate self-harm (DSH) in young prison inmates through personality disorder. *Journal of Forensic Sciences, 49,* 137–140.

Monroe, S. M., & Simons, A. D. (1991). Diathesis-stress theories in the context of life stress research. *Psychological Bulletin, 110,* 406–425.

Morrell, S., Page, A., & Taylor, R. (2002). Birth cohort effects in New South Wales suicide, 1865–1998. *Acta Psychiatrica Scandinavia, 106,* 365–372.

Morriss, R., Gask, L., Webb, R., Dixon, C., & Appleby, L. (2005). The effects on suicide rates of an educational intervention for front-line health professionals with suicidal patients (the STORM Project). *Psychological Medicine, 35,* 957–960.

Motto, J. A., & Bostrom, A. G. (2001). A randomized controlled trial of postcrisis suicide prevention. *Psychiatric Services, 52,* 828–833.

Mulder, R. T. (2002). Personality pathology and treatment outcome in major depression: A review. *American Journal of Psychiatry, 159,* 359–371.

Mulder, R. T., Joyce, P. R., & Luty, S. E. (2003). The relationship of personality disorders to treatment outcome in depressed outpatients. *Journal of Clinical Psychiatry, 64,* 259–264.

Murphy, G. E. (2000). Psychiatric aspects of suicidal behavior: Substance abuse. In K. Hawton & K. van Heeringen (Eds.), *The international handbook of suicide and attempted suicide* (pp. 135–146). New York: Wiley.

Murphy, G. E., & Wetzel, R. D. (1980). Suicide risk by birth cohort in the United States, 1949 to 1974. *Archives of General Psychiatry, 37,* 519–523.

Nelson, E. E., Leibenluft, E., McClure, E. B., & Pine, D. S. (2005). The social re-orientation of adolescence: A neuroscience perspective on the process and its relation to psychopathology. *Psychological Medicine, 35,* 163–174.

Newton-Howes, G., Tyrer, P., & Johnson, T. (2006). Personality disorder and the outcome of depression: Meta-analysis of published studies. *British Journal of Psychiatry, 188,* 13–20.

Nickel, M. K., Nickel, C., Mitterlehner, F. O., Tritt, K., Lahmann, C., Leiberich, P. K., et al. (2004). Topiramate treatment of aggression in female borderline personality disorder patients: A double-blind, placebo-controlled study. *Journal of Clinical Psychiatry, 65,* 1515–1519.

Offer, D., & Offer, J. (1975). Three developmental routes through normal male adolescence. *Adolescent Psychiatry, 4,* 121–141.

Oldham, J. M., Gabbard, G. O., Goin, M. K., Gunderson, J., Soloff, P., Spiegel, D., et al. (2001). Practice guideline for the treatment of borderline personality disorder. *American Journal of Psychiatry, 158*(Suppl.), 1–52.

O'Leary, K. M. (2000). Borderline personality disorder: Neuropsychological testing results. *Psychiatric Clinics of North America, 23,* 41–60.

Olfson, M., Shaffer, D., Marcus, S. C., & Greenberg, T. (2003). Relationship between antidepressant medication treatment and suicide in adolescents. *Archives of General Psychiatry, 60,* 978–982.

Orbach, I. (2003). Mental pain and suicide. *Israel Journal of Psychiatry & Related Sciences, 40,* 191–201.

Orbach, I. (2003). Mental pain and suicide. *Israel Journal of Psychiatry & Related Sciences, 40,* 191–201.

Orlinsky, D. E., Ronnestad, M. H., & Willutski, U. (2004). Fifty years of psychotherapy process–outcome research: Continuity and change. In M. J. Lambert (Ed.), *Bergin and Garfield's handbook of psychotherapy and behavior change* (pp. 307–390). New York: Wiley.

Osuch, E. A., Noll, J. G., & Putnam, F. W. (1999). The motivations for self-injury in psychiatric inpatients. *Psychiatry, 62,* 334–346.

Packman, W. L., & Harris, E. A. (1998). Legal issues and risk management in suicidal patients. In B. Bongar, A. L. Berman, R. W. Maris, M. M. Silverman, E. A. Harris, & W. L. Packman (Eds.), *Risk management with suicidal patients* (pp. 150–186). New York: Guilford.

Page, A., Morrell, S., & Taylor, R. (2002). Suicide differentials in Australian males and females by various measures of socio-economic status, 1994–98. *Australian & New Zealand Journal of Public Health, 26,* 318–324.

Pajonk, F. G., Gruenberg, K. A., Moecke, H., & Naber, D. (2002). Suicides and suicide attempts in emergency medicine. *Crisis: Journal of Crisis Intervention & Suicide, 23,* 68–73.

Pao, N. P. (1967). The syndrome of deliberate self-cutting. *British Journal of Medical Psychology, 42,* 195–206.

Paris, J. (1994). *Borderline personality disorder: A multidimensional approach.* Washington, DC: American Psychiatric Press.

Paris, J. (1996). *Social factors in the personality disorders.* New York: Cambridge University Press.

Paris, J. (1998). *Working with traits.* Northvale, NJ: Aronson.

Paris, J. (1999). *Nature and nurture in psychiatry: A predisposition-stress model.* Washington, DC: American Psychiatric Press.

Paris, J. (2000). *Myths of childhood.* Philadelphia: Brunner/Mazel.

Paris, J. (2002a). Chronic suicidality in borderline personality disorder. *Psychiatric Services, 53,* 738–742.

Paris, J. (2002b). Implications of long-term outcome research for the management of patients with borderline personality disorder. *Harvard Review of Psychiatry, 10,* 315–323.

Paris, J. (2003). *Personality disorders over time.* Washington, DC: American Psychiatric Press.

Paris, J. (2004a). Borderline or bipolar? Distinguishing borderline personality disorder from bipolar spectrum disorders. *Harvard Review Psychiatry, 12,* 140–145.

Paris, J. (2004b). Half in love with easeful death: The meaning of chronic suicidality in borderline personality disorder. *Harvard Review of Psychiatry, 12,* 42–48.

Paris, J. (2004c). Is hospitalization useful for suicidal patients with borderline personality disorder? *Journal of Personality Disorders, 18,* 240–247.

Paris, J. (2004d). Sociocultural factors in the treatment of personality disorders. In J. Magnavita (Ed.), *Handbook of personality disorders: Theory and practice* (pp. 135–147). New York: Wiley.

Paris, J. (2005a). Borderline personality disorder. *Canadian Medical Association Journal, 172,* 1579–1583.

Paris, J. (2005b). Diagnosing borderline personality disorder in adolescence. *Adolescent Psychiatry, 29,* 237–247.

Paris, J. (2005c). *The fall of an icon: Psychoanalysis and academic psychiatry.* Toronto, Canada: University of Toronto Press.

Paris, J. (2005d). Recent advances in the treatment of borderline personality disorder. *Canadian Journal of Psychiatry, 50,* 435–441.

Paris, J. (2005e). Understanding self-mutilation in borderline personality disorder. *Harvard Review of Psychiatry, 13,* 179–185.

Paris, J., Brown, R., & Nowlis, D. (1987). Long-term follow-up of borderline patients in a general hospital. *Comprehensive Psychiatry, 28,* 530–553.

Paris, J., Nowlis, D., & Brown, R. (1989). Predictors of suicide in borderline personality disorder. *Canadian Journal of Psychiatry, 34,* 8–9.

Paris, J., & Zweig-Frank, H. (2001). A twenty-seven-year follow-up of borderline patients. *Comprehensive Psychiatry, 42,* 482–487.

Paris, J., Zweig-Frank, H., & Guzder, J. (1994). Psychological risk factors for borderline personality disorder in female patients. *Comprehensive Psychiatry, 35,* 301–305.

Paris, J., Zweig-Frank, H., Ng, F., Schwartz, G., Steiger, H., & Nair, V. (2004). Neurobiological correlates of diagnosis and underlying traits in patients with borderline personality disorder compared with normal controls. *Psychiatry Research, 121,* 239–252.

Parker, G. (2005). Beyond major depression. *Psychological Medicine, 35,* 467–474.

Pazzagli, A., & Monti, M. R. (2000). Dysphoria and aloneness in borderline personality disorder. *Psychopathology, 33,* 220–226.

Pelkonen, M., & Marttunen, M., (2003). Child and adolescent suicide: Epidemiology, risk factors, and approaches to prevention. *Paediatric Drugs, 5,* 243–265.

Pepper, C. M., Klein, D. N., Anderson, R. L., Riso, L. P., Ouimette, P. C., & Lizardi, H. (1995). DSM–III–R Axis II comorbidity in dysthymia and major depression. *American Journal of Psychiatry, 152,* 239–247.

Pfeffer, C. (2000). Suicidal behavior in children: An emphasis on developmental influences. In K. Hawton, & K. van Heeringen (Eds.), *The international handbook of suicide and attempted suicide* (pp. 237–248). New York: Wiley.

Pfeffer, C. R., Klerman, G. L., Hurt, S. W., Lesser, M., Peskin, J. R., & Siefker, C. A. (1991). Suicidal children grow up: Demographic and clinical risk factors for adolescent suicide attempts. *Journal of the American Academy of Child & Adolescent Psychiatry, 30,* 609–616.

Philgren, H. (1995). Depression and suicide in Gotland. *Journal of Affective Disorders, 35,* 147–152.

Pinto, A., Grapentine, W. L., Francis, G., & Picariello, C. M. (1996). Borderline personality disorder in adolescents: Affective and cognitive features. *Journal of the American Academy of Child & Adolescent Psychiatry, 35,* 1338–1343.

Pinto, C., Dhavale, H. S., Nair, S., Patil, B., & Dewan, M. (2000). Borderline personality disorder exists in India. *Journal of Nervous and Mental Disease, 188,* 386–388.

Pinto, O. C., & Akiskal, H. S. (1998). Lamotrigine as a promising approach to borderline personality: An open case series without concurrent DSM–IV major mood disorder. *Journal of Affective Disorders, 51,* 333–343.

Piper, W. E., Azim, H. A., Joyce, A. S., & McCallum, M. (1991). Transference interpretations, therapeutic alliance, and outcome in short-term individual psychotherapy. *Archives of General Psychiatry, 48,* 946–953.

Piper, W. E., Rosie, J. S., & Joyce, A. S. (1996). *Time-limited day treatment for personality disorders: Integration of research and practice in a group program.* Washington, DC: American Psychological Association.

Pirkola, S., Isometsa, E., & Lonnqvist, J. (2003). Do means matter? Differences in characteristics of Finnish suicide completers using different methods. *Journal of Nervous & Mental Disease, 191,* 745–750.

Plath, S. (1966). *Ariel.* New York: Harper & Row.

Plomin, R., DeFries, J. C., McClearn, G. E., & Rutter, M. M. (2000). *Behavioral genetics: A primer* (3rd ed.). New York: W. H. Freeman.

Pokorny, A. D. (1983). Prediction of suicide in psychiatric patients: Report of a prospective study. *Archives of General Psychiatry, 40,* 249–257.

Rachlin, H. (2000). *The science of self control.* Cambridge, MA: Harvard University Press.

Rachlin, S. (1984). Double jeopardy: Suicide and malpractice. *General Hospital Psychiatry, 6,* 302–307.

Reiss, D., Hetherington, E. M., & Plomin, R. (2000). *The relationship code.* Cambridge, MA: Harvard University Press.

Rey, J. M., Singh, M., Morris-Yates, A., & Andrews, G. (1997). Referred adolescents as young adults: The relationship between psychosocial functioning and personality disorder. *Australian and New Zealand Journal of Psychiatry, 31,* 219–226.

Rich, C. L., Fowler, R. C., Fogarty, L. A., & Young, D. (1988). San Diego suicide study: Relationships between diagnoses and stressors. *Archives of General Psychiatry, 45,* 589–594.

Rinne, T., van den Brink, W., Wouters, L., & van Dyck, R. (2002). SSRI treatment of borderline personality disorder: A randomized, placebo-controlled clinical trial for female patients with borderline personality disorder. *American Journal of Psychiatry, 159,* 2048–2054.

Robins, E. (1981). *The final months: A study of the lives of 134 persons who committed suicide*. New York: Oxford University Press.

Robins, L. N. (1966). *Deviant children grown up*. Baltimore: Williams & Wilkins.

Robins, L. N., Schoenberg, S. P., & Holmes, S. J. (1985). Early home environment and retrospective recall: A test for concordance between siblings with and without psychiatric disorders. *American Journal of Orthopsychiatry, 55,* 27–41.

Rogers, J. H., Widiger, T. A., & Krupp, A. (1995). Aspects of depression associated with borderline personality disorder. *American Journal of Psychiatry, 152,* 268–270.

Rosenzweig, S. (1936). Some implicit common factors in diverse methods of psychotherapy. *American Journal of Orthopsychiatry, 6,* 412–415.

Rudd, M. D., Joiner, T., & Rajab, M. H. (1996). Relationships among suicide ideators, attempters and multiple attempters in a young-adult sample. *Journal of Abnormal Psychology, 105,* 541–550.

Rudd, M. D., Joiner, T. E., Jr., & Rumzek, H. (2004). Childhood diagnoses and later risk for multiple suicide attempts. *Suicide & Life-Threatening Behavior, 34,* 113–125.

Rutter, M. (1987). Temperament, personality, and personality disorder. *British Journal of Psychiatry, 150,* 443–448.

Rutter, M., & Smith, D. J. (1995). *Psychosocial problems in young people.* Cambridge, England: Cambridge University Press.

Sakinofsky, I. (2000). Repetition of suicidal behavior. In K. Hawton & K. van Heeringen (Eds.), *The international handbook of suicide and attempted suicide* (pp. 385–404). New York: Wiley.

Samuels, J., Eaton, W. W., Bienvenu, J., Clayton, P., Brown H., Costa, P.T., et al. (2002). Prevalence and correlates of personality disorders in a community sample. *British Journal of Psychiatry, 180,* 536–554.

Sanderson, C., Swenson, C., & Bohus, M. (2002). A critique of the American Psychiatric Association practice guideline for the treatment of patients with borderline personality disorder. *Journal of Personality Disorders, 16,* 122–129.

Sato, T., & Takeichi, M. (1993). Lifetime prevalence of specific psychiatric disorders in a general medicine clinic. *General Hospital Psychiatry, 15,* 224–233.

Scarr, S., & McCartney, K. (1983). How people make their own environments: A theory of genotype–environment effects. *Child Development, 54,* 424–435.

Scheel, K. R. (2000). The empirical basis of dialectical behavior therapy: Summary, critique, and implications. *Clinical Psychology: Science & Practice, 7,* 68–86.

Schneidman, E. S. (1973). *Deaths of man*. New York: Quadrangle/New York Times.

Schwartz, D. A. (1979). The suicidal character. *Psychiatric Quarterly, 51,* 64–70.

Schwartz, D. A., Flinn, D. E., & Slawson, P. F. (1974). Treatment of the suicidal character. *American Journal of Psychotherapy, 28,* 194–207.

Shaffer, D., Gould, M. S., Fisher, P., Trautman, P., Moreau, D., Kleinman, M., et al. (1996). Psychiatric diagnosis in child and adolescent suicide. *Archives of General Psychiatry, 53,* 339–348.

Shea, M. T., Pilkonis, P. A., Beckham, E., Collins, J. F., Elikin, E., Sotsky, S. M., et al. (1990). Personality disorders and treatment outcome in the NIMH Treatment of Depression Collaborative Research Program. *American Journal of Psychiatry, 147,* 711–718.

Siever, L. J., & Davis, K. L. (1991). A psychobiological perspective on the personality disorders. *American Journal of Psychiatry, 148,* 1647–1658.

Silk, K. R., & Yager, J. (2003). Suggested guidelines for e-mail communication in psychiatric practice. *Journal of Clinical Psychiatry, 64,* 799–806.

Silver, D., & Cardish, R. (1991, May). *BPD outcome studies: Psychotherapy implications.* Paper presented at the American Psychiatric Association, New Orleans.

Simeon, D., Stanley, B., Frances, A., Mann, J. J., Winchel, R., & Stanley, M. (1992). Self mutilation in personality disorders: Psychological and biological correlates. *American Journal of Psychiatry, 149,* 221–226.

Skodol, A. E., Buckley, P., & Charles, E. (1983). Is there a characteristic pattern in the treatment history of clinic outpatients with borderline personality? *Journal of Nervous and Mental Diseases, 171,* 405–410.

Skodol, A. E., Pagano, M. E., Bender, D. S., Shea, M. T., Gunderson, J. G., Yen, S., et al. (2005). Stability of functional impairment in patients with schizotypal, borderline, avoidant, or obsessive–compulsive personality disorder over two years. *Psychological Medicine, 35,* 443–451.

Skogman, K., Alsen, M., & Ojehagen, A. (2004). Sex differences in risk factors for suicide after attempted suicide—A follow-up study of 1,052 suicide attempters. *Social Psychiatry & Psychiatric Epidemiology, 39,* 113–120.

Soloff, P. (2000). Psychopharmacological treatment of borderline personality disorder. *Psychiatric Clinics of North America, 23,* 169–192.

Soloff, P. H., Cornelius, J., George, A., Nathan, S., Perel, J. M., & Ulrich, R. F. (1993). Efficacy of phenelzine and haloperidol in borderline personality disorder. *Archives of General Psychiatry, 50,* 377–385.

Soloff, P. H., Lynch, K. G., & Kelly, T. M. (2002). Childhood abuse as a risk factor for suicidal behavior in borderline personality disorder. *Journal of Personality Disorders, 16,* 201–214.

Soloff, P. H., Lynch, K. G., Kelly, T. M., Malone, K. M., & Mann, J. J. (2000). Characteristics of suicide attempts of patients with major depressive episode and borderline personality disorder: A comparative study. *American Journal of Psychiatry, 157,* 601–608.

Solomon, M. I., & Hellon, C. P. (1980). Suicide and age in Alberta, Canada, 1951 to 1977: A cohort analysis. *Archives of General Psychiatry, 37,* 511–513.

Spirito, A., Valeri, S., Boergers, J., & Donaldson, D. (2003). Predictors of continued suicidal behavior in adolescents following a suicide attempt. *Journal of Clinical Child & Adolescent Psychology, 32,* 284–289.

Stanley, B., Gameroff, M. J., Michalsen, V., & Mann, J. J. (2001). Are suicide attempters who self-mutilate a unique population? *American Journal of Psychiatry, 158,* 427–432.

Statham, D. J., Heath, A. C., Madden, P. A., Bucholz, K. K., Bierut, L., Dinwiddie, S. H., et al. (1998). Suicidal behaviour: An epidemiological and genetic study. *Psychological Medicine, 28,* 839–855.

Stern, A. (1938). Psychoanalytic investigation of and therapy in the borderline group of neuroses. *Psychoanalytic Quarterly, 7,* 467–489.

Stevenson, A. (1988). *Bitter fame. A life of Sylvia Plath.* Boston: Houghton Mifflin.

Stevenson, J., & Meares, R. (1992). An outcome study of psychotherapy for patients with borderline personality disorder. *American Journal of Psychiatry, 149,* 358–362.

Stone, M. H. (1990). *The fate of borderline patients.* New York: Guilford.

Sudak, H. S., Ford, A. B., & Rushforth, N. B. (1984). *Suicide in the young.* Boston: Wright.

Suokas, J., Suominen, K., Isometsa, E., Ostamo, A., & Lonnqvist, J. (2001). Long-term risk factors for suicide mortality after attempted suicide—Findings of a 14-year follow-up study. *Acta Psychiatrica Scandinavica, 104,* 117–121.

Suominen, K., Isometsa, E., Haukka, J., & Lonnqvist, J. (2004). Substance use and male gender as risk factors for deaths and suicide—A 5-year follow-up study after deliberate self-harm. *Social Psychiatry & Psychiatric Epidemiology, 39,* 720–724.

Suominen, K. H., Isometsa, E. T., Henriksson, M. M., Ostamo, A. I., & Lonnqvist, J. K. (2000). Suicide attempts and personality disorder. *Acta Psychiatrica Scandinavica, 102,* 118–125.

Suominen, K., Isometsa, E., Ostamo, A., & Lonnqvist, J. (2004). Level of suicidal intent predicts overall mortality and suicide after attempted suicide: A 12-year follow-up study. *BMC Psychiatry, 4,* 11.

Suominen, K., Isometsa, E., Suokas, J., Haukka, J., Achte, K., & Lonnqvist, J. (2004). Completed suicide after a suicide attempt: A 37-year follow-up study. *American Journal of Psychiatry, 161,* 563–564.

Suyemoto, K. (1998). The functions of self-mutilation. *Clinical Psychology Review, 18,* 531–554.

Tollefson, G. D., Fawcett, J., Winokur, G., Beasley, C. M., Jr., Potvin, J. H., Faries, D. E., et al. (1993). Evaluation of suicidality during pharmacologic treatment of mood and nonmood disorders. *Annals of Clinical Psychiatry, 5,* 209–224.

Torgersen, S., Kringlen, E., & Cramer, V. (2001). The prevalence of personality disorders in a community sample. *Archives of General Psychiatry, 58,* 590–596.

Torgersen, S., Lygren, S., Oien, P. A., Skre, I., Onstad, S., Edvardsen, J., et al. (2000). A twin study of personality disorders. *Comprehensive Psychiatry, 41,* 416–425.

Townsend, E., Arensman, E., Gunnell, D., Hazell, P., House, A., & van Heeringen, K. (2000). Psychosocial versus pharmacological treatments for deliberate self harm. *Cochrane Database of Systematic Reviews, 2,* CD001764.

Tritt, K., Nickel, C., Lahmann, C., Leiberich, P. K., Rother, W. K., Loew, T. H., et al. (2005). Lamotrigine treatment of aggression in female borderline patients: A randomized, double-blind, placebo-controlled study. *Journal of Psychopharmacology, 19,* 287–291.

Trivedi, M. H., & Kleiber, B. A. (2001). Using treatment algorithms for the effective management of treatment-resistant depression. *Journal of Clinical Psychiatry, 62*(Suppl. 18), 25–29.

Trull, T. J., & Sher, K. J. (1994). Relationship between the five-factor model of personality and Axis I disorders in a nonclinical sample. *Journal of Abnormal Psychology, 103,* 350–360.

Tyrer, P. (2002). Practice guideline for the treatment of borderline personality disorder: A bridge too far. *Journal of Personality Disorders, 16,* 113–118.

Tyrer, P., Coid, J., Simmonds, S., Joseph, P., & Marriott, S. (2000). Community mental health teams (CMHTs) for people with severe mental illnesses and disordered personality. *Cochrane Database of Systematic Reviews, 2,* CD000270.

Vajda, J., & Steinbeck, K. (2000). Factors associated with repeat suicide attempts among adolescents. *Australian & New Zealand Journal of Psychiatry, 34,* 437–445.

van den Bosch, L. M., Verheul, R., Schippers, G. M., & van den Brink, W. (2002). Dialectical behavior therapy of borderline patients with and without substance use problems: Implementation and long-term effects. *Addictive Behaviors, 27,* 911–923.

van Praag, H. M. (2003). A stubborn behaviour: the failure of antidepressants to reduce suicide rates. *World Journal of Biological Psychiatry, 4,* 184–191.

Verheul, R., van den Bosch, L. M. C., Maarten, W. J., de Ridder, M. A. J., Stijnen, T., & van den Brink, W. (2003). Dialectical behaviour therapy for women with borderline personality disorder: 12-month, randomised clinical trial in The Netherlands. *British Journal of Psychiatry, 182,* 135–140.

Verkes, R. J., & Cowen, P. J. (2000). Pharmacotherapy of suicidal ideation and behavior. In K. Hawton & K. van Heeringen (Eds.), *The international handbook of suicide and attempted suicide* (pp. 487–502). New York: Wiley.

Von Egmond, N., & Diekstra, R. F. (1990). The predictability of suicidal behavior: The results of a meta-analysis. *Crisis, 11,* 57–84.

Waldinger, R. J., & Gunderson, J. G. (1984). Completed psychotherapies with borderline patients. *American Journal of Psychotherapy, 38,* 190–201.

Wampold, B. E. (2001). *The great psychotherapy debate: Models, methods, and findings.* Mahwah, NJ: Lawrence Erlbaum Associates.

Weissman, M. M., Bland, R. C., Canino, G. J., & Faravelli, C. (1996). Cross-national epidemiology of major depressive and bipolar disorder. *Journal of the American Medical Association, 276,* 298–299.

Weissman, M. M., Bland R. C., Canino, G. J., Greenwald, S., Hwu, H. G., Joyce, P. R., et al. (1999). Prevalence of suicide ideation and suicide attempts in nine countries. *Psychological Medicine, 29,* 9–17.

Weissman, M. M., Leaf, P. J., Tischler, G. L., Blazer, D. G., Karno, M., Bruce, M. L., et al. (1988). Affective disorders in five United States communities. *Psychological Medicine, 8:* 141–153.

Welch, S. S. (2001). A review of the literature on the epidemiology of parasuicide in the general population. *Psychiatric Services, 52,* 368–375.

Westen, D., Novotny, C. M., & Thompson-Brenner, H. (2004). The empirical status of empirically supported psychotherapies: Assumptions, findings, and reporting in controlled clinical trials. *Psychological Bulletin, 130,* 631–663.

White, C. N., Gunderson, J. G., Zanarini, M. C., & Hudson, J. I. (2003). Family studies of borderline personality disorder: A review. *Harvard Review of Psychiatry, 11,* 118–119.

Wilkinson, D. G. (1982). The suicide rate in schizophrenia. *British Journal of Psychiatry, 140,* 138–141.

Wilkinson, G. (1994). Can suicide be prevented? *British Medical Journal, 309,* 860–862.

Wilkinson-Ryan, T., & Westen, D. (2000). Identity disturbance in borderline personality disorder: An empirical investigation. *American Journal of Psychiatry, 157,* 528–541.

Williams, J. M. G. (1997). *Cry of pain: Understanding suicide and self-harm.* London: Penguin.

Williams, L. (1998). A "classic" case of borderline personality disorder. *Psychiatric Services, 49,* 173–174.

Willis, L. A., Coombs, D. W., Drentea, P., & Cockerham, W. C. (2003). Uncovering the mystery: Factors of African American suicide. *Suicide & Life-Threatening Behavior, 33,* 412–429.

Winchel, R. M., & Stanley, M. (1991). Self-injurious behavior: A review of the behavior and biology of self-mutilation. *American Journal of Psychiatry, 148,* 306–317.

Wixom, J., Ludolph, P., & Westen, D. (1993). The quality of depression in adolescents with borderline personality disorder. *Journal of the American Academy of Child & Adolescent Psychiatry, 32,* 1172–1177.

Yen, S., Shea, M. T., Sanislow, C. A., Grilo, C. M., Skodol, A. E., Gunderson, J. G., et al. (2004). Borderline personality disorder criteria associated with prospectively observed suicidal behavior. *American Journal of Psychiatry, 161,* 1296–1298.

Yeomans, F., Clarkin, J. F., & Kernberg, O. F. (2002). *A primer of transference-based psychotherapy.* Northvale, NJ: Aronson.

Young, J. E. (1999). *Cognitive therapy for personality disorders: A schema focused approach* (3rd ed.). Sarastoa, FL: Professional Resource Press.

Zahl, D. L., & Hawton, K. (2004). Repetition of deliberate self-harm and subsequent suicide risk: Long-term follow-up study of 11,583 patients. *British Journal of Psychiatry, 185,* 70–75.

Zanarini, M. C. (2000). Childhood experiences associated with the development of borderline personality disorder. *Psychiatric Clinics of North America, 23,* 89–101.

Zanarini, M. C., & Frankenburg, F. R. (2003). Omega-3 fatty acid treatment of women with borderline personality disorder: A double-blind, placebo-controlled pilot study. *American Journal of Psychiatry, 160,* 167–169.

Zanarini, M. C., Frankenburg, F. R., Dubo, E. D., Sickel, A. E., Trikha, A., Levin, A., et al. (1998). Axis I comorbidity of borderline personality disorder. *American Journal of Psychiatry, 155,* 1733–1739.

Zanarini, M. C., Frankenburg, F. R., Hennen, J., & Silk, K. R. (2003). The longitudinal course of borderline psychopathology: 6-year prospective follow-up of the phenomenology of borderline personality disorder. *American Journal of Psychiatry, 160,* 274–283.

Zanarini, M. C., Frankenburg, F. R., Khera, G. S., & Bleichmar, J. (2001). Treatment histories of borderline inpatients. *Comprehensive Psychiatry, 42,* 144–150.

Zelkowitz, P., Paris, J., Guzder, J., Feldman, R., & Rosval, L. (2006). *A five-year follow-up of children with borderline pathology of childhood.* Manuscript submitted for publication.

Zimmerman, M., Rothschild, L., & Chelminski, I. (2005). The prevalence of DSM–IV personality Disorders in psychiatric outpatients. *American Journal of Psychiatry, 162,* 1911–1918.

Zweig-Frank, H., & Paris, J. (2002). Predictors of outcomes in a 27-year follow-up of patients with borderline personality disorder. *Comprehensive Psychiatry, 43,* 103–107.

Zweig-Frank, H., Paris, J., & Guzder, J. (1994). Psychological risk factors for disssociation and self-mutilation in female patients with personality disorders. *Canadian Journal of Psychiatry, 39,* 259–265.

Author Index

Subject Index